BONDS, GUARANTEES AND PERFORMANCE SECURITY IN THE CONSTRUCTION INDUSTRY

BONDS, GUARANTEES AND PERFORMANCE SECURITY IN THE CONSTRUCTION INDUSTRY

Paul Newman MA(Cantab), FCI Arb
Barrister, Gray's Inn

JORDANS
1999

Published by
Jordan Publishing Limited
21 St Thomas Street
Bristol BS1 6JS

British Library Cataloguing-in-Publication Data
A catalogue record for this book is available from the British Library.

ISBN 0 85308 415 7

Typeset by Mendip Communications Ltd, Frome, Somerset
Printed by MPG Books Ltd, Bodmin, Cornwall

Preface

Writing a book is always a Herculean task, needing to be accommodated alongside the author's day job and family commitments. Long-suffering editors presumably learn to endure the unanswered telephone calls and delayed time-scales with fortitude. This signals my gratitude to Stephen Honey and Martin West of Jordans for their encouragement and gentle cajoling when necessary. I am also grateful to my wife, Veronica, for her tolerant support and have noted with wry amusement the behaviour of my son, David, who, when I was checking the proofs, decided to sit down beside me, taking most of the table, to amend documents of his own.

So why was this book written? I felt there was a role for a book which was not another account of insolvency in the construction industry but which identified some of the underlying issues relating to methods of security over payment and other obligations. Having originally intended simply to consider the legal questions, precedents were included after discussions with Stephen Honey. The precedents are included as illustrative examples of particular types of documents and are derived from my experience as a practising lawyer. My slowness to complete has forced me to consider the Housing Grants, Construction and Regeneration Act 1996 and the recently published amendments to the JCT contracts.

My last thanks go to the kindness and support of Richard Davis of Masons who has provided a number of materials which might otherwise have gone unnoticed.

Paul Newman
Cardiff
October 1999

Contents

Table of Cases

References are to paragraph numbers; *italic* references are to Appendix page numbers.

Table of Statutes

References are to paragraph numbers; *italic* references are to Appendix page numbers.

Table of Statutory Instruments

References are to paragraph numbers; *italic* **references are to Appendix page numbers.**

Table of Building Bonds, Contracts, etc

References are to paragraph numbers; *italic* **references are to Appendix page numbers.**

Table of Abbreviations

ABI	Association of British Insurers
BCSA	British Constructional Steelwork Association
BPF	British Property Federation
CASEC	Committee of Associations of Specialist Engineering Contractors
CEDR	Centre for Dispute Resolution
CCSJC	Conditions of Contract Standing Joint Committee
FASS	Federation of Associations of Specialists and Sub-Contractors
FCEC	Federation of Civil Engineering Contractors
IATA	International Air Transport Association
ICE	Institution of Civil Engineers
IFC	Intermediate Form of Building Contract
JCT	Joint Contracts Tribunal
NEC	New Engineering Contract
RIBA	Royal Institute of British Architects
RSC	Rules of the Supreme Court 1965
TeCSA	Technology and Construction Solicitors Association
the 1996 Act	Housing Grants, Construction and Regeneration Act 1996
the 1998 Regulations	Scheme for Construction Contracts (England and Wales) Regulations 1998

Chapter 1

PAYMENT ISSUES IN THE CONSTRUCTION INDUSTRY

Introduction – Lump sum payments and 'entire' contracts – Certified monies – Arbitration Act 1996, section 9 – Housing Grants, Construction and Regeneration Act 1996 – Contractual set-off – Legal and equitable set-off – Abatement – Pay when paid – The Latham Report – Response to the Latham Report – Appendix

INTRODUCTION

1.1   The purpose of this chapter is not to provide a critique of the payment provisions found in standard form building contracts but to consider some of the broader questions relating to payment. It is obviously difficult to fix a price for building work. Anyone who has had building work carried out at home knows that the final price may not bear any relation to the price originally quoted by the contractor. Building is full of imponderables. First, the client may require extensive additional works (or indeed omissions from the works) and, secondly, various things may be discovered during the course of the construction which add complexity and increase the construction costs. Traditionally, in England and Wales building work has been priced by reference to bills of quantities. These list on an elemental basis the works to be carried out against which the contractor inserts a unit price. Under JCT contracts, the contractor works to a contract sum specifically mentioned in the contract, although the out-turn cost may be greater or less than the sum specified. The final contract sum is ascertained by adding the value of variations or deducting, as the case may be, the value of omissions from the original contract sum. Civil engineering contracts operate on a different basis – that of so-called admeasurement. Although the scope of the works will be delineated by reference to the contract drawings and bills of quantities, it is expressly stated in the conditions of contract that the works set out in the bills of quantities are merely an estimate, meaning that the quantity of work actually executed may go up or down. What happens is that the contractor's work output is measured, usually on a monthly cycle, and the engineer will certify the value of work properly carried out by the contractor during the payment period. Admeasurement reflects the particular problems of civil engineering contracts. Until the work is commenced, and indeed carried out, it is difficult to anticipate the actual amount of work required to complete the works. This leads to great uncertainty in budgeting and disgruntled clients who find that they have spent more than they originally anticipated.

LUMP SUM PAYMENTS AND 'ENTIRE' CONTRACTS

1.2   Although the above principles apply to more sophisticated contracts, quite often a contractor will agree to build the works for a lump sum and the contract is an 'entire' one. A contract is 'entire' if complete performance by one party is a condition precedent to payment by the other. This means that, if the contractor abandons the works before completion, he is not entitled to payment. However, this rule will be mitigated in certain circumstances. In a late 19th century case, *Sumpter v Hedges*,[1] a contractor had agreed to erect buildings on the defendant's land for a lump sum. Partway through the work, he stopped because of a lack of money. The court held that he was not entitled to any payment at all. The starkness of this rule was mitigated in subsequent litigation. If the contractor has provided the client with a benefit, the contractor is entitled to payment less the costs of making good defects and omissions. In *Hoenig v Isaacs*,[2] the plaintiff was employed to decorate and furnish a flat for £750, the payment terms being 'net cash as work proceeds; balance on completion'. The defendant, having paid £400 by instalments, refused to pay the balance on the ground that the work was defective. The Court of Appeal held that the contract had been substantially performed with the defendant liable to pay, less the cost of making good defects. More recently, the law was reviewed by His Honour Judge John Newey QC, in *Holland Hannen & Cubitts (Northern) Limited v Welsh Health Technical Services Organisation*:[3]

'(1)   An entire contract is one in which what is described as "complete performance" by one party is a condition precedent to the liability of the other party: *Cutter v Powell* (1795) 6 TR 320, and *Munro v Butt* (1858) 8 EB 739.

(2)   Whether a contract is an entire one is a matter of construction; it depends upon what the parties agreed. A lump sum contract is not necessarily an entire contract. A contract providing for interim payments, for example, as work proceeds, but for retention money to be held until completion is usually entire as to the retention moneys, but not necessarily the interim payments: Denning LJ in *Hoenig v Isaacs* [1952] 2 All ER 176, at pp 180 and 181.

(3)   The test of complete performance for the purposes of an entire contract is in fact "substantial performance": *H Dakin & Co Ltd v Lee* [1916] 1 KB 566, and *Hoenig v Isaacs*.

(4)   What is substantial is not to be determined on a comparison of cost of work done and work omitted or done badly: *Kiely & Sons Ltd v Medcraft* [1965] 109 SJ, 829 and *Bolton v Mahadeva* [1972] 1 WLR 1009.

(5)   If a party abandons performance of the contract, he cannot recover payment for work which he has completed: *Sumpter v Hedges* [1898] 1 QB 673.

(6)   If a party has done something different from that which he contracted to perform, then, however valuable his work, he cannot claim to have performed substantially: *Forman & Co Proprietary Ltd v The Ship "Liddesdale"* [1900] AC 190.

---

1   [1898] 1 QB 673.
2   [1952] 2 All ER 176.
3   (1981) 18 BLR 89 at 122 and 123.

(7)   If a party is prevented from performing his contract by default of the other party, he is excused from performance and may recover damages: dicta, by Blackburn J in *Appleby v Myers* (1866) 2 CP 651, at p 661; *Mackay v Dick* [1880] AC 251.

(8)   Parties may agree that, in return for one party performing certain obligations, the other will pay to him a *quantum meruit.*

(9)   A contract for payment of a *quantum meruit* may be made in the same way as any other type of contract, including conduct.

(10)   A contract for a *quantum meruit* will not readily be inferred from the actions of a landowner in using something which has become physically attached to his land: *Munro v Butt.*

(11)   There may be circumstances in which, even though a special contract has not been performed there may arise a new or substituted contract; it is a matter of evidence: *Whitaker v Dunn* (1886) 3 TLR 602.'

1.3   The tightness of cash flow and financial planning beset both contractors and employers. Employers, particularly in the late 1980s and early 1990s, took on speculative developments. They were only as good as the last draw-down from the funding institution and contractors often found themselves in the position where the employer was 'robbing Peter to pay Paul'. This led to many and various (and often spurious) set-offs being raised against contractors and other claims being made in abatement. Equally, contractors have on occasions been keen to buy work and have tendered for work at unrealistically low rates. This has been most acute in the context of local authority and other publicly funded works, where lowest tender wins. Here, contractors have deployed a number of techniques to counteract uneconomic tendering. First, the allowance for profit has almost been eradicated, with the contractor looking to make good the shortfall under a variety of heads, including delay and disruption. Secondly, in order to accelerate cash flow, contractors have 'front-loaded' their contract bills, perhaps without any specific link to the value of work executed.

CERTIFIED MONIES

1.4   Whatever the contract, the usual principle under building contracts is that work carried out during the requisite valuation period is certified by the engineer or architect, who, although appointed by and working for the employer, carries out an independent audit. Once the architect or engineer has made his deliberation, this is incorporated in a certificate which is passed to the employer as an indication of those monies which, in the professional opinion of the architect or engineer, are due to be paid to the contractor. In the construction industry, there has been much confusion regarding the status of certificates. However, a combination of case-law, which has demonstrated that the mere issue of an architect's or engineer's certificate is no bar to cross-claims being raised on behalf of the employer, and the wording of standard form contracts, has made the question of easy recovery of certified monies under standard form contracts (traditionally by summary judgment) a legal minefield. Further, the problems have now been compounded by the provisions of the Arbitration Act 1996 calling for the mandatory stay of proceedings to arbitration wherever the contract contains an arbitration clause. Section 9 of the Arbitration Act 1996 reads as follows:

'(1) A party to an arbitration agreement against whom legal proceedings are brought (whether by way of a claim or counterclaim) in respect of a matter which under the agreement is to be referred to arbitration may (upon notice to the other parties to the proceedings) apply to the court in which the proceedings have been brought to stay the proceedings so far as they concern that matter.

(2) An application may be made notwithstanding that the matter is to be referred to arbitration only after the exhaustion of other dispute resolution procedures.

(3) An application may not be made by a person before taking the appropriate procedural steps (if any) to acknowledge the legal proceedings against him or after he has taken any steps in those proceedings to answer the substantive claim.

(4) On an application under this section the court shall grant a stay unless satisfied that the arbitration is null and void, inoperative or incapable of being performed.'

ARBITRATION ACT 1996, SECTION 9

1.5   How to interpret s 9 of the Arbitration Act 1996 arose in a Queen's Bench Division (Admiralty Court) decision, *Halki Shipping Corporation v Sopex Oils Limited*,[1] a decision of Clark J. The shipowners chartered a vessel to the charterers on a tanker voyage charter party with an arbitration clause. After discharge of the cargo, the owner claimed demurrage as a result of the charterers' failure to load and discharge the vessel within the laytime. The charterers did not admit the claim and the owners brought an action in demurrage. The charterers sought a stay under s 9 of the 1996 Act, while the owners applied for summary judgment under Rules of the Supreme Court (RSC) Ord 14. The judge held that save in very limited circumstances, all disputes fell within the arbitration clause and had to be referred to arbitration. Even claims for which there was obviously no answer in fact or law were no longer justifiable by legal process and had to be referred to arbitration. This decision was upheld by the Court of Appeal.[2] All this is bad news for potential claimants under building contracts (which contain an arbitration clause, although the Joint Contracts Tribunal (JCT) in its latest suite of contracts, including JCT 48, have discarded arbitration) who might otherwise have made summary judgment or interim payment applications under RSC Ord 14 or RSC Ord 29 respectively. Parties, requiring a quick release of monies, will now rely principally upon s 39 of the Arbitration Act 1996, which leaves the parties under contracts, where there is an arbitration clause, free to agree that the arbitral tribunal shall have power to make provisional awards (ie early release of monies in favour of one or other of the parties).

HOUSING GRANTS, CONSTRUCTION AND REGENERATION ACT 1996

1.6   Legislation was brought in for the construction industry in the Housing Grants, Construction and Regeneration Act 1996 (the 1996 Act). By virtue of s 108 of this Act, a disgruntled party to a construction contract (construction contracts being defined by a combination of s 104 and s 105 of the 1996 Act to encompass most

---

1   [1996] 3 All ER 833.
2   [1998] 2 All ER 23.

construction activities, with the exception of domestic building contracts and some mechanical plant contracts) may invoke an adjudication procedure. Adjudication is not arbitration and is a form of expert decision-making. Under the 1996 Act, the adjudicator will adhere to a very rapid timetable (not more than 42 days) in order to come to a decision which is binding upon the parties until they agree to resolve their dispute in a different manner, the matter has been litigated or the matter has gone to final arbitration. The process reflects the fact that 'cash flow is the lifeblood of the construction industry' and contractors need to be protected from the ravages of the litigation system with its delays and high costs. Various professional bodies, eg the Construction Industry Council, the Official Referees' Solicitors Association (now the Technology and Construction Solicitors Association (TeCSA)), the Centre for Dispute Resolution (CEDR) and the Institution of Civil Engineers (ICE), have all produced their own adjudication codes. In addition, for those parties who forget to include appropriate dispute-resolution procedures in their contracts or whose own procedures are contrary to the spirit of the Act, the legislature has produced the Scheme for Construction Contracts (England and Wales) Regulations 1998 (the 1998 Regulations),[1] which came into force on 1 May 1998. Much has been written in the construction press and in books dedicated to dispute resolution on the desirability of the legislation and the impact it will have on a contractor's ability to recover outstanding monies quickly.[2]

It is open to an employer on a contractor's application for payment of sums certified or apparently due and owing to raise all manner of cross-claims. This has resulted in complex case-law. For a time, an architect's certificate was 'as good as cash' and actions on unpaid certificates were treated in the same manner as those on dishonoured cheques. The authority for this proposition was Lord Denning MR in *Dawnays Ltd v FG Minter Ltd*.[3] The case was overruled by the House of Lords in *Gilbert Ash Northern Ltd v Modern Engineering (Bristol) Ltd*[4] and confirmed in *Mottram Consultants Ltd v Sunley & Sons Ltd*.[5] There are no special rules relating to cross-claims in the construction industry. Further, given that building is not an exact science, this provided a severe limit on the ability of contractors to obtain summary judgment or interim payments (a position now made even worse by the Arbitration Act 1996). In the words of Lord Salmon in *Gilbert Ash* (at p 223):

> 'The [JCT] provisions relating to interim certificates as a rule ensure a steady cash flow in normal conditions ... when, however, a bona fide dispute arises, I do not think [they are] designed to put the Plaintiff Contractors or Sub-contractors in a fundamentally better position than any ordinary Plaintiffs or the Defendants in any worse position than any ordinary Defendants.'

---

1 SI 1998/649.
2 The court has supported statutory adjudication in *Macob Civil Engineering Limited v Morrison Construction Limited* (1999) CILL 1470.
3 [1971] 2 All ER 389.
4 [1973] 3 All ER 195.
5 (1974) 2 BLR 28.

CONTRACTUAL SET-OFF

1.7   So what pre-emptive strikes can a contractor make? Sometimes contracts allow specifically for the contractor to determine his own employment in the event of non-payment. A suitable power was found in clause 28.1.1 of JCT 80, which listed as a ground for determination the employer's failure to pay the amount properly due to the contractor on any certificate within 14 days of its issue. However, it was a two-stage process. The contractor must issue a notice stating that he would determine his own employment unless payment was made within seven days of receipt of the notice, such notice to be served by registered or recorded delivery post. A similar power of determination was found under the standard sub-contract form, DOM/1, clause 30.1.1.3. JCT 80 Amendment 18 and JCT 98 have added the statutory right to suspend.

1.8   At common law, the contractor has no right, in the absence of a specific contract provision, to suspend performance for non-payment, although the case of *Jefco Mechanical Services Ltd v London Borough of Lambeth*[1] seems to suggest that repeated late payment or underpayment of a contractor might 'so shatter the contractor's confidence' in the ability of the other party to perform his contractual obligations as to give rise to a right to consider the continued non-payment as a repudiatory breach of contract. Under a contract, in the old form JCT 63, the Court of Appeal held in *JM Hill & Sons v London Borough of Camden*[2] that the contractor had, by effecting a 'go-slow', been guilty of a repudiatory breach of contract. Although the provision was frequently deleted by main contractors, clause 21.6 of DOM/1 permitted the sub-contractor to suspend completion of his work in the event of non-payment by the main contractor. The problem of achieving regular stage payments has been addressed in the Housing Grants, Construction and Regeneration Act 1996, and is discussed later in this chapter. This Act provided a statutory right to suspend, as found in clause 21.6 of DOM/1 and clause 30.1.4 of JCT 98.

1.9   Traditionally, sub-contractors appear to have come off badly when chasing monies from main contractors. Leaving to one side the complex law of set-off, many main contractors have traditionally produced an array of amendments to standard form contracts. These have included removal of the right to suspend performance for non-payment, adjusting the date of release of retention monies to a date long after the sub-contractor may have completed his work, removing the protections in standard form contracts against arbitrary set-off (ie prior written notice of the intended set-off with a detailed quantification) and frequent use of the so-called 'pay when paid' principle.

1.10   Construction contracts tend to set out very specifically the terms upon which monies can be withheld. Common requirements were found in most of the standard form sub-contracts, even prior to the 1996 Act:

-    the amount to be set off had to have been quantified in advance with reasonable accuracy;

---

1   (1983) 24 BLR 1.
2   (1981) 18 BLR 31.

- the contractor had to give written notice of his intention to set off to the sub-contractor;
- the notice of set-off had to indicate the grounds upon which the set-off was being made;
- the notice had to be given a specified number of days before the day on which the sum otherwise payable to the sub-contractor became due.

Most, if not all, contracts indicate that the rights of set-off were exclusively as set out in the contract and any other rights which might arise at common law are specifically excluded.

1.11 It is important to identify particular procedural hurdles in specific contracts forms. For instance, clause 35.15.1 of JCT 80 states that an architect's certificate is required as a precondition to the contractor's right to set off monies against a nominated sub-contractor. Particular problems are caused by contract forms which allow the set-off of sums based on a bona fide estimate rather than a strict calculation of losses incurred. A notable example of the latter was the cluster of cases arising out of the so-called Broadgate litigation. However, the more typical form of set-off provision was of the type encountered in clause 23 of DOM/1:

'The Contractor shall be entitled to set-off against any money (including any Sub-Contractor's retention) otherwise due under the Sub-Contract, the amount of any claim for loss and/or expense which has actually been incurred by the Contractor by reason of any breach of, or failure to observe the provisons of the Sub-Contract by the Sub-Contractor providing:

1. the amount of such set-off has been quantified in detail and with reasonable accuracy by the Contractor; and

2. the Contractor has given to the Sub-Contractor notice in writing specifying his intention to set-off the amount quantified in accordance with Clause 23.2.1 and the grounds on which set-off is claimed to be made. Such notice shall be given not less than 20 days before the money from which the amount or part thereof is to be set-off becomes due and payable to the Sub-Contractor.'

1.12 Any amount set off under clause 23.2 of DOM/1 was without prejudice to the rights of the contractor or sub-contractor in any subsequent negotiations, arbitration proceedings or litigation to seek to vary the amount claimed and set off by the contractor under clause 23.2. Further, clause 23.4 of DOM/1 stated that the rights of the parties in respect of set-off were fully set out in the sub-contract. This excluded the use of other set-off rights that might otherwise arise at law. This was not, however, the position under all contract forms. For instance, under the civil engineering Blue Form, the standard FCEC sub-contract, for use with the ICE Conditions of Contract, clauses 15(3)(b) and 15(3)(d) expressly preserved common law rights of set-off: *NEI Thompson Limited v Wimpey Construction UK Limited.*[1] Again, in *Tubeworkers Limited v Tilbury Construction Limited,*[2] the Court of Appeal upheld the contract machinery as being exclusionary of any other rights of set-off. Tubeworkers were structural steel sub-contractors to Tilbury Construction and suffered a deduction of monies otherwise due which was not made in accordance with the contract conditions.

---

1   (1987) 39 BLR 65.
2   (1985) 30 BLR 67.

The contract was the old nominated sub-contract form for use with JCT 63, the so-called NFBTE/FASS Green Form. Clause 13A(4) provided:

> '(4) The rights of the parties to this Sub-Contract in respect of set-off are fully set out in these Conditions and no other rights whatsoever shall be implied as terms of this Sub-Contract.'

1.13   The importance of disregarding future contingent liabilities was demonstrated in *Chatbrown Limited v Alfred McAlpine Construction (Southern) Limited*.[1] Here, the Court of Appeal considered the NFBTE/FASS/CASEC form of domestic sub-contract,[2] for use with JCT 63. Clause 15(2) allowed the contractors to set off against any money otherwise due under the sub-contract 'the amount of money claimed for loss and/or expense which has actually been incurred by the contractor by reason of any breach of, or failure to observe the provisions of, the sub-contract by the sub-contractor'. Sub-clause (4) limited the rights of set-off to those provided by the contract. The defendant complained that the plaintiff had been late in completing its sub-contract works and on 8 March 1985 gave notice of intention to deduct, in accordance with clause 15(2), and an assessment of additional costs incurred. The assessment included 'general site costs, 16 weeks at £14,490 per week . . . equals £231,844'. The plaintiff subsequently issued a writ claiming £231,844. At first instance, the Official Referee, Judge Fox-Andrews QC, gave judgment for the plaintiff holding that:

> 'It was not enough that they [the plaintiff] be under a liability to the defendants but the defendants had actually to incur the loss or expenses alleged and they had not done so at the date of the notice.'

The defendant appealed to the Court of Appeal on other grounds. Although strictly *obiter*, Kerr LJ referred (at p 52) to the interpretation of clause 15(2):

> 'He [Judge Fox-Andrews QC] concluded that it was not sufficient that a liability should have been incurred which would, or was liable to, lead to loss and/or damage in the future, but that it was necessary that loss and/or expense should actually have been incurred prior to the notice and be covered by the notice in the terms required under sub-clause (2). . . . I had no doubt, on reading the papers, that his construction was perfectly correct, and nothing that has been said since this appeal was opened this morning had led me to any different conclusion.'

The current position under DOM/1 is to require, under clause 21.3.3, written notice of set-off, five days before the final date for payment, with a right to late payment under clause 21.3.4. Clause 30.1.1.4 of JCT 98 similarly requires five days' prior notification of set-off.

LEGAL AND EQUITABLE SET-OFF

Legal set-off

1.14   Under legal set-off, both the claim and the cross-claim have to be for liquidated demands (ie debts about which there is no dispute). They must not be for

---

1   (1986) 35 BLR 44.
2   1971 edn (July 1978 Revision).

damages, whether liquidated or unliquidated. This means that the principle has limited relevance in the construction industry. Furthermore, the exclusion of rights of set-off in standard form contracts (other than those guaranteed by the contract provisions) imposes additional limitations on its usefulness. In *B Hargreaves Limited v Action 2000 Limited*,[1] one of the contractor's arguments was that the alleged overpayment on two out of nine sub-contracts came within the principle of mutual debts (ie sums of monies indisputedly owed and not merely claimed). The judge rejected this proposition. The alleged overpayment on the two sub-contracts did not establish a legal set-off. It was not a liquidated sum which could be taken into account in assessing monies due on the remaining seven sub-contracts. It was only the quantity surveyor's assessment and could not become a liquidated sum due until such time that it was agreed or decided upon by the court. Again, in *Axel Johnson Petroleum AB v MG Mineral Group AG*,[2] the Court of Appeal considered the availability of summary judgment where there was a liquidated cross-claim. The plaintiff bought a cargo of oil from the defendant under a joint venture arrangement at a price to be calculated by adding a fixed amount per metric tonne to the price paid by the defendant to the supplier. Subsequently, the plaintiff paid a price, expressed in US dollars, which was considerably less than the defendant's own calculations. The defendant pleaded the outstanding balance as a set-off to a claim by the plaintiff against the defendant for demurrage arising out of a later contract, albeit while under the general joint venture arrangement. On the plaintiff's application for summary judgment under RSC Ord 14, the judge refused leave to defend and gave judgment to the plaintiff. On appeal, the Court of Appeal held that the defendant's cross-claim was for a liquidated sum and was therefore capable of being set off at law against the plaintiff's claim. There was a triable issue on the cross-claim and therefore the defendant was entitled to unconditional leave to defend. In the words of Leggatt LJ (at p 274):

> 'The plaintiffs dispute their liability on the grounds that they were only obliged to pay the defendants what the defendants were bound to pay to [the suppliers], and that the defendants were not bound to pay to [the suppliers] as much as they did pay. The difference between what the defendants did pay and what the plaintiffs claim the defendants were bound to pay represents the amount of the defendant's cross-claim; whether they are entitled to recover it constitutes a triable issue.
>
> Since equitable set-off has not been argued before us I will say no more about it than it also looks to be arguable that there was by virtue of the joint venture agreement such a connection between the respective contracts, which founded the claim and counter-claim, as would make it inequitable to insist on the plaintiffs' claim without taking the defendants' cross-claim into account.
>
> I would add, in the circumstances of this case, the comment that the state of the law is unsatisfactory that allows a set-off at law of debts which were liquidated, even if unconnected, and in equity of debts which are connected, even if unliquidated, but not a set-off of debts which are both unliquidated and unconnected.'

Equitable set-off

1.15 Equitable set-off occurs where a cross-claim arises out of the same transaction as the claim or out of a transaction that is so closely related to the claim,

---

1   (1993) 62 BLR 72.
2   [1992] 1 WLR 270.

and the cross-claim is so closely connected with the money claim made by the plaintiff as to make it unfair that the defendant should pay the plaintiff without deducting the amount of the cross-claim. Significantly, neither the claim nor cross-claim need to be for a liquidated (ie definite and fixed) amount. It is a common occurrence for employers who have a number of contracts with a particular contractor to attempt to set off one contract against another. This is done despite the fact that there is no link between the various contracts apart from there being a common employer and contractor.

1.16   Two leading Court of Appeal cases are *Anglian Building Products Limited v W & C French (Construction) Limited*,[1] and *AB Contractors Limited v Flaherty Brothers Limited*.[2] In *Anglian Building Products*, Anglian had supplied prestressed beams for use in motorway works on the M3, M4 and M6 motorways. Following a summary judgment application, Anglian was awarded the monies due on the M4 and M6 beams. W & C French sought a stay of execution of the judgment because of an alleged quantifiable set-off on the M3 contract. A stay was refused, because the Court of Appeal could find no nexus between the contracts to establish a right of equitable set-off. A similar result was reached in *AB Contractors*, which involved two contracts on two different sites.

Just because the claim and the cross-claim arise from the same transaction, this does not mean that the law of set-off will necessarily apply:

> 'It may even be insufficient that claim and cross-claim arise out of the same contract or transaction, unless they are so inseparably connected that the one ought not to be enforced without taking account of the other.'[3]

1.17   An interesting example of a failed attempt to establish equitable set-off in a construction insolvency was part of the decision in *B Hargreaves Limited v Action 2000 Limited*.[4] Hargreaves' receivers claimed £58,569 in respect of work undertaken by Hargreaves as a sub-contractor for Action 2000. There were nine identical sub-contracts, each of which made reference to the main contract. Following the receiver's appointment, legal proceedings were commenced for unpaid works. In the absence of any contractual set-off provisions, Action 2000 argued that it was entitled to set off sums from related overpayments on two of the nine sub-contracts against the value of monies outstanding to Hargreaves on the remaining seven sub-contracts. Although all nine sub-contracts were in the Midlands and the North West, the judge was not persuaded that the claim and cross-claim were so closely connected as to give rise to an equitable set-off.

ABATEMENT

1.18   In addition, main contractors have often found themselves, when all else fails, assisted by the common law doctrine of abatement. Standard form

---

1   (1972) 16 BLR 1.
2   (1978) 16 BLR 8.
3   *Dole Dried Fruit & Nut Company Limited v Trustin Kerwood Limited*, [1990] 2 Lloyd's Rep 309, cited, but not reported in full, in [1990] CILL 594.
4   (1993) 62 BLR 72.

sub-contracts, even if not amended, have been full of such phrases as 'the sub-contractor is entitled to the value of work properly carried out'. The courts have held such phraseology to mean that a contractor who may have breached the strict set-off rules under standard form contracts is nonetheless able to rely upon the common law doctrine of abatement. Although abatement is not strictly a form of set-off, and indeed independent of it, it often provides similar results. It was explained in *Mondel v Steel*[1] in the following way:

> 'It is competent for the defendant ... not to set-off as a set-off by a proceeding in the nature of a cross action the amount of damages which he has sustained by breach of the contract, but simply to defend himself by showing how much less the subject matter is worth by reason of the breach of contract.'

1.19   Abatement is a deduction to take account of the reduction in value of goods or work carried out because of the breaches of contract by the supplier of the goods or of the persons carrying out the works. Although abatement is an ideal mechanism to deal with defective work or instances of overvaluation, it cannot be used to reduce the payment of professional fees or to take account of potential latent defects.[2] All seemed well for sub-contractors when an Official Referee, Judge Esyr Lewis QC, decided in *BWP (Architectural) Limited v Beaver Building Systems Limited*[3] that the effect of clause 21 of the NAM/SC standard sub-contract, for use with IFC 84, was that unless the contractor complied with the strict terms in regard to set-off, the contractor could not then:

-   resist a summary judgment application on the grounds that work had not been properly executed; or
-   challenge the sub-contractor's application for payment on the ground of arithmetical error.

1.20   What followed were notorious examples of the application of abatement in case-law. In *Acsim (Southern) Ltd v Danish Contracting and Development Co Ltd*,[4] it was held that the contractor was entitled to defend the sub-contractor's claim on the basis that the sub-contractor was, because of his defective performance, entitled to a lesser sum than the one claimed. Here, the sub-contract used was the NFBTE/FASS/CASEC domestic sub-contract[5] (the Blue Form). Clause 15 required proper notice of set-off to be given by the contractor before the due date for payment. The sub-contractor believed that the contractor had failed to apply properly the set-off procedures in clause 15, thereby entitling the sub-contractor to the release of £221,018.03 which had been withheld. The contractor contended that, regardless of any procedural breaches in making the set-off, the true value of outstanding monies owed to the sub-contractor was £36,952. The Court of Appeal held that clause 15 only defined the parties' rights in set-off. Under clause 13, the sub-contractor was entitled in his monthly interim payments only to 'the total value of the Sub-contract Works properly executed' (subject to retention and any discount) within 14 days of the application. The contractor had, therefore, a right to defend a claim for any interim

1   (1841) 1 BLR 108.
2   *Slater v Duquemin* (1992) 29 Con LR 24.
3   (1988) 42 BLR 86.
4   (1989) 47 BLR 55.
5   (1978 Revision).

payment by demonstrating that the claim included sums to which the sub-contractor was not entitled, either because certain work had not been done or because the work was rendered worthless because of the sub-contractor's breaches of contract.

1.21   Similarly, in *A Cameron Ltd v John Mowlem and Company plc*,[1] the Court of Appeal decided that the contractor could dispute the amount due to the sub-contractor on the grounds that the sub-contractor's valuation had included sums for work not 'properly executed'. Clause 21.4.1.1 of DOM/1 entitled the sub-contractor to be paid 'the total value of the Sub-contract work on site properly executed'. The courts have continued to review the application of the principle of abatement under building contracts. In *Mellowes Archital Limited v Bell Projects Limited*,[2] the Court of Appeal considered the question of abatement under DOM/1. The respondent to the appeal engaged the appellant as sub-contractor. The appellant had issued an application for summary judgment in respect of monies due under two interim certificates. The respondent claimed against the appellant, not on the basis that the works were defective, but that there had been delay in the performance of the sub-contractor which had given rise to damages being suffered by the main contractor. The Official Referee had held at first instance that the main contractor had failed to comply with the time periods for notice contained in clause 23.2 and therefore any right of set-off failed. However, the Official Referee also held that the main contractor could rely upon the option of abatement. However, the Court of Appeal held this to be wrong. The cases on abatement were concerned with the reduced value of works and not with collateral or consequential loss arising from delay in performance. According to Buxton LJ (at p 1322):

> 'That rule [the principle in *Mondel v Steel*] does not apply to claims based on delay. I do not see any oddity or inconvenience in that. The difference between abatement and set-off is only of significance in very particular situations ...'

According to Hobhouse LJ (at p 1323):

> 'It is therefore clear that, for a party to be able to rely upon the common law right to abate the price which he pays for goods supplied or work done, he must be able to assert that the breach of contract has directly affected and reduced the actual value of the goods or work – "the thing itself". In other words any other loss or damage, if it is to be relied upon by way of answer to a claim for the price, has to arise from the principle of equitable set-off. In most contractual relationships there would be no need to draw a distinction between the two types of defence. But under DOM/1 it is necessary to do so.'

1.22   The question of reducing the monies payable to a sub-contractor under DOM/1 was also considered by His Honour Judge Esyr Lewis QC in *Barrett Steel Building Limited v Amec Construction Limited*.[3] Amec was main contractor for building works at a hospital, with Barrett Steel as sub-contractor for the design, supply and erection of the structural steelwork. The sub-contract was based on DOM/2 (in all material respects the same as DOM/1). On Amec's refusal to pay certain interim applications, Barrett applied to the courts for summary judgment and/or an interim payment in accordance with RSC Ord 14 or RSC Ord 29 respectively. Amec alleged that the design of the steelwork was defective and the steelwork was unfit for its

---

1   (1990) 52 BLR 24.
2   [1997] CILL 1320.
3   [1997] 15 CLD 10–07.

purpose. Necessary remedial works cost £47,845, exclusive of VAT. Amec alleged that it could defend on the following grounds:

- the sub-contract price could be abated by reason of the defects in the floor slab;
- clause 23.2 of DOM/2 permitted a set-off against the sub-contractor's applications for payment;
- payment of the sums claimed by the sub-contractor was not due as the work was not 'properly executed' as required by clause 21.1.4.1 of DOM/2.

The sub-contractor argued that there was no defence to Barrett's claim for the following reasons:

- there was no difference between the so-called abatement as pleaded and the claim to set off the costs of the remedial works. If the main contractor was correct, this rendered the sub-contractor's right to argue non-compliance with the set-off provisions in the sub-contract an illusory protection;
- the set-off was invalid, not having been quantified in detail and with reasonable accuracy as provided for by clause 23.2.2 of DOM/2;
- there was no loss and/or expense and/or damage at the date of the purported notice and, on the facts of the particular case, the set-off had been retracted in correspondence.

The Official Referee concluded that a contractor might effectively have three lines of defence. These were:

- an abatement of the sub-contractor's claim by deducting a sum of money corresponding to the reduction in value of the defective works;
- a set-off for remedial works in accordance with the relevant provisions under the sub-contract;
- contractually, the contractor was only obliged to pay for those works properly carried out.

1.23   However, the courts do not always throw the contractor a lifeline when he has failed to apply the set-off provisions properly. In *Hermcrest plc v G Percy Trentham Limited*,[1] Trentham, having misapplied the set-off provisions under clause 23 of DOM/1 in attempting to sustain a cross-claim for alleged delay caused by the sub-contractor, relied on clause 12 of DOM/1 to defend its actions. Under clause 12.2 the sub-contractor 'shall pay or allow to the contractor a sum equivalent to any loss or damage suffered or incurred by the contractor'. Trentham argued unsuccessfully before the Court of Appeal that this created an independent right of set-off that did not require qualification or notice under clause 23.

1.24   It may be that the somewhat arcane law of abatement assisting a contractor in his dispute with a sub-contractor may now be of lesser importance with the coming into force of the Housing Grants, Construction and Regeneration Act 1996 and the Scheme for Construction Contracts (England and Wales) Regulations 1998, which are discussed more fully at **1.33** et seq.

---

1   (1991) 53 BLR 104.

PAY WHEN PAID

1.25   One of the more acutely perceived contractual abuses, at least in the eyes of sub-contractors and long discussed in the construction industry press, has been that of pay when paid. This recognises that many contractors are little more than managers, with over 80 per cent of work on site carried out by sub-contractors. One argument is that it is only fair that main contractors should have no greater liability to sub-contractors than the value of monies they have received from a client or funder of a particular project. Why should the main contractor, who is at the mercy of monies received from the client, owe any greater liability than to pass on monies to the extent that he has received them from the client? Unfortunately, there is great potential for abuse. First, many contractors set up a variety of claims (often spurious) against sub-contractors and, secondly, with an absence of contractual links between client and sub-contractor, sub-contractors are not in a position to request and obtain details from clients as to monies received by the main contractor which may not have been passed on to the sub-contractors. This means that sub-contractors can provide a generous interest-free loan to main contractors.

1.26   There is case-law on the practice of pay when paid, much of which has emanated from the Far East. In *Brightside Mechanical and Electrical Services Group Ltd v Hyundai Engineering and Construction Co Ltd*,[1] clause 11(b) of the sub-contract stated:

> 'Within 5 days of the receipt by the Contractor of the sum included in any Certificate of the Architect the Contractor shall notify and pay to the Sub-contractor the total value certified therein ... less ... any sum to which the Contractor may be entitled in respect of the delay in completion of the Sub-contract Works or any section thereof.'

The architect certified a sum of some $1.6 million as being due to the plaintiff sub-contractor which, following permitted deductions, meant a sum for payment of $924,711. The employer failed to pay the defendant main contractor because of claims relating to late completion. This led to the main contractor refusing to pay monies otherwise due to the sub-contractor, who sued the main contractor, bringing summary judgment proceedings. The main contractor's argument was simple. In the absence of any monies received from the client, there was no liability to the sub-contractor. The proceedings were stayed to arbitration and the sub-contractor appealed to the Singapore High Court. Here, Thean J dismissed the sub-contractor's appeal. Clause 11(b) of the sub-contract contemplated the actual receipt by the main contractor of the sum included in the certificate; therefore, the main contractor was not obliged to pay until he had actually received monies from the employer. The rigours of the Far East approach may be absent in other jurisdictions. According to *Keating on Building Contracts*:[2]

> 'In the United States, such a clause [pay when paid] has been construed as postponing payment by a main contractor for a reasonable period of time but not as disentitling a sub-contractor from payment where the employer becomes insolvent and the main contractor remains unpaid.'

---

1   (1988) 41 BLR 111.
2   6th edn (Sweet & Maxwell, 1995) p 323.

1.27   Two US decisions are cited in *Keating*: *Thomas J Dyer Co v Bishop International Engineering Co*[1] and *Aesco Steel Incorporated v JA Jones Construction Company and Fidelity and Deposit Company of Maryland*.[2] The editors of *Keating* suggest that an English court might consider a pay when paid clause, in the context of the Unfair Contract Terms Act 1977, to be subject to the requirement of reasonableness. They also mention, in passing, the decision of the High Court of New Zealand, *Smith & Smith Glass Ltd v Winstone Architectural Cladding Systems Ltd*,[3] a decision of Master Towle delivered on 4 October 1991, in which he considered a number of US and Far Eastern cases. In this particular case, Winstone were sub-contractors for the curtain walling for a development in Auckland, New Zealand, with Smith & Smith as their sub-contractor and, in the contractual framework, a sub-sub-contractor for the supply and fixing of glass and related works. Winstone defended proceedings brought by Smith & Smith, not on the basis of any alleged defects in the work carried out, but solely on the principle of pay when paid, the circumstances for which it was alleged had not occurred. The relevant contract clauses provided:

> 'Payment will be made in accordance with the Contract documents. Before any progress payment is made the necessary Public Liabiity Insurance, Note 6, shall be delivered to the office of Angus Construction Ltd [the Main Contractor]. Payments will be made within 5 working days of receipt of the Client's cheque.

> Payment shall be made by the 20th of the month following the month in which the invoice is sent to the Sub-contractor. No lien or maintenance retentions are to be held on supply only contracts. The only permissible deductions shall be:
> Any deductions necessary to comply with the Wages Protection and Contractor's Liens Act 1979.
> Any deductions to cover maintenance retentions in accordance with the NZIA General Conditions of Contract.

> Detailed progress claims in accordance with the attached format are to be in our hands by the 21st of each month (with diary entries attached – see item 10) for the calendar month preceeding. We will endeavour (this is not to be considered a guarantee) to pay these claims within 5 days after payment to Winstone Architectural Ltd of monies claimed on behalf of the Sub-contractor. If your claim is not received by the 21st of the month, it may be included in the following month's claim.'

1.28   Master Towle concluded that it may be possible to include in contracts clear and unambiguous conditions which need to be met before payment is made. Clauses needed to be analysed to see if they fell within the category of 'pay when paid' or 'pay if paid'. According to Master Towle:

> 'It seems however that if the parties wish to regulate their liability to pay the party with whom they are in sub-contract and to prescribe that their liability arises only insofar as they themselves receive payment from the Owner or Head Contractor they must do so by express agreement...'

He continued:

---

1   303 F2d 655 (6th Circuit) 1962.
2   (1988) 4 Const LJ 310.
3   (1993) CILL 894.

'For myself I believe that unless the condition precedent is spelt out in clear and precise terms and accepted by both parties, then clauses such as the two particular ones identified in this proceeding do no more than identify the time at which certain things are required to be done, and should not be extended into the "if" category to prevent a Sub-contractor who has done the work from being paid merely because the party with whom he contracts has not been paid by someone higher up the chain.'

1.29   Although counsel had referred the judge to the Singaporean decision in *Brightside Mechanical & Electrical Services Group*,[1] he was able to distinguish that decision because the matter was not dealt with on a final basis. The court reached the conclusion that in the Singapore jurisdiction the plaintiff was not entitled to summary judgment without the matter being considered fully. He did concede that two Hong Kong decisions, *Hong Kong Teakwood Ltd v Shui On Construction Co Ltd*[2] and *Schindler Lips (Hong Kong) Ltd v Shui On Construction Co Ltd*,[3] not followed by him, lent some weight to the defendant's argument on the interpretation of pay when paid clauses.

1.30   There has been only limited discussion in England of the status of pay when paid clauses. The question arose in *Maidenhead Electrical Services Limited v Johnson Control Systems Limited*,[4] a decision of Mr Recorder Knight QC sitting on Official Referee's Business. The case may be of relatively limited general application, given the specially drafted nature of the contract in question. Glaxo had employed a contractor to construct a new research campus at Stevenage. Johnson Control Systems was sub-contractor for the installation of building management and control systems, with Johnson employing Maidenhead Electrical as its own sub-contractor for electrical installation work. The sub-contract between Johnson and Maidenhead was based on Johnson's purchase order and the terms of the principal sub-contract. When Maidenhead sought payment Johnson refused on the basis of pay when paid. Matters proceeded by way of a preliminary issue before the recorder. Johnson relied upon clause 17 which stated:

'17 PAYMENTS ... Within 14 days of the receipt by the Company of any payment pursuant to such applications the Company [Johnson] shall account to the Contractor [Maidenhead] for all monies properly due hereunder to the Contractor in respect of the Works less any sums which may be deducted from such payments ...'

The wording of the clause was not such as to create a pay when paid obligation.

THE LATHAM REPORT

1.31   An understanding that all was not well with the construction industry led to the appointment of Sir Michael Latham to report on the ills of the industry in a government-sponsored move. Sir Michael produced two reports. The first, in December 1993, Sir Michael's interim report, was *Trust and Money*, the two factors continually lacking in the construction industry. Subsequently, in July 1994, he

---

1   (1988) 41 BLR 111.
2   [1984] Hong Kong LR 235.
3   (1984) 29 BLR 95.
4   [1997] 15 CLD 10–03.

produced his final report, *Constructing the Team*. The twin pillars of the Latham report were repairing relationships, partly through a greater emphasis on partnering at the front end of projects, and short-order dispute-resolution mechanisms (particularly adjudication) during the currency of projects, to nip problems in the bud as and when they arose. Sir Michael also considered particular changes to existing insolvency law, including, on the insolvency of the employer, conferring the status of preferential creditor on an unpaid contractor. Importantly for contractors and sub-contractors, Sir Michael recommended in *Constructing the Team* (para 10.8) that payment should be subject to a trust arrangement to protect the interests of the contractor, sub-contractors and particular suppliers. The employer would set money aside in a trust fund, with the various monies held on trust for the contractor to be paid in accordance with the contract. On the contractor's insolvency, prior to completion of the works, the primary trust would fail and a secondary trust would immediately arise in favour of the sub-contractors and suppliers. Such a trust would place monies outside the strict *pari passu* rules. Sub-contractors favoured, however, what has been described as the cascade system under which money received by the contractor is held on trust by the contractor to pay himself and his sub-contractors and suppliers. Similarly, the sub-contractor, on receiving money, holds those monies on trust for himself and his own sub-contractors and suppliers down the line. This system operates in most of Canada and applies even if the trust is not written into the particular contract. Contractors disliked the cascade system, believing that such a system would reduce the amount of capital available to fund construction in the UK. Banks would not lend money to contractors if they lost control over the contractor's contract debts which became subject to trust status.

1.32   With the exception of certain ad hoc arrangements, one being that based on the principle established in *Lovell Construction Ltd v Independent Estates plc*,[1] the best-known examples of trusts of the contract sum are the little-used form published by the Electrical Contractor's Association in 1993 and the New Engineering Contract (NEC).[2] Under the first, the contract sum is placed in an account from which the contractor and sub-contractors are paid by the employer. The employer is denied all rights of set-off against the account. The New Engineering Contract includes an optional clause which allows the use of the trust fund. A useful comparative table of provisons of the *Lovell*, SEACC and NEC trusts is to be found at Appendix II, pp 31 to 47 inclusive, in *Contemporary Issues in Construction Law, Volume 1 – Security for Payment*.[3]

RESPONSE TO THE LATHAM REPORT

1.33   The statutory response to *Constructing the Team* has been limited and is found in the Housing Grants, Construction and Regeneration Act 1996 (the 1996 Act). The provisions of this Act which affect the construction industry are found in Part II. Most excitedly discussed were the provisions relating to statutory adjudication. Provisions relating to payment are to be found in ss 109 to 113 inclusive. Under s 104,

---

1   [1994] 1 BCLC 31.
2   2nd edn (1995).
3   Davis and Odams (eds) (Construction Law Press, 1996).

the 1996 Act applies only to construction contracts which are, according to s 104(1)(a), contracts for the 'carrying out of construction operations'. Construction operations are defined in s 105 of the 1996 Act and cover most forms of contract which would ordinarily be anticipated to be of a construction nature. Those categories of work excluded from the ambit of the Act are set out in s 105(2) and include oil and gas, mining, process engineering, and contracts for the manufacture and supply of goods and materials. Domestic building contracts are also excluded from the 1996 Act under s 106. Section 107 makes it clear that the 1996 Act applies only to contracts which are evidenced in writing. Under s 109, the contractor is entitled to stage payments unless the works are to last less than 45 days. The parties are free to agree the amounts of the payments and the intervals at which and circumstances in which they fall due. Under s 111, there is a statutory prohibition on the withholding of monies against stage payments unless the party wishing to set off/deduct has given the prescribed notice to the recipient of the intended set-off/deduction and the grounds of the proposed set-off/deduction. In essence, this replicated many of the provisions found in standard form sub-contracts used in the construction industry and now extended. The 1996 Act studiously avoids the word 'set-off', as do the Scheme for Construction Contracts (England and Wales) Regulations 1998 (the 1998 Regulations). Section 111 refers to the withholding of payment, and the same terminology is replicated in the 1998 Regulations, which apply if the contract does not comply with the 1996 Act. Regulation 10 is prefaced 'Notice of intention to withhold payment', with the protection against arbitrary deduction being guaranteed by reg 9, which states that the party to suffer the deduction must have prior warning of the deduction. The only reference to the word 'abatement' is found in reg 9, which states:

> 'A party to a construction contract shall, not later than five days after the date on which any payment –
> (a)   becomes due from him, or
> (b)   would have become due if –
>   (i)   the other party had carried out his obligations under the contract,
>   (ii)   no set-off or abatement was permitted by reference to any sum claimed to be due under one or more other contracts,
> give notice to the other party to the contract specifying the amount (if any) of the payment he has made or proposed to make, specifying to what the payment relates and the basis on which that amount is calculated.'

Regulation 10 reads:

> 'Any notice of intention to withhold payment mentioned in Section 111 of the Act should be given not later than the prescribed period, which is to say not later than seven days before the final date for payment determined either in accordance with the construction contract, or where no such provision is made in the contract, in accordance with paragraph 8 above.'

1.34   The net result of the 1998 Regulations appears to be that claims based on abatement will similarly be regulated in the manner already found in regard to set-off provisions. Contractors will not be at the mercy of an *ex post facto* reliance on abatement. Unfortunately, the Act is not a model of clarity. There is a tendency both in s 111 of the 1996 Act and in the 1998 Regulations to refer to 'final date for payment'. However, it does seem from the general context that 'final date' actually refers to any interim or stage payment rather than the final certified sum due under the contract.

Support for this is found in reg 8, which refers to 'a final date for payment in relation to any sum which becomes due under a construction contract'. Again, the right to suspend performance for non-payment is expressly recognised in s 112 of the 1996 Act, provided notice is given of the intention in advance, and this was carried forward into standard form building contracts, as previously noted. Section 113 of the 1996 Act has been much praised by sub-contractor groups as representing an effective prohibition on the pay when paid principle, described in the 1996 Act as 'conditional payment provisions'. According to s 113(1):

> 'A provision making payment under a construction contract conditional on the payer receiving payment from a third person is ineffective, unless that third person, or any other person payment by whom is under the contract (directly or indirectly) a condition of payment by that person, is insolvent.'

The insolvency bar is an important limitation given that many developers, particularly in the late 1980s and early 1990s, became readily insolvent.

1.35   Government, conscious of possible non-compliance with the provisions of the 1996 Act, produced, after a couple of attempts that were subject to criticism, draft schemes for construction contracts which apply in the event that a contract offends against the necessary principles. The final Scheme was brought into law under the 1998 Regulations. The provisions in the Act and the Scheme relating to payment are replicated in the Appendix to this chapter.

1.36   Even if the construction industry has not, over the last 30 years or so, been an exercise in total failure, there is a feeling that the industry does need to change if it is not to go the same way as the British car industry. The industry has over-capacity; it lurches between the existence of work and a lack of work and, with many contractors fulfilling a managerial role, high capitalisation is not necessary. Employers do not assist with their desire for a 'bargain', and lawyers and quantity surveyors, the latter with a legal bent, have perhaps assisted the adversarial nature of the industry. The 1996 Act may not work, it may be unwieldy and, in practice, ill-thought-out, but it does represent a plea that things need to change. Finally, what must be of concern is, given the looseness of the 1996 Act and the potentially cumbersome nature of the Scheme, the prospect that lawyers and quantity surveyors will spend their time trying to subvert its basic principles.

Appendix

HOUSING GRANTS, CONSTRUCTION AND REGENERATION ACT 1996

. . .

PART II

. . .

Adjudication

108 Right to refer disputes to adjudication

(1) A party to a construction contract has the right to refer a dispute arising under the contract for adjudication under a procedure complying with this section.

For this purpose 'dispute' includes any difference.

(2) The contract shall –

- (a) enable a party to give notice at any time of his intention to refer a dispute to adjudication;
- (b) provide a timetable with the object of securing the appointment of the adjudicator and referral of the dispute to him within 7 days of such notice;
- (c) require the adjudicator to reach a decision within 28 days of referral or such longer period as is agreed by the parties after the dispute has been referred;
- (d) allow the adjudicator to extend the period of 28 days by up to 14 days, with the consent of the party by whom the dispute was referred;
- (e) impose a duty on the adjudicator to act impartially; and
- (f) enable the adjudicator to take the initiative in ascertaining the facts and the law.

(3) The contract shall provide that the decision of the adjudicator is binding until the dispute is finally determined by legal proceedings, by arbitration (if the contract provides for arbitration or the parties otherwise agree to arbitration) or by agreement.

The parties may agree to accept the decision of the adjudicator as finally determining the dispute.

(4) The contract shall also provide that the adjudicator is not liable for anything done or omitted in the discharge or purported discharge of his functions as adjudicator unless the act or omission is in bad faith, and that any employee or agent of the adjudicator is similarly protected from liability.

(5) If the contract does not comply with the requirements of subsections (1) to (4), the adjudication provisions of the Scheme for Construction Contracts apply.

(6) For England and Wales, the Scheme may apply the provisions of the Arbitration Act 1996 with such adaptations and modifications as appear to the Minister making the scheme to be appropriate.

For Scotland, the Scheme may incude provision conferring powers on courts in relation to adjudication and provision relating to the enforcement of the adjudicator's decision.

Payment

109   Entitlement to stage payments

(1) A party to a construction contract is entitled to payment by instalments, stage payments or other periodic payments for any work under the contract unless –

    (a)   it is specified in the contract that the duration of the work is to be less than 45 days, or

    (b)   it is agreed between the parties that the duration of the work is estimated to be less than 45 days.

(2) The parties are free to agree the amounts of the payments and the intervals at which, or circumstances in which, they become due.

(3) In the absence of such agreement, the relevant provisions of the Scheme for Construction Contracts apply.

(4) References in the following sections to a payment under the contract include a payment by virtue of this section.

110   Dates for payment

(1) Every construction contract shall –

    (a)   provide an adequate mechanism for determining what payments become due under the contract, and when, and

    (b)   provide for a final date for payment in relation to any sum which becomes due.

The parties are free to agree how long the period is to be between the date on which a sum becomes due and the final date for payment.

(2) Every construction contract shall provide for the giving of notice by a party not later than five days after the date on which a payment becomes due from him under the contract, or would have become due if –

    (a)   the other party had carried out his obligations under the contract, and

    (b)   no set-off or abatement was permitted by reference to any sum claimed to be due under one or more other contracts.

specifying the amount (if any) of the payment made or proposed to be made, and the basis on which that amount was calculated.

(3) If or to the extent that a contract does not contain such provision as is mentioned in subsection (1) or (2), the relevant provisions of the Scheme for Construction Contracts apply.

111   Notice of intention to withhold payment

(1) A party to a construction contract may not withhold payment after the final date for payment of a sum due under the contract unless he has given an effective notice of intention to withhold payment.

The notice mentioned in section 110(2) may suffice as a notice of intention to withhold payment if it complies with the requirements of this section.

(2) To be effective such a notice must specify –

    (a)   the amount proposed to be withheld and the ground for withholding payment, or

(b) if there is more than one ground, each ground and the amount attributable to it,

and must be given not later than the prescribed period before the final date for payment.

(3) The parties are free to agree what that prescribed period is to be.

In the absence of such agreement, the period shall be that provided by the Scheme for Construction Contracts.

(4) Where an effective notice of intention to withhold payment is given, but on the matter being referred to adjudication it is decided that the whole or part of the amount should be paid, the decision shall be construed as requiring payment not later than –

(a) seven days from the date of the decision, or
(b) the date which apart from the notice would have been the final date for payment,

whichever is the later.

112 Right to suspend performance for non-payment

(1) Where a sum due under a construction contract is not paid in full by the final date for payment and no effective notice to withhold payment has been given, the person to whom the sum is due has the right (without prejudice to any other right or remedy) to suspend performance of his obligations under the contract to the party by whom payment ought to have been made ('the party in default').

(2) The right may not be exercised without first giving to the party in default at least seven days' notice of intention to suspend performance, stating the ground or grounds on which it is intended to suspend performance.

(3) The right to suspend performance ceases when the party in default makes payment in full of the amount due.

(4) Any period during which performance is suspended in pursuance of the right conferred by this section shall be disregarded in computing for the purposes of any contractual time limit the time taken, by the party exercising the right or by a third party, to complete any work directly or indirectly affected by the exercise of the right.

Where a contractual time limit is set by reference to a date rather than a period, the date shall be adjusted accordingly.

113 Prohibition of conditional payment provisions

(1) A provision making payment under a construction contract conditional on the payer receiving payment from a third person is ineffective, unless that third person, or any other person payment by whom is under the contract (directly or indirectly) a condition of payment by that third person, is insolvent.

(2) For the purposes of this section a company becomes insolvent –

(a) on the making of an administration order against it under Part II of the Insolvency Act 1986,
(b) on the appointment of an administrative receiver or a receiver or manager of its property under Chapter I of Part III of that Act, or the appointment of a receiver under Chapter III of that Part,
(c) on the passing of a resolution for voluntary winding-up without a declaration of solvency under section 89 of that Act, or

    (d)   on the making of a winding-up order under Part IV or V of that Act.

(3) For the purpose of this section a partnership becomes insolvent –

    (a)   on the making of a winding-up order against it under any provision of the Insolvency Act 1986 as applied by an order under section 420 of that Act, or
    (b)   when sequestration is awarded on the estate of the partnership under section 12 of the Bankruptcy (Scotland) Act 1985 or the partnership grants a trust deed for its creditors.

(4) For the purposes of this section an individual becomes insolvent –

    (a)   on the making of a bankruptcy order against him under Part IX of the Insolvency Act 1986, or
    (b)   on the sequestration of his estate under the Bankruptcy (Scotland) Act 1985 or when he grants a trust deed for his creditors.

(5) A company, partnership or individual shall also be treated as insolvent on the occurrence of any event corresponding to those specified in subsection (2), (3) or (4) under the law of Northern Ireland or of a country outside the United Kingdom.

(6) Where a provision is rendered ineffective by subsection (1), the parties are free to agree other terms for payment.

In the absence of such agreement, the relevant provisions of the Scheme for Construction Contracts apply.

Supplementary provisions

114   The Scheme for Construction Contracts

(1) The Minister shall by regulations make a scheme ('the Scheme for Construction Contracts') containing provision about the matters referred to in the preceding provisions of this Part.

(2) Before making any regulations under this section the Minister shall consult such persons as he thinks fit.

(3) In this section 'the Minister' means –

    (a)   for England and Wales, the Secretary of State, and
    (b)   for Scotland, the Lord Advocate.

(4) Where any provisions of the Scheme for Construction Contracts apply by virtue of this Part in default of contractual provision agreed by the parties, they have effect as implied terms of the contract concerned.

(5) Regulations under this section shall not be made unless a draft of them has been approved by resolution of each House of Parliament.

115   Service of notices, etc

(1) The parties are free to agree on the manner of service of any notice or other document required or authorised to be served in pursuance of the construction contract or for any of the purposes of this Part.

(2) If or to the extent that there is no such agreement the following provisions apply.

(3) A notice or other document may be served on a person by any effective means.

(4) If a notice or other document is addressed, pre-paid and delivered by post –

  (a) to the addressee's last known principal residence of, if he is or has been carrying on a trade, profession or business, his last known principal business address, or

  (b) where the addressee is a body corporate, to the body's registered or principal office,

it shall be treated as effectively served.

(5) This section does not apply to the service of documents for the purposes of legal proceedings, for which provision is made by rules of court.

(6) References in this Part to a notice or other document include any form of communication in writing and references to service shall be construed accordingly.

SCHEME FOR CONSTRUCTION CONTRACTS (ENGLAND AND WALES) REGULATIONS 1998, SI 1998/649

. . .

PART II

PAYMENT

Entitlement to and amount of stage payments

1. Where the parties to a relevant construction contract fail to agree –

   (a) the amount of any instalment or stage or periodic payment for any work under the contract, or
   (b) the intervals at which, or circumstances in which, such payments become due under that contract, or
   (c) both of the matters mentioned in sub-paragraphs (a) and (b) above,

the relevant provisions of paragraphs 2 to 4 below shall apply.

2. (1) The amount of any payment by way of instalments or stage or periodic payments in respect of a relevant period shall be the difference between the amount determined in accordance with sub-paragraph (2) and the amount determined in accordance with sub-paragraph (3).

(2) The aggregate of the following amounts –

   (a) an amount equal to the value of any work performed in accordance with the relevant construction contract during the period from the commencement of the contract to the end of the relevant period (excluding any amount calculated in accordance with sub-paragraph (b)),
   (b) where the contract provides for payment for materials, an amount equal to the value of any materials manufactured on site or brought onto site for the purposes of the works during the period from the commencement of the contract to the end of the relevant period, and
   (c) any other amount or sum which the contract specifies shall be payable during or in respect of the period from the commencement of the contract to the end of the relevant period.

(3) The aggregate of any sums which have been paid or are due for payment by way of instalments, stage or period payments during the period from the commencement of the contract to the end of the relevant period.

(4) An amount calculated in accordance with this paragraph shall not exceed the difference between –

   (a) the contract price, and
   (b) the aggregate of the instalments or stage or periodic payments which have become due.

Dates for payment

3. Where the parties to a construction contract fail to provide an adequate mechanism for determining either what payments become due under the contract, or when they become due for payment, or both, the relevant provisions of paragraphs 4 to 7 shall apply.

4. Any payment of a kind mentioned in paragraph 2 above shall become due on whichever of the following dates occurs later –

    (a) the expiry of 7 days following the relevant period mentioned in paragraph 2(1) above, or

    (b) the making of a claim by the payee.

5. The final payment payable under a relevant construction contract, namely the payment of an amount equal to the difference (if any) between –

    (a) the contract price, and

    (b) the aggregate of any instalment or stage or periodic payments which have become due under the contract,

shall become due on the expiry of –

    (a) 30 days following completion of the work, or

    (b) the making a claim by the payee,

whichever is the later.

6. Payment of the contract price under a construction contract (not being a relevant construction contract) shall become due on

    (a) the expiry of 30 days following the completion of the work, or

    (b) the making of a claim by the payee,

whichever is the later.

7. Any other payment under a construction contract shall become due

    (a) on the expiry of 7 days following the completion of the work to which the payment relates, or

    (b) the making of a claim by the payee,

whichever is the later.

Final date for payment

8. (1) Where the parties to a construction contract fail to provide a final date for payment in relation to any sum which becomes due under a construction contract, the provisions of this paragraph shall apply.

(2) The final date for the making of any payment of a kind mentioned in paragraphs 2, 5, 6 or 7, shall be 17 days from the date that payment becomes due.

Notice specifying amount of payment

9. A party to a construction contract shall, not later than 5 days after the date on which any payment –

    (a) becomes due from him, or

    (b) would have become due, if –

        (i)   the other party had carried out his obligations under the contract, and

        (ii)   no set-off or abatement was permitted by reference to any sum claimed to be due under one or more other contracts

    give notice to the other party to the contract specifying the amount (if any) of the payment he has made or proposes to make, specifying to what the payment relates and the basis on which that amount is calculated.

Notice of intention to withhold payment

10. Any notice of intention to withhold payment mentioned in section 111 of the Act shall be given not later than the prescribed period, which is to say not later than 7 days before the final date for payment determined either in accordance with the construction contract, or where no such provision is made in the contract, in accordance with paragraph 8 above.

Prohibition of conditional payment provisions

11. Where a provision making payment under a construction contract conditional on the payer receiving payment from a third person is ineffective as mentioned in section 113 of the Act, and the parties have not agreed other terms for payment, the relevant provisions of –

(a) paragraphs 2, 4, 5, 7, 8, 9 and 10 shall apply in the case of a relevant construction contract, and

(b) paragraphs 6, 7, 8, 9 and 10 shall apply in the case of any other construction contract.

Interpretation

12. In this Part of the Scheme for Construction Contracts –

'claim by the payee' means a written notice given by the party carrying out work under a construction contract to the other party specifying the amount of any payment or payments which he considers to be due and the basis on which it is, or they are calculated;

'contract price' means the entire sum payable under the construction contract in respect of the work;

'relevant construction contract' means any construction contract other than one –

(a) which specifies that the duration of the work is to be less than 45 days, or

(b) in respect of which the parties agree that the duration of the work is estimated to be less than 45 days;

'relevant period' means a period which is specified in, or is calculated by reference to the construction contract or where no such period is so specified or is so calculable, a period of 28 days;

'value of work' means an amount determined in accordance with the construction contract under which the work is performed or where the contract contains no such provision, the cost of any work performed in accordance with that contract together with an amount equal to any overhead or profit included in the contract price;

'work' means any of the work or services mentioned in section 104 of the Act.

Chapter 2

RETENTION FUNDS

Introduction – Retention under main building contracts – Separate bank accounts – Sub-contracts – Mutual debits and credits – Injunctions – Administrative receivership – Assignment of rights – Nominated sub-contractor retention money – Retention provisions under the management contract, JCT 87 – The New Engineering Contract – Retention bonds – Appendix

INTRODUCTION

2.1   The retention fund, although heavily maligned, remains an intrinsic part of UK contracting methods. As long ago as 1964, the government-commissioned Banwell Report[1] recommended its abolition. More recently, it has received sustained criticism from, among others, specialist sub-contracting groups. It is a source of concern to both main and sub-contractors that the retention fund may not be immune from the effects of employer insolvency. Sir Michael Latham, in his report, *Constructing the Team*, considered the question of retention:

> 'The retention system is supposed to be a mechanism whereby clients can build up a fund during the course of a project which will act as an inducement to the contractor to remedy any defect during the liability period. The idea in principle is a sound one, though in practice the system no longer operates in that manner. A better option would be to replace it in the contracts with retention [An argument used against retention bonds is that they might be much more expensive than retention, and might tempt the client's quantity surveyor to undervalue interim work as a precaution. (CIEC final report). The former would presumably depend upon the reputation of the contractor, and the latter could be referred to an adjudicator, or be overcome by the use of milestones/activity schedules] reducing in value as each milestone section of the work is completed. Some clients may prefer a cash retention system, and that option should also be available for them, provided that the money is retained in a secure trust fund.' (para 11.1, p 99)

2.2   The retention clause, which is found in most standard form construction contracts, permits employers to withhold a percentage of sums due which would otherwise be payable to the contractor, as security against the contractor's performance. Under the standard building contracts, JCT 80, JCT CD 81 and IFC 84, including the 1998 editions, under which the previous principles have not been changed, the retention is released to the contractor in two portions: at practical completion and at making good of defects. The principal civil engineering contracts, ICE 6th edition and ICE Design and Construct Conditions of Contract operate in an identical manner, with one half of the retention released at substantial completion and

---

1   The report of the Committee on the Placing and Management of Contracts for Building and Civil Engineering Works, chaired by Sir Harold Banwell.

the second half at the expiry of the defects correction period. Those involved in the administration of construction contracts know that the principle of retention is frequently abused by employers. Retention monies are not released to the contractor strictly in accordance with the contractual provisions. Some employers, who consider that they have a legitimate claim against the contractor, illegally withhold retention monies pending the resolution of claims for which, strictly speaking, the retention is not held as security. That said, contractors sometimes forget that, notwithstanding clauses in the JCT contracts that state that the employer's interest in the retention is fiduciary as trustee for the contractor, a wide range of set-off rights remains vested in the employer. According to clause 30.1.1.2 of JCT 98 (similar provisions being found in clause 30.1.1.2 of JCT 80 and clause 30.4.3 of JCT CD 81 and 98):

> 'Notwithstanding the fiduciary interest of the Employer in the Retention as stated in clause 30.5.1 the Employer is entitled to exercise any right under this Contract of withholding and/or deduction from monies due or to become due to the Contractor against any amount so due under an Interim Certificate whether or not any Retention is included in that Interim Certificate by the operation of clause 30.4.'

2.3   On occasions, it is inconvenient for particular employers to set up separate bank accounts for retention monies. If the employer is a UK subsidiary of an overseas group, it may not have authority to set up bank accounts without the consent of an overseas parent, which might require numerous explanations and create delay. In those instances, an escrow account may be preferable along the lines indicated in the Appendix to this chapter.

RETENTION UNDER MAIN BUILDING CONTRACTS

2.4   The status of retention money is clearly established in law as far as JCT contracts are concerned. In JCT 80, JCT CD 81 and IFC 84 and the 98 versions, it is clear that 'the employer's interest in the retention is fiduciary as trustee for the contractor' (clause 30.5.1 of JCT 80; clause 30.4.2.1 of JCT CD 81; and, provided the employer is not a local authority, clause 4.4 of IFC 84). With the exception of IFC 84, which is silent on the point, the retention is to be placed in a separate bank account if the contractor so requests (clause 30.5.3 of JCT 80, excluding the local authorities' version in clause 30.4.2.2 of JCT CD 81). The operation of a separate bank account may be crucial to a contractor in the event of the employer's insolvency. Clause 4.2 of MW 80 makes no reference to the employer's interest in the retention being fiduciary as trustee for the contractor, and in this regard parallels the position under the civil engineering contracts. Therefore, subject to tracing remedies in equity the contractor is at serious risk in the event of the employer's insolvency.

2.5   As referred to above, clause 30.5.1 of JCT 80 states that 'The Employer's interest in the Retention is fiduciary as trustee for the Contractor and for any Nominated Sub-Contractor'. Identical wording is found in clause 30.4.2.1 of JCT CD 81, and similar wording is found in clause 4.4 of IFC 84. Clause 4.8 of JCT 87 (management contract) states that 'The Employer's interest in the Retention is fiduciary as trustee for the Management Contractor and for any Works Contractor'.

SEPARATE BANK ACCOUNTS

2.6   A series of decisions show that the standard JCT clause obliges the employer to set aside retention monies in a separate trust fund: *Rayack Construction Ltd v Lampeter Meat Company Ltd;*[1] *Re Arthur Sanders Ltd;*[2] *Wates Construction (London) Ltd v Franthom Property Ltd.*[3] In *Rayack Construction*, counsel on behalf of the employer suggested that there were no specific words in JCT contracts requiring the retention monies to be set aside in a separate bank account. Counsel argued that there was at least a triable issue whether such a provision could be implied. However, Vinelott J held:

> '... condition 30(4), construed in the context of the articles of agreement as a whole, does impose an obligation on an employer to appropriate and set aside as a separate trust fund a sum equal to that part of the sum certified in any interim certificate as due in respect of work completed which the employer is entitled to retain during the defects liability period
> ...
>
> If sub-clauses (3) and (4) of condition 30 are read together, it is in my judgment clear that the purpose of the provisions for retention under the terms of condition 30(4)(a) is to protect both employer and contractor against the risk of insolvency of the other. The employer is protected by his right to retain a proportion of the sum certified as due in respect of work done against the risk that claims in respect of any failure to carry out the architect's instructions or in respect of delay or other breaches of the contractor's obligations will, in the event of the contractor's insolvency, rank as unsecured debts. The contractor is protected by the provisions of condition 30(4)(a) against the risk that his claim for payment of monies retained by the employer will similarly rank as an unsecured debt, save only for the *lien* confirmed by the proviso to condition 26(2). Thus, both are protected if and to the extent that the employer carries out his obligation to set aside as a separate trust fund the sum equal to the retention monies. The contractor must be exposed to some degree of risk jeopardy if that is not done.'[4]

SUB-CONTRACTS

2.7   The principle established in *Rayack* was extended in *Re Arthur Sanders Ltd.* Here, the trial judge, Nourse J, held that the main contract, JCT 63, and the sub-contract, the NFBTE/FASS sub-contract (the Green Form) were 'back to back' and extended the retention trust protection in favour of a nominated sub-contractor. In the words of Nourse J:[5]

> 'Clause 30(4)(a) creates ... a trust of the retention moneys in favour of the contractor. It is then necessary to go to Clause 27, which deals with nominated sub-contractors. Although the employer's agent nominates the sub-contractors, it is the contractor who contracts with them ... no sub-contractor can be nominated who will not (save where the parties otherwise agree) enter into a sub-contract which provides for the matters set out in the nine paragraphs of sub-clause (a). The only one of those paragraphs with which this case

---

1   (1981) 12 BLR 30.
2   (1981) 17 BLR 125.
3   (1991) 53 BLR 23.
4   (1981) 12 BLR 30 at 37–38.
5   (1981) 17 BLR 125 at 137–138.

is directly concerned is (viii), which provides that the contractor shall hold a due proportion of the retentions on trust for the sub-contractor. That gives to the sub-contractor a right corresponding to that given to the contractor by Clause 30(4)(a) of the RIBA Conditions. . . .

The sub-contract therefore takes effect as an assignment to the sub-contractor, made with the authority and with the knowledge of the employer, of a due proportion of the contractor's beneficial interest in the retention moneys under Clause 30(4)(a) of the main contract. In my judgment there can be no doubt that that is the effect of Clause 11(h) of the FASS Sub-contract. If authority be needed for that it can be found in the decision of Parry J in *Re Tout and Finch*.'[1]

MUTUAL DEBITS AND CREDITS

2.8   Nourse J felt obliged to comment on the decision of the House of Lords in *British Eagle International Airlines Ltd v Compagnie Nationale Air France*,[2] even if simply to state that the decision in *British Eagle* (at p 140) 'has nothing to do with this kind of case, and indeed the contrary was not suggested in argument'. It had been suggested in *Hudson on Building and Engineering Contracts*[3] that the retention trust decisions, existing at the date of publication of the book, gave inadequate consideration to the decision in *British Eagle*. In that case, the House of Lords analysed the lawfulness of the arrangement for mutual credits and debits between international airlines (under which no monies ever changed hands) in the light of s 302 of the Companies Act 1948 (the predecessor of s 107 of the Insolvency Act 1986). The scheme was held invalid as against British Eagle's liquidator, who sought release from claims by Air France. The monies were required to be released to creditors of British Eagle under the *pari passu* principle. In *British Eagle*, the International Air Traffic Association (IATA) merely performed the function of a clearing house for the inter-airline debts with the monies never being vested in the IATA.

Monies on trust for third parties

2.9   The principle of monies that could fall outside those available to a liquidator was discussed by Gibson J in *Carreras Rothmans Ltd v Freeman Mathews Treasure Ltd*.[4] A employed B to promote A's product, with B acting via third party sub-contractors. With B in financial difficulties, A and B agreed that a special account would be opened into which A would pay a sum equivalent to the monies due to the third parties. Subsequently, B went into liquidation, with monies remaining in the special account. A paid the third parties direct and took an assignment of the third parties' debts covered by the special account. It was A's argument against B's liquidator that monies in the special account were held on trust for the purpose of paying the third parties, with B contending that the arrangement was contrary to s 302 of the Companies Act 1948. The judge held that the monies were held on trust for the third parties and referred to Lord Wilberforce in *Quistclose Investments Ltd v Rolls*

---

1   [1954] 1 WLR 178.
2   [1975] 1 WLR 758.
3   11th edn (Sweet & Maxwell, 1994), paras 8.081–086, 13.131, 14.045, 16.031, 16.055–058.
4   [1985] 1 Ch 207.

Razer Ltd,[1] who said that: 'A relationship of a fiduciary character or trust in favour, as a primary trust, of the creditors, and secondarily, if the primary trust fails, of the third person . . .'

Interim certificate

2.10 As soon as the contractor requests (which he can do at any time) that the retention is held separately, the employer is bound to set it aside in the sense of physically placing it in a separately identifiable bank account. An interim certificate that states the existence of retention monies is insufficient identification of the retention: *Wates Construction (London) Ltd v Franthom Property Ltd*.[2] According to Beldam LJ:

> 'The second argument put forward on behalf of the employer was that he was only bound to appropriate a sum to the fund and was not bound to set it aside in the sense of placing it in a separately identifiable account. It was argued that the statement in the interim certificates which had been issued was a sufficient appropriation of the fund for that purpose. . . . the first duty of the trustee, [which] is to safeguard the fund in the interests of the beneficiaries. It would be, in my judgment, a breach of trust for any trustee to use the trust fund in his own business, and there can be found a clear instance of that in the case of *Re Davies*[3] where the trustee who, from the best of motives, used the trust fund for the purpose of providing the beneficiary with an increased income and to reduce the overdraft of a business in which he had an interest, conceded that that was not a proper investment or use to make of a trust fund. . . .
>
> It is further argued that the interest of the beneficiaries in the retention fund, that is to say the contractors and sub-contractors, was sufficiently protected provided the sum was identifiable because they would have a right in equity to trace. That, of course, depends on the ability to identify a fund into which the money had been placed, albeit a mixed fund. It is of no value whatever if the money was, for example, paid away to the general creditors of the employer's business who had given value without notice of any trust. Consequently, it seems to me that the right to trace would in many instances be of no value to the contractor and sub-contractors should the employer use the retention fund in his own business and for one reason or another become insolvent, the fund being unable to be traced.'[4]

2.11 Again, in *Wates Construction*, the trust principle survived although the parties had agreed to delete clause 30.5.3 from the version used of JCT 80. The contractor retained a right to compel the employer to set up a separate trust account for the retention monies and simple removal of the clause was insufficient. In the words of the Court of Appeal:

> 'The words of clause 30.5.1 under which the trust is created are quite clear. Secondly, the fact of deletion in the present case is of no assistance because the parties in agreeing to the deletion of clause 30.5.3 may well have had different reasons for doing so and it is not possible to draw from the deletion of that clause a settled intention of the parties common to each of them that the ordinary incidence of the duties of trustee clearly created by clause 30.5.1 were to be modified or indeed removed. It may have been thought by one of the

---

1 [1970] AC 567 at 581.
2 (1991) 53 BLR 23.
3 [1902] 2 Ch 314.
4 (1991) 53 BLR 23 at 31–32.

parties to have been unnecessary to have included clause 30.5.3. It may have been that one of them thought that the employer should have been liable to account for any interest to the contractor if the retention fund was placed in a separate account. But there may be various reasons, which it is not possible to set out in full, why the clause was deleted and it is quite impossible to draw any clear inference from the fact of deletion. I therefore would reject an argument based upon the fact of deletion and can see no ambiguity upon which reference to that deleted clause could assist.'[1]

The decision in *Wates Construction* caused consternation among local authorities, which were concerned that the policy of using retention monies held against contractors to finance future public works was under threat. As a result, some local authorities started to amend standard form contracts to remove all references to trust status for retention monies.

Interim payments

2.12   Once a contractor has asked for the trust fund to be constituted, standard JCT clauses, such as clause 30.4.2 of JCT CD 81 and clause 30.5.3 of JCT 80, do not oblige the contractor to repeat a request for retention monies to be set aside in a trust account each time an interim payment is made and the employer exercises his right to retention: *JF Finnegan v Ford Sellar Morris Developments Ltd*.[2] According to the Official Referee, His Honour Judge Esyr Lewis QC:

'For Ford Sellar, [counsel] has submitted, in essence, that in the present case clause 30.4.2.2, on its proper construction, requires the contractor, each time that an interim payment is made and the employer exercises his right of retention, and only then, to request the employer to pay the retention into a separate bank account and no such request was ever made. In short, he submits that the request made by Finnegan's solicitors in April 1991 was too late as the contract prescribes the timing of the requests. In any event, he submits that the construction he contends for is an arguable one and that the court should not therefore grant a mandatory injunction in an interlocutory application. He places emphasis on the word "then" in the phrase "if the contractor then so requests" and seeks to link this phrase directly with the words "at the time of each interim payment". He also submits that in the *Wates* case the deletion of the clause entitling the contractor to request the retention money be paid into a separate banking account left the court free to decide that the clause declaring the employer to have a fiduciary interest in the retention money as trustee for the contractor imported an obligation on the employer to open a separate banking account, since there was no contractual clause explicitly defining the circumstances in which the contractor could require the employer to open a separate banking account as there is in the present case. ... I do not consider that a construction of clause 30.4.2.2 which requires the contractor to make a request every time the employer made a retention on an interim payment makes good sense. In any event, I do not accept that the phrase "if the contractor then so requests" relates to the phrase "at the time of each interim payment". In my view the earlier phrase is linked to the words "to the extent that the Employer exercises his right under Clause 30.4". I consider, therefore, that once the employer indicates that he is exercising his right to retain a percentage of the sum due to the contractor when making an interim payment, the contractor is entitled at any time to request the employer to place the retention in a separate banking account and he is not obliged to make repetitive requests that this should be done each time an interim payment

---

1   (1991) 53 BLR 23 at 36.
2   (1991) 53 BLR 38.

is made. This interpretation of clause 30.4.2.2, in my judgment, accords with the purpose of clause 30.4.2.1, which makes the employer a trustee of the retention money for the benefit of the contractor alone, although the employer has the right of recourse to the retention under the provisions of clause 30.4.3. If the employer does not place the retention in a separate banking account "so designated as to identify the amount that is the retention held by the employer on trust" … the object of clause 30.4.2.1 could be frustrated by the bankruptcy or liquidation of the employer.'[1]

INJUNCTIONS

2.13   For contractors, it became common knowledge in the early 1990s that, if the employer failed or refused to open a separate bank account for retention monies, the contractor's rights could be enforced by way of a court injunction: *JF Finnegan v Ford Sellar Morris Developments Ltd* (above). On the facts of the case, the employer was not put at risk by having to set the retention monies aside, whereas the contractor was potentially prejudiced if the employer could use the retention monies during the ordinary course of his business. Ford Sellar had argued that Finnegan was not entitled to a mandatory injunction because the employer had a right to deduct liquidated and ascertained damages, exceeding the value of the retention monies. The judge chose to attach limited significance to the employer's notice, under clause 24 of JCT 80, of intention to deduct liquidated damages. The employer's rights over the retention fund remained speculative. This situation can be distinguished from one where the employer has an indisputable right of deduction which exceeds the outstanding retention monies. In *Henry Boot Building Ltd v Croydon Hotel & Leisure Co Ltd*,[2] the employer, under a JCT 63 contract (July 1977 Revision), had a right to deduct liquidated and ascertained damages because of late completion by the contractor. The employer's right to claim as liquidated and ascertained damages a sum somewhat greater than the outstanding retention monies is sufficient to foil the contractor's application for a mandatory injunction. In the judgment of Nourse LJ:

> 'It is clear that if the architect issues a certificate under that clause [clause 22] the employer may deduct the stated amount of the liquidated and ascertained damages from the sums retained by him by virtue of clause 30(3) since those sums are "monies … to become due to the Contractor under this Contract". … it seems to me to be clear that if, as here, the court is asked to grant an injunction at a time when the employer is entitled to deduct a greater amount of liquidated and ascertained damages, no injunction can be granted for the simple reason that there is no subsisting obligation to appropriate and set aside. In *Rayack* no certificate had been issued under clause 22.'[3]

2.14   *Henry Boot* was discussed by His Honour Judge Esyr Lewis QC in *JF Finnegan* (above). Adopting the argument of Finnegan's counsel, he concluded:

> '… there is a difference between the certificate issued by the architect under the contract conditions under consideration in *Henry Boot*, which have had a binding effect unless and until set aside by the arbitrator, and the giving of notice by the employer under clause 24 of the conditions in the present case. I have come to the conclusion that he [counsel] is

---

1   (1991) 53 BLR 38 at 48–49.
2   (1986) 36 BLR 41.
3   (1986) 36 BLR 41 at 46.

right. It is not suggested that there is any provision in the standard conditions here, except the provisions of clause 24 itself, which would give the employers' notice in writing under clause 24 a binding effect. The architect's certificate in *Henry Boot* under the conditions of the contract could only be set aside by an arbitrator. I find nothing in clause 24 itself which gives the employers' notice binding effect where, as here, there is a bona fide dispute as to their validity.'[1]

Proceedings claiming sums due on interim certificates

2.15   The Official Referee was also referred to the decision of Rhind J in *Concorde Construction Co Ltd v Colgan Co Ltd*,[2] decided in the High Court of Hong Kong. There, the contractor commenced proceedings claiming sums due on interim certificates, with the employer counter-claiming in the proceedings on the grounds of alleged defects which needed to be rectified. The employer's claims exceeded those of the contractor. The contract was in the Standard Form of Building Contract for use in Hong Kong (1976 edition) (With Quantities) which contained provisions comparable to those in JCT contracts. According to Rhind J:

'I do not think that an employer is entitled to have recourse on the trust fund of retention monies simply on the strength of his own belief that he has a good claim which entitles him to such monies. The court cannot countenance a situation where the employer would, in effect, be the judge in his own cause and able to say when he would make deductions from the retention monies. Allowing the employer to free the retention monies from the trust whenever the employer claimed entitlement to a set-off would drive a coach and horses through the whole system of protection ...

As a matter of common sense, the employer can only be permitted to deduct substantiated claims for liquidated amounts from the retention monies. How the employer will substantiate his claims depends on the circumstances. The best substantiation of all will be whether the contractor admits the money is due to the employer. In these circumstances it is clearly right that the employer should have immediate recourse to the trust money. ....
... the employer has an arguable case, judging from the material so far before the court, but nonetheless, its contentions about the main contractor's responsibility for defects and in relation to the other disputed matters are "speculative" in the sense that it is a matter for speculation whether the employer will ultimately succeed in proving its contentions. In the *Rayack* case, the court would not allow what is described as a "speculative" set-off to defeat the contractor's request that the retention monies should be set aside as a separate trust fund.'[3]

Employer claims on a sub-contractor

2.16   In another Hong Kong case, *Hsin Chong Construction Co Ltd v Yaton Realty Co Ltd*,[4] Hunter J, in the High Court of Hong Kong, considered the impact of employer claims on a sub-contractor. Again, the contract was the Standard Form of Building Contract for use in Hong Kong (1976 edition), not materially dissimilar to JCT 63. The architect issued a certificate under clause 22, the effect of which was to enable Yaton to deduct liquidated and ascertained damages. The contractor gave

---

1   (1986) 36 BLR 41 at 51–52.
2   (1984) 29 BLR 120.
3   Ibid, at 133.
4   (1986) 40 BLR 119.

notice of arbitration and also applied to the court for a mandatory order requiring Yaton to place all retention monies withheld from interim certificates in a trust account. At trial, the contractor conceded the employer's right to have recourse to the retentions insofar as they related to the value of work carried out by the contractor, but contended that the employer could not use money retained in respect of nominated sub-contractor work. The court held that clause 30(3) of the main contract created a single retention fund in relation to which the employer had rights irrespective of the ultimate destination of the monies retained. According to Hunter J:

> 'What is in issue is the circumstances in which such an obligation [to set aside] ceases. The *Henry Boot* decision shows that the obligation ceases if a clause 22 certificate exists for a sum in the liquidated damages exceeding the retention monies. Such a certificate binds the parties unless and until set aside by an arbitrator ...
>
> ... No attempt seems to have been made in argument in *Henry Boot* to split the retention fund or to draw the distinction sought to be drawn here between the two portions of it. This, the employer asserts, is because such a distinction is not valid. I think there is very considerable force in this submission that a split or division of the fund would run counter to the rationale of privity created by the contract. Clause 30(3) creates a single fund ...'[1]

He continued:

> 'Accordingly in my judgment, the employer's right of recourse under clause 30(4) extends to the whole retention fund, and no valid distinction can be drawn between the main contractor's and the nominated subcontractor's proportions of it. Such recourse may be based upon a right to deduct arising under any term of the contract ...'[2]

Defective works corrected by other contractors

2.17   In *GPT Realisations Ltd (In Liquidation) v Panatown Ltd*,[3] the Official Referee, His Honour Judge Bowsher QC, concluded that where the employer had a set-off which was a substantial claim overtopping the amount of the retention monies, there could be no obligation to set the retention monies aside. In that case, on two out of three contracts the employer had had defective works corrected by other contractors in accordance with clause 4.1.2 of JCT CD 81. Although this had not occurred on the third contract, nevertheless the Official Referee was satisfied that the employer had a potential right of set-off sufficient to defeat any obligation to have the retention monies with regard to that particular contract set aside. The judge accepted that the lengthy affidavit evidence filed by the employer was sufficient, on an interlocutory application, to satisfy him that, for the purposes of the summonses, there were substantial claims, as well as relying on clause 4.1.2 of JCT JD 81. The judge accepted that there was a general right of set-off on the principles set out in *Modern Engineering Ltd v Gilbert Ash*.[4] In addition, the judge found against the granting of an interlocutory injunction on the following grounds:

–   there was a delay in making the application;
–   there was an inability to offer an acceptable cross-undertaking as to damages;

---

1   (1986) 40 BLR 119 at 127.
2   Ibid at 129.
3   61 BLR 88.
4   [1974] AC 689.

– the risk of injustice favoured the employer.

Delay by contractors

2.18   Although the Official Referee was able to decide in *GPT Realisations* that an application for a mandatory injunction was, among other reasons, defeated through delay on the contractor's part, other courts have held that delay does not necessarily preclude the court from granting a mandatory injunction. The question of delay was raised in *JF Finnegan v Ford Sellar Morris Ltd.*[1] Dealing with this issue, the Official Referee stated:

> '. . . it would be inappropriate to grant a mandatory injunction to Finnegan in this interlocutory proceeding on the grounds that they are guilty of inordinate delay in requesting Ford Sellar to place the retention money into a separate banking account. Finnegan could obviously have made their request that Ford Sellar should do so as soon as Ford Sellar indicated they would exercise their right to make retentions from interim payments. However . . . I do not consider that clause 30.4.2.2 contains any time restriction on a request by Finnegan to Ford Sellar to place the retention money in a separate banking account.'[2]

Therefore, the question of delay will be a subjective issue to be considered by the particular judge. Also, in *JF Finnegan* the Official Referee dealt with the 'hardship' argument in the granting of injunctions. The judge referred to counsel's submission in this regard:

> '. . . a mandatory injunction is an exceptional form of relief and [counsel] has drawn my attention to what Megarry J said in *Shepherd Houses Ltd v Sandam*:[3]

> > "Third, on a motion, as contrasted with a trial, the court is far more reluctant to grant a mandatory injunction than it would be to grant a comparable prohibitory injunction. In a normal case the court must, inter alia, feel a high degree of assurance that at the trial it will appear that the injunction was rightly granted, and this is a higher standard than is required for a prohibitory injunction." '[4]

Placing the existing case-law in the context of retention funds, the Official Referee stated:

> 'In my view, the withholding of a mandatory injunction in the circumstances of this case carries a greater risk of injustice than the granting of it. Ford Sellar will not lose the retention fund or their right to have recourse to it if they eventually establish that right in the trial of the action . . . Under clause 30.4.2.1 Ford Sellar's interest in the retention is only that of a trustee. I consider that a higher risk of injustice being done arises if this primary status of the retention is undermined by a refusal to grant a mandatory injunction now when Ford Sellar's right to have recourse to the retention fund is subject to a bona fide challenge. If the fund is used for the ordinary purposes of Ford Sellar's business, Finnegan's beneficial interest in the trust fund must be subject to the risks and hazards which must inevitably attach to the use of such funds in a business.'[5]

---

1   (1991) 53 BLR 38; see also **2.12**.
2   Ibid, at 53.
3   [1971] Ch 340 at 351.
4   (1991) 53 BLR 38 at 53.
5   Ibid, at 55.

ADMINISTRATIVE RECEIVERSHIP

2.19   Some may ask, so why all this fuss about having retention money set aside in a separately identifiable bank account? The answer lies in the decision in *Mac-Jordan Construction Ltd v Brookmount Erostin Ltd (in Administrative Receivership)*.[1] Here, the employer, a property developer, had failed, prior to going into administrative receivership, to place the retention monies on a JCT 80 project in a separately identifiable bank account. The bank had a floating charge over the employer's assets which crystallised on 4 March 1991 on the appointment of receivers. By January 1991, the amount which should have been set aside in the retention fund was £109,247. The bank had express notice of the building contract and its provisions when it took the floating charge. The Court of Appeal held that the bank's rights under the floating charge prevailed over those of the contractor in the absence of a specifically set up retention fund. The right of the contractor to have the money set aside in the retention fund was a bare contractual one. The retention monies acquired no trust status (which protects them from seizure by receivers or a liquidator) until a contractual right to have them set aside had been exercised. According to Scott LJ:

> 'Once the floating charge has crystallised with the advent of the receivership, the receivers have statutory duties imposed by the Insolvency Act 1986 that they must discharge. They must apply the assets of the company in paying preferential debts (see section 40(2) of the 1986 Act). The unsatisfied contractual right of the plaintiff under clause 30.4.2.1 cannot deprive preferential creditors of their rights.'[2]

He further commented:

> 'In a case where the employer is insolvent when the application for a mandatory order is made, the mandatory order would, assuming it were complied with, give preference to the contractor as against other unsecured creditors. I do not see any reason why the court should do such a thing. If the directors of an insolvent company were, pursuant to a clause such as clause 30.4.2.1, to set aside a retention fund for the benefit of a building contractor, questions of preference might well arise (see section 239 of the Insolvency Act 1986). So far as preference is concerned, the appropriation of assets to constitute the retention fund would be no different, in my opinion, from the payment of any other contract debt. So I question whether in a case where the employer is insolvent the court would necessarily make a mandatory order for the setting up of the retention fund. If, in the present case, there had been funds available for unsecured creditors of Brookmount, I do not follow why the plaintiff should, in respect of the indebtedness due to it for retentions, be in any better position than other unsecured creditors. The position would, of course, subject to section 239 have been otherwise if a retention fund had already been duly constituted by an appropriation and setting aside of assets.'[3]

Order to enforce former contractual rights

2.20   Two other arguments were canvassed in *Mac-Jordan*. First, the receiver argued that, since the contractor had terminated his own employment under the building contract, he was no longer entitled to an order to enforce former contractual rights. The Court of Appeal rightly held that it was the contractor's employment under

1   (1991) 56 BLR 1.
2   Ibid, at 14.
3   Ibid, at 16.

the contract which had been terminated, and when this occurred this was, in any event, 'without prejudice to the accrued rights of either party'. Secondly, it was argued by the receiver that the contractor could be properly protected only if its interest was registered in accordance with s 395 of the Companies Act 1985, as its claim was in the nature of a floating charge as against the bank if it was not registered. According to Scott LJ:

> 'If it were right that, upon each deduction and retention being made in each interim certificate, the plaintiff required an equitable interest in the assets of Brookmount for the time being, the equitable interest being the right to have a sum equal to the amount of the deduction raised out of those assets and appropriated to a retention fund, with Brookmount retaining the right until the requisite amount had been raised and appropriated of using all its assets in the ordinary course of its business, there would, I think, be some force to the argument.

> But I do not see any reason why the contractual obligation to be implied from clause 30.4.2.1 should be anything more complex than a contractual obligation to appropriate and set aside the requisite sum in a retention fund. That contractual obligation does not, in my opinion, carry with it any equitable interest of a security character in the assets for the time being of the employer. So the floating charge point does not, in my opinion, arise.'[1]

In *Mac-Jordan*, the Court of Appeal endorsed comments of Nourse J in *Re Jartray Developments Ltd*:[2]

> 'It is clear both in principle and on authority that clause 30(4)(a) of the RIBA conditions imposed an obligation on Jartray to appropriate and set aside the £23,009 retentions as a separate trust fund, and that if RPW had made an application before Jartray went into liquidation the court would have made a mandatory order to that effect [see *Rayack*]. However it is equally clear in principle that that relief ceased to be available to RPW on the commencement of the liquidation. Accordingly there being no evidence that any part of the retentions were appropriated or set aside before liquidation commenced, RPW cannot now claim to be treated as if it had.'[3]

Reluctance of courts to endorse security arguments

2.21   The reluctance of the courts to endorse security arguments is also seen in *Lovell Construction Ltd v Independent Estates plc*.[4] Here, the parties had entered into a standard JCT contract, although alongside it stood an escrow account controlled by their respective solicitors into which payments were to be made to fund the works as they progressed. The monies in the account were to enjoy trust status in favour of the contractor, with the interest earned on the account to be for the benefit of the employer. His Honour Judge Fox-Andrews QC was asked to consider that the escrow account was a security interest operating by way of charge, which, being unregistered, was void as against the liquidator of the employer. He rejected any such contention.

---

1   (1991) 56 BLR 1 at 17.
2   (1982) 22 BLR 134 at 141.
3   (1991) 56 BLR 1 at 14.
4   [1994] 1 BCL 31.

ASSIGNMENT OF RIGHTS

2.22   Another issue which may arise is: what happens following the assignment by an employer of his interest in a building contract to a third party? This question was dealt with by His Honour Judge Esyr Lewis QC in *JF Finnegan v Ford Sellar Developments Ltd (No 2)*.[1] The contract was in the form JCT 80 Private with Approximate Quantities, although, prior to the contract, Ford Sellar had entered into a development agreement with Allied Dunbar Assurance plc to finance the project. With Finnegan's consent, as required by clause 19.1.2 of JCT 80, Ford Sellar had entered into an undated deed of assignment intended to become effective after practical completion (which occurred on 14 February 1991). The assignment of the contract to Allied Dunbar did not release Ford Sellar from its obligation to hold the retention as trustee for Finnegan, because, first, there was no evidence that the deed of assignment was dated and made operative before the date of Finnegan's request and, secondly, the obligation created by clause 30.5 was not 'a benefit of the contract' and was not within the assignment. According to the Official Referee:

> 'I do not accept that the assignment deed executed by Finnegan released Ford Sellar from their obligation to hold the retention as trustees for Finnegan. First, there is no evidence to show that Allied Dunbar dated the deed and made it operative before the date when the request was made by Finnegan to Ford Sellar that they should place the retention in a separate banking account. However, there is, in my judgment a fundamental reason why the assignment did not have this effect. The deed of assignment assigned "all the benefits of the contract and the works executed thereunder together with the right to bring proceedings against the contractor . . .". This provision may be wider than the provisions of clause 19.1.2 of the building contract, which would entitle any assignee "to bring proceedings in the name of the employer . . . to enforce any of the terms of this contract for the benefit of the employer hereunder", but the essential right assigned by the deed of assignment is "all the benefits of the contract". I do not regard the obligation created by clause 30.5 of the building contract to be a term for the benefit of the employer. The retention rights granted to the employer under clause 30.4 of the building contract are part and parcel of the employer's obligation contained in clause 30 to make payments to the contractor and its overall effect is to confirm a benefit on the contractor and to create obligations for the employer.'[2]

Draw down of monies from a funding institution

2.23   In *JF Finnegan (No 2)*, the Official Referee dealt with an argument common among developers in the early 1990s. Many developers argued that draw-down of monies from a funding institution was always made net of retentions and, therefore, such retentions were never in the hands of the developer to set aside in a bank account. His Honour Judge Esyr Lewis QC had little sympathy for this argument:

> 'I turn to [counsel's] penultimate argument. This is that it is now impossible for Ford Sellar to comply with a mandatory injunction requiring Ford Sellar to pay the retention into a separate banking account as Ford Sellar have asked Allied Dunbar to give them the retention money so that they may do so and Allied Dunbar have refused to do so. This submission cannot survive my conclusion that the obligation to pay the retention into a

---

1   (1991) 27 Conv LR 41.
2   Ibid, at 50.

separate banking account is and remains that of Ford Sellar. ... the contractual arrangements between Ford Sellar and Allied Dunbar are not binding on Finnegan. Finnegan are, in my judgment, entitled to enforce the provisions of clause 30.5.3 of the building contract against Ford Sellar without regard to the terms of the development agreement.'[1]

NOMINATED SUB-CONTRACTOR RETENTION MONEY

2.24   The position in regard to nominated sub-contractor retention monies has already been indicated in general terms, but requires further explanation. Protection given to sub-contractors is much more limited. Although the employer and contractor hold the nominated sub-contractor retention as fiduciary as trustee (clause 21.9 of NSC/4 and clauses 4.19 and 4.22 of NSC/C), such protection has never been extended to domestic sub-contractors. In the case of nominated sub-contractors, the contractor is fiduciary as trustee of their retention monies, without obligation to invest. If the contractor attempts or purports to mortgage or charge his interest in the retention (except by way of floating charge) he is bound to set aside immediately (and act as trustee of) a sum equivalent to the retention which is payable to the nominated sub-contractor on demand. As a beneficiary of a properly drafted clause, the nominated sub-contractor can assert rights of direct payment over those of other relevant parties.

The 'Green Form'

2.25   In *Re Tout & Finch Ltd*,[2] it was held that clause 11(h) of the NFBTE/FASS nominated sub-contract (the Green Form) placed retention monies attributable to nominated sub-contractor work outside the assets available to creditors on the main contractor's liquidation. The liquidator was obliged to pass on the nominated sub-contractor's retention when this was received from the employer. The same principle is valid for NSC/4 and NSC/C. The standard form main contract and standard form nominated sub-contract trust retention provisions, when read together, operate as an assignment to the nominated sub-contractors of the contractor's right to receive their retention. This point was made in *Re Arthur Sanders Ltd*.[3] If the contractor, having received the nominated sub-contractor's retention, becomes insolvent without paying the retention over to the nominated sub-contractors, the employer is at risk of being required to pay twice. The nominated sub-contractors may, because of the assignment, be able to claim direct payment of the outstanding retention. The question of direct payment is considered further in Chapter 3. A release of retention made direct to the nominated sub-contractors may interfere with the contractor's rights under clause 23 of NSC/4 (clause 4.27.1 of NSC/C). A contractor, subject to quantification with reasonable accuracy and the giving of proper notice, has a right of set-off 'against any money otherwise due under the Sub-Contract from the Contractor to the Sub-Contractor including any Sub-Contractor's retention notwithstanding the fiduciary obligation of the Contractor' (clause 4.27.1 of NSC/C).

---

1   (1991) 27 Conv LR 41 at 52.
2   [1954] 1 WLR 178.
3   (1981) 17 BLR 125; see also **2.6–2.7**.

However, on the authority of *Re Arthur Sanders*, the employer cannot use the sub-contractor's retention to satisfy claims against the contractor. In that case, the main contractor became insolvent and went into liquidation. The employer could not use the sum of £1,374, held as retention against nominated sub-contractors (out of a total retention of £11,086), to meet a set-off that the employer had against the contractor on another contract. According to Nourse J:

> '... once a sub-contract has been entered into, the contractor no longer has a beneficial interest in the sub-contractor's due proportion of the retention. At this stage, his only interest in that proportion is as trustee for the sub-contractor, a state of affairs for which express provision is made in both clause 27(a)(viii) of the RIBA Conditions and clause 11(a) of the FASS sub-contract. Secondly, once that stage is reached I do not see how the proportion in question can really be said to be "due" to the contractor at all. It may strictly still be payable to him under the terms of the main contract, but he must immediately pay it over under the sub-contract.'[1]

2.26 However, these *dicta* were expressly disapproved by Hunter J in *Hsin Chong Construction* :

> 'I regret that I do not find this passage persuasive [the *dicta* in *Re Arthur Sanders*] and am unable to follow it. Nowhere in his judgment does the learned judge refer to clause 13 of the sub-contract. This, I regard as a crucial provision. It affords the main contractor a right of "deduction or set-off more widely framed than the right of recourse in clause 30(4)". He is by no means a bare trustee: one whose "only interest ... is as a trustee". ....
> [I]n my judgment, the employer's right of recourse under clause 30(4) extends to the whole retention fund ...'[2]

Certified payments

2.27 In an Irish case, *Glow Heating Ltd v Eastern Health Board and Another*,[3] the main contractor had, prior to liquidation, received a certified payment of £6,617 in regard to nominated sub-contract work. Monies had not been passed to the nominated sub-contractor. The nominated sub-contractor argued that he was entitled to a direct payment. The monies could be deducted from the retention held against the main contractor. The liquidator accepted the general validity of retention trust clauses but maintained that they could not oust the general *pari passu* distribution of assets required by s 275 of the Companies Act 1963. There were, additionally, outstanding retention monies and monies for work carried out but to be certified after the date of the liquidation. The Irish court held that a sum could be deducted from monies due to the main contractor to meet the certified amount of £6,617 without any implications under general insolvency law. The nominated sub-contractor was also entitled to a full release of retention monies to the value of work executed which would be passed on by the liquidator to the nominated sub-contractor when received.

---

1   (1981) 17 BLR 125 at 139–140.
2   (1984) 29 BLR 120 at 128–129.
3   (1992) 8 Const LJ 56.

RETENTION PROVISIONS UNDER THE MANAGEMENT CONTRACT, JCT 87

2.28   There has been less judicial consideration of the retention provisions under the management contract, JCT 87. The question was considered, in regard to an amended management contract, by the Court of Appeal in *Herbert Construction (UK) Ltd v Atlantic Estates plc*.[1] On issue of the architect's interim certificate number 30, dated 2 May 1991, it was revealed that the client was withholding £171,291 in respect of retention monies. Later the same year, the contractor requested the client to pay the retention monies into a separate bank account in accordance with clause 4.8 of JCT 87. The client refused, whereupon the contractor issued proceedings to oblige the client to pay the sum into a separate bank account. Following certain agreements between the parties, His Honour Judge Wilcox QC, sitting as a Deputy Official Referee, ordered the client to pay the sum of £165,167, held by way of retention, together with all future retention monies, into a separate bank account. The client appealed to the Court of Appeal. Of importance was the division of works contracts into 'existing tenders' and 'future works' contractors. The client maintained that there was no obligation to set aside retention monies in regard to the 'future works' contractors, and its liability was limited to £46,313 for 'existing tenders'.

2.29   The amended clause 4.8 read as follows:

'1. The Employer's interest in the Retention is fiduciary and as trustee for the Management Contractor and for any Works Contractor *whose work is comprised in any of the existing tenders* (but without obligation to invest).

. . .

3. Except where the Employer is a local authority the Employer shall if the Management Contractor or through the Management Contractor any Works Contractor so requests at the date of payment of each interim certificate place the Retention held thereby in a separate banking account (so designated as to identify the amount of Retention held by the Employer on trust as provided in clause 4.8.1) . . .

4. If the Employer exercises the right to deduct referred to in clause 4.3.3 against any Retention he shall include, in the written information to the Management Contractor . . . details of any deduction from either the Retention held in respect of the Management Contractor or the Retention held for any Works Contractor . . .'

The Court of Appeal, Stuart-Smith LJ dissenting, held that the object of the relevant amendments was to distinguish between works contractors whose work was comprised in any existing tenders from works contractors whose work was not so included. Therefore, the amount to be set aside was £46,313.

2.30   In a Scottish case, *Balfour Beatty v Britannia Life*,[2] a decision under the Scottish equivalent of JCT 87, the management contractor had gone into receivership. The works contractor sought to obtain a payment of its retention monies direct from the employer. The court held it was not entitled to these monies; the withholding of the retention by the management contractor did not create a fund in the hands of the employer with trust status under Scots law.

---

1   (1993) CILL 858.
2   1997 SLT 10, OH.

2.31 The question of retention funds under management contracts was also considered in *PC Harrington Contractors Ltd v Co Partnerships Ltd*,[1] a Court of Appeal decision. Co Partnerships entered into a contract, as employer, under JCT 87 with the contractor for a development in London. PC Harrington was a works contractor appointed under Works Contract/2. PC Harrington carried out their works and payments were made, subject to deductions for retention. Practical completion was certified on 3 August 1991, with the defects liability period expiring one year later. The Final Account was agreed in March 1992. In December 1992, the final defects inspection took place, but before the making good of defects certificate could be issued, the management contractor went into administrative receivership and his contract was automatically determined. Eventually, the loss to the employer, resulting from the management contractor's insolvency, was ascertained in the sum of £659,672. The employer was withholding £288,166. The employer claimed to be entitled to the whole of the retention, which was held in a separate bank account at Barclays Bank in diminution of the management contractor's indebtedness to the employer. The retention contained, however, some £22,695, due to the works contractor as retention. The works contractor brought proceedings before Mr Michael Tugendhat QC, sitting as an additional judge of the Queen's Bench Division, claiming that the employer held the sum of £22,695 in trust for the works contractor and it was not available to off-set the indebtedness of the management contractor. The deputy judge held that the monies were, in fact, held on trust by virtue of clauses 4.8.1 of the management contract and 4.29 of the works contract. The employer appealed to the Court of Appeal which dismissed the appeal following a detailed analysis of the provisions in the management and works contracts. According to Morritt LJ:

'Though the Management Contract and the Works Contract are both detailed and complicated the overall effect is, in my view, clear. The sums deducted by the Management Contractor from the sums due to the Works Contractor and retained by the Employer pursuant to clause 4.23 of the Works Contract and clause 4.8.1 of the Management Contract were never due or payable by the Employer to the Management Contractor.

Down to the date of practical completion there were two parallel provisions for retentions, namely the retentions under the Management Contract … and the retentions under the Works Contract … The latter retentions never had been money due to the Management Contractor … Those retentions had not been and never became money due to the Management Contractor. They were held by the Employer in trust for the Works Contractor … At all times since the Works Contract retentions had been made they had been held by the Employer in trust for the Works Contractor.'[2]

THE NEW ENGINEERING CONTRACT

2.32 The approach of the New Engineering Contract (NEC) (2nd edn), now the Engineering and Construction Contract, to retention is fundamentally different. Under the NEC (Option), retention of monies due to the contractor is a secondary option rather than one of the so-called core clauses. Clause P1.1 does not permit

---

1   (1998) 88 BLR 44.
2   Ibid, at 54.

the deduction of retention until valuations have reached a certain level. The obvious intention is to assist contractors with cash flow in the early stages of a project. In principle, the retention-free amount should be entered in the contract data. If no amount is included, or the stated amount is nil, deduction will start immediately. Again, the retention percentage needs to be fixed by the employer and entered in the contract data. To enter a blank will have the same effect as entering a nil deduction. Brian Eggleston states, in *The New Engineering Contract – a Commentary*:[1]

> 'One aspect of clause P1.1 which may cause some concern to contractors is that retention is apparently held against sums valued for compensation events. This seems to follow from the definition of the price for work done to date. However, it is hardly equitable that the employer should be entitled to retention on an amount payable to the contractor in respect of any compensation event which is a breach of contract by the employer.'

On the release of retention, the NEC is not radical. According to clause P1.2, half the retention is released on completion, with the second half released on issue of the defects certificate. The NEC is silent on the possible trust status of retention monies, and it is debatable that such monies are subject to trust status. It is pushing a point too far to suggest, as Eggleston does,[2] that the obligation under clause 10.1 of the core clauses could be brought into play. The duty to co-operate does not realistically provide sufficient substance for such a conclusion.

RETENTION BONDS

2.33   As an alternative to the vagaries of the retention fund, there has been much support, at least in principle, for retention bonds or guarantees, which are particularly used in international contracting, but which domestically have been promoted by the British Constructional Steelwork Association (BCSA). These can be held either throughout the contract period or in substitution for the early release of retention monies. With contractors often on very low profit margins, it may be to a contractor's advantage to provide a retention bond instead of having monies tied up in the employer's bank account. Examples of retention bonds are set out in the Appendix to this chapter. The terminology can be modified to suit a wide range of construction contracts. It is usual for the value of the bond to reduce automatically by 50 per cent at practical completion. The bond otherwise remains in force, pending the issue of the Certificate of Making Good Defects.

A selection of retention bonds is set out in the Appendix to this chapter. These will not be construed as construction contracts for the purposes of the Housing Grants, Construction and Regulation Act 1996 and statutory adjudication will not apply to disputes under them.

1   (Blackwell Science, 1996) pp 34–35.

2   Ibid, at p 35.

Appendix

VERSION 1
ON DEMAND RETENTION BOND

To: [*name and address of Beneficiary*]

From: [*name and address of Bank* **or** *Insurance Company providing the Bond*]

We understand that [*name of Contractor*] ('the Contractor') has entered into an agreement with you dated 199 ('the Building Contract') for works comprising [*short description of works*] ('the Works').

Terms used in this Bond shall be interpreted as they are defined in the Building Contract. Under the terms of the Building Contract a Retention Bond is required.

WE undertake to pay you an amount not exceeding in the aggregate 5% of the sum stated in Schedule [   ] to the Building Contract on our receiving your written demand if such demand is accompanied by:

A written notice from the Architect appointed under the Building Contract confirming that the Contractor is in default under the Building Contract in relation to a defect in the Works which is attributable to the Contractor's workmanship or materials not being in accordance with the Building Contract.

Every demand under this Bond shall be signed by one of your directors or the Company Secretary for the time being and shall be settled by us subject to satisfactory authentication of costs claimed and on you establishing the Contractor's default.

This Bond shall be irrevocable.

Our liability under this Bond shall not be discharged or affected by any arrangements made between you and the Contractor or by any alteration in the Contractor's obligations under the Building Contract or by any forbearance whether as to payment, time, performance or otherwise (whether or not such arrangement, alteration or forbearance is made with our knowledge or consent).

The value of this Bond shall automatically reduce by 50% on the date of issuing the Certificate of Practical Completion under clause [   ] of the Building Contract and thereafter shall be valid and effective until the issue of the Certificate of Making Good Defects under clause [   ] of the Building Contract whereupon it shall extinguish. If a Certificate of Making Good Defects is not issued under the Building Contract our liability shall cease [   ] years after the date of Practical Completion of the Works.

This Bond is personal to yourselves and is not transferable or assignable.

This Bond shall be governed by and construed in accordance with the laws of England and Wales.

(The Bond is to be executed as a Deed)

VERSION 2

RETENTION BOND WITH PROVISION FOR ALL FOLLOWING UNSATISFIED JUDGMENTS OR ARBITRATION AWARDS

To: [*name and address of Beneficiary*]

From: [*name and address of Bank* **or** *Insurance Company providing the Bond*]

We understand that [*name of Contractor*] ('the Contractor') has entered into an agreement with you dated 199 ('the Building Contract') for works comprising [*short description of works*] ('the Works').

Terms used in this Bond shall be interpreted as they are defined in the Building Contract. Under the terms of the Building Contract a Retention Bond is required.

WE undertake to pay you an amount not exceeding in the aggregate 5% of the sum stated in Schedule [   ] to the Building Contract on our receiving your written demand if such demand is accompanied by:

A certified copy of a Judgment of a Court or Arbitrator's Award relating to the Building Contract together with your statement that such Judgment or Arbitrator's Award has not been fully satisfied in relation to a defect in the Works which is attributable to the Contractor's workmanship or materials not being in accordance with the Building Contract, or

A decision of the Architect appointed under the Building Contract confirming that the Contractor is in default under the Building Contract in relation to a defect in the Works which is attributable to the Contractor's workmanship or materials not being in accordance with the Building Contract.

Every demand under this Bond shall be signed by one of your directors or where there are no directors by someone authorised to sign.

This Bond shall be irrevocable.

Our liability under this Bond shall not be discharged or affected by any arrangements made between you and the Contractor or by any alteration in the Contractor's obligations under the Agreement or by any forbearance whether as to payment, time, performance or otherwise (whether or not such arrangement, alteration or forbearance is made with our knowledge or consent).

The value of this Bond shall automatically reduce by 50% on the date of Practical Completion as evidenced in accordance with the Building Contract and thereafter shall be valid and effective until [*date*] whereupon it shall extinguish.

This Bond is personal to yourselves and is not transferable or assignable.

This Bond shall be governed by and construed in accordance with the laws of England and Wales.

(The Bond is to be executed as a Deed)

VERSION 3
BRITISH CONSTRUCTIONAL STEELWORK ASSOCIATION RETENTION BOND

THIS BOND is made as a deed on [*date*]

BETWEEN:

(1)   [*name and registered office address of Main Contractor*] ('Main Contractor'); and

(2)   [*name and registered office address of Surety*] ('Surety'); and

(3)   [*name and registered office address of BCSA Member*] ('Specialist')

WHEREAS:

(A)   By a Sub-Contract for [*describe sub-contract*] dated [*date*] entered into between the Main Contractor and the Specialist ('Sub-Contract') the Specialist has agreed to execute Works ('Works') for the Main Contractor at a price of £[   ] ('Sub-Contract Sum').

(B)   The Main Contractor has agreed that in consideration of the provision of this Bond by the Surety to the Main Contractor at the request of the Specialist, the Main Contractor will not make any deduction of sums by way of retentions from payments to be made to the Specialist under the terms and conditions of the Sub-Contract.

NOW THIS DEED WITNESSES as follows:

1   Subject to the provisions of this Bond, the Surety hereby guarantees to the Main Contractor the due and punctual performance by the Specialist of the obligations on its part to be performed contained in Clause [*defects liability/maintenance clause*] of the Sub-Contract so that in the event of any default thereunder on the part of the Specialist, the Surety shall pay any damages actually and reasonably sustained by the Main Contractor subject to the limitations set out in clause 2 hereof.

2   (a)   Subject to the provisions of 2(b) hereof, the liability of the Surety under this Bond shall not exceed such sum as, but for the provision of this Bond, would otherwise have been held by the Main Contractor by way of retention at the time of any breach of Clause [*defects liability/maintenance clause*] of the Sub-Contract, but in any event the maximum aggregate liability of the Surety hereunder shall not exceed whichever is the lesser of either an amount equivalent to 3% of the Sub-Contract Sum or £[   ].

       (b)   The maximum aggregate liability of the Surety hereunder shall automatically be reduced to an amount equivalent to 1½ % of the Sub-Contract Sum on [*date*] which is the anticipated date of (practical completion) of the Works.*

---

*   Note: For flexibility, an additional number of weeks may be added, in which case, the words 'plus [   ] weeks' should be added here.

3   There shall be no obligation on the part of the Surety to discharge any claim made by the Main Contractor hereunder unless the Main Contractor submits together with such claim a certified true copy of a decision of an adjudicator under the Sub-Contract that the Specialist is in default of Clause [   ] of the Sub-Contract.

4   Neither this Deed nor any rights arising under or in connection with it may be assigned without the prior written consent of the Surety and the Specialist.

5   The Surety covenants and agrees that without limitation any of the actions by the Main Contractor which are set out below may be made and done without notice to or the consent of the Surety and without in any way affecting, changing, or releasing the Surety from its obligations hereunder or affecting the liability of the Surety hereunder. The actions are:

   (a)   waiver by the Main Contractor of any of the terms, provisions, conditions, obligations and agreements of the Sub-Contract or any failure to make demand upon or take action against the Specialist;
   (b)   any modification or changes to the Sub-Contract;
   (c)   the giving by the Main Contractor of any consent to an assignment or the making of any assignment of the Sub-Contract;
   (d)   the granting of extensions of time to the Specialist; and
   (e)   the release of any Co-Surety.

6   This Deed shall be governed by and construed in accordance with English law and shall be subject to the exclusive jurisdiction of the English Courts.**

7   This Deed shall finally expire and cease to be of effect on [*date*].***

IN WITNESS whereof this Bond has been executed as a Deed delivered the day and year first before written by:

The Common Seal of [*Surety*]
was hereunto affixed in the presence of:

....
[*name*] Director/Secretary

The Common Seal of [*Specialist*]
was hereunto affixed in the presence of:

....
[*name*] Director

....
[*name*] Director/Secretary

OR

**   Substitute 'Scots Law' and 'Scottish Courts' as appropriate.
***   Note: This should be a date six months after the date in Clause 2(b).

[*Surety*]
acting by two directors/a director and its secretary, namely:

....
[*name*] Director

....
[*name*] Director/Secretary

[*Specialist*]
acting by two directors/a director and its secretary, namely:

....
[*name*] Director

....
[*name*] Director/Secretary

[*Reproduced by kind permission of the British Constructional Steelwork Association.*]

SPECIMEN FORM OF STANDARD GUARANTEE ON DEMAND IN LIEU OF RETENTION

We [*name*] ('the Guarantor') [jointly and severally] understand that you [*name*] ('the Purchaser') intend to enter [or have entered] into a Contract with [*name*] ('the Contractor') for services relating to the design, engineering, procurement and construction of [specify type of plant] at [*address*]

In consideration therefore of your paying the Contractor in full settlement of his invoices without any deduction by way of retention[1]

WE HEREBY IRREVOCABLY[2] GUARANTEE to pay on your first demand the sum of £[   ] subject to the following conditions.

1   Your demand shall be in writing and shall state

    (i)   You have given the Contractor 14 days' notice in writing of your intention under this guarantee.[3]

2   The giving of time by you or the neglect or forebearance by you in enforcing the said Contract or the granting by you of any other indulgence shall not in any way prejudice our obligation under this guarantee.

3   Our maximum liability under this agreement is limited to £[   ].

4   This guarantee shall expire on [*date*] and thereafter shall be wholly null, void and unenforceable.

5   Upon expiry this guarantee shall be returned to us for cancellation.

NOTES:

1   The guarantee may be made under seal, in which case a further condition '6 This guarantee has been made under seal' should be added and the words 'in consideration ... retention' may be deleted because a guarantee under seal is binding without consideration. If the guarantee is given under hand only there must be some consideration to make it binding; the words in the specimen will usually suffice but may need adapting to the circumstances.
2   If there is more than one surety, here insert 'jointly and severally'.
3   Here insert precise details of the contents to be inserted in the demand to ensure, in the absence of bad faith, that payment is only made on the happening of the event justifying payment; possible words are as follows:
    (a)   Down Payment Bonds
        (ii) The said Contract has been terminated by reason of [*specify*] effective on [*date*].
        In the case of down payment bonds the words stating the amount to be paid need to be adapted to show by how much and on what dates or events the amount payable reduces. If the amounts reduce on the happening of the events then insert also:
        (iii) Which, if any, of the events referred to above have happened and the date(s) when they happened.
    (b)   Performance Bonds
        (ii) The Contractor has failed to perform his contractual obligations with full details of all such alleged failures and the relevant clauses in the Contract *or* that an arbitration

award has been made in your favour in which case the arbitration award must be enclosed with your demand.

(c) Damages Bonds

    (ii) Liquidated damages are payable to you under the Contract with full particulars of the damages due and the reasons why they are due.

(d) Bonds in lieu of retention

Delete all the words in condition (1) after 'shall be in writing'.

Chapter 3

DIRECT PAYMENT TO NOMINATED SUB-CONTRACTORS

Introduction – The legitimacy of direct payment – Direct payment provisions in standard form building contracts – Nominated sub-contractor agreements – Appointment of administrative receiver or administrator – Preferential payment to nominated sub-contractors – JCT Amendment 18 (1998) and JCT 98 – Appendix

INTRODUCTION

3.1   It has been estimated that over 90 per cent of the total value of the site process is carried out by sub-contractors, nominated/named and domestic. Statistics are found in Table 3.3 of the Construction and Housing Statistics 1990,[1] which indicated that most sub-contracts were domestic (45.7 per cent), relatively few nominated (approximately 11.23 per cent), with 9.04 per cent named sub-contractors under NAM/SC (for use with IFC 84). More anecdotal evidence, prepared by leading firms of quantity surveyors in particular, seems to point to similar conclusions.

3.2   Although the use of nominated sub-contractors has been common within the construction industry for a period of approximately 100 years (although the use of such sub-contractors may now be declining with their lesser involvement in local authority work), it has been difficult for lawyers, if they consider the problem, to justify contract clauses and legal decisions which have allowed employers to make direct payments to nominated sub-contractors, potentially in disregard of general insolvency law. The problem usually arises where the contractor is in liquidation and the employer makes direct payments to nominated sub-contractors. In these circumstances, it is arguable that such payments are illegal, being in apparent contravention of the *pari passu* principle that all unsecured creditors rank equal (s 107 of the Insolvency Act 1986, formerly s 302 of the Companies Act 1948). From the employer's point of view, direct payment clauses are of practical worth. They can help to prevent delays on a project in the event that the main contractor either fails to make regular payments to the sub-contractors or fails to pass on the sub-contractors' monies when certified to them. The risk the employer runs in making direct payments to nominated sub-contractors is that, if such payments are subsequently held to be illegal, he will still have to pay the main contractor's liquidator.

---

1   (Department of the Environment, 1992).

THE LEGITIMACY OF DIRECT PAYMENT

3.3   In the absence of back-to-back provisions in both the main contract and sub-contracts, contractually the employer cannot pay a sub-contractor direct (in the absence of a direct warranty), regardless of the possible impact of the insolvency legislation. This is part of the general privity of contract rules. If A and B are parties to the contract, they cannot ordinarily seek to provide C with a benefit arising under the contract between A and B. For instance, in *Re Holt ex parte Gray*,[1] the employer tried unsuccessfully to bypass the contractor's insolvency by direct payment to the nominated sub-contractor.

Bankruptcy/insolvency

3.4   For many years, it was well-established law (either by direct judicial decisions or due to a tendency to view building contracts differently from other contracts and as, somehow, not subject to the general laws of insolvency) that, under Royal Institution of British Architects (RIBA) and Joint Contracts Tribunal (JCT) contracts, provisions for direct payment to nominated sub-contractors (ie contractors whose employment was forced on the main contractor by the employer) did not infringe bankruptcy or insolvency legislation. One noteworthy decision of the courts was *Re Wilkinson ex parte Fowler*.[2] Here, the court was able, on a public authority development, to uphold the use of direct payment clauses, following the main contractor's bankruptcy, on grounds of 'public policy'. Direct payment provisions assisted the satisfactory completion of public works contracts and were of mutual benefit to employer and sub-contractor in that they created a mutual sense of trust and confidence in performance and payment.

3.5   *Re Tout and Finch Ltd*[3] is another inadequate analysis by the courts of the legitimacy of direct payment clauses. The main contractor went into liquidation after practical completion of the works but before the issue of the architect's final certificate. Sums were due to sub-contractors under interim certificates previously issued by the architect. The nominated sub-contractors argued that the then current RIBA form of building contract (a predecessor to JCT 63) permitted the employer to make direct payments to them. One nominated sub-contractor sought a declaration that the sum of £600 certified in his favour but unpaid by the main contractor could be the subject of a direct payment by the employer under clause 21(c) of the contract. The nominated sub-contractor further sought release of a sum of £787 held by the employer as retention in respect of nominated sub-contractor work. The court found for the nominated sub-contractor on both counts. The second count, which concerns release or the retention, is a more satisfactory decision and mirrors the general law on retention monies, which was discussed in Chapter 2. As far as the entire repayment of money certified but not paid is concerned, the decision attracts less confidence. The court does not appear to have considered the general provisions of the insolvency legislation. The contractual power to pay direct was treated as an authority irrevocable

---

1   (1888) 58 LJQB 5.
2   [1905] 2 KB 713.
3   [1954] 1 WLR 178.

even on insolvency. Based on *dicta* of Bigham J in *Re Wilkinson ex parte Fowler* (above):

'It is an authority which, in my opinion, it was not competent for the bankrupt to withdraw, and it was never contemplated he should withdraw it; and, indeed, it is not contended on behalf of the trustee that the authority was one that could be lawfully withdrawn. It is an authority, therefore, which the bankruptcy of the contractor did not annul.'[1]

Despite the trustee arguing that direct payments did not bind him, the court concluded:

'... as that power or authority never was revoked, in my opinion it binds the trustee in bankruptcy just as much as it would have bound the contractor himself if he had never been made a bankrupt.'[2]

3.6   A similar position was adopted in Australia where, in *Re Monkhouse Proprietary Ltd*,[3] the Australian courts concluded that monies due to sub-contractors were subject to the express provisions of the contract and:

'... the payment of the building owner cannot be described as a payment made out of the building owner's own moneys for the builder. It is a payment made out of the building owner's own moneys which, if the contract were strictly carried out, would never become due to the builder.'

3.7   Despite the seemingly casual attitude of judges in certain construction law cases, other legal authority has stated that the bankruptcy rules for the distribution of an insolvent's estate should take precedence over contrary contractual provisions. For instance, in *Ex parte Mackay*[4] James LJ said:

'... a man is not allowed, by stipulation with a creditor, to provide for a different distribution of his effects in the event of bankruptcy from that which the law provides.'

In the same case, Mellish LJ stated:

'A person cannot make it a part of his contract that, in the event of bankruptcy, he is then to get some additional advantage which prevents his property being distributed under the bankruptcy laws.'[5]

International case-law

3.8   How to deal with nominated sub-contractors has also been considered in South Africa. In *Administrator (Natal) v Magill, Grant & Nell (Pty) Ltd (In Liquidation)*,[6] Ogilvy Thompson JA said:

'... although the defendant's payment to the nominated sub-contractors was made pursuant to the election conferred upon him without apparent qualification, by clause 21(b) of the contract, the exercise of that election after liquidation had supervened disturbed both the realisation and distribution of the plaintiff's company's assets as prescribed by the law relating to liquidations. Were this Court now to uphold the validity

---

1   [1905] 2 KB 713 at 720.
2   Ibid, at 721.
3   (1968) P2 NSW 238.
4   (1873) LR 8 Ch App 643 at 647.
5   Ibid, at 648.
6   (1969) (1) SA 660 (A) at 672.

of the election exercised by the defendant in the present case, the door would be opened to contractual stipulations expressly designed to accord, on insolvency or liquidation, preference to selected creditors who would otherwise be merely concurrent.'

Therefore, in South Africa the court refused to follow the English authorities, *Re Wilkinson ex parte Fowler* and *Re Tout and Finch*.

3.9   Similarly, in the Far East, courts have been less willing to allow direct payment provisions to operate and apparently to oust the general law of insolvency. Two such decisions are *Re Right Time Construction Co Ltd (in Liquidation)*[1] and *Jo Yee Construction Pty Ltd v Diethelm Industries Pty Ltd.*[2]

3.10   In the first case, Right Time Construction was the main contractor to Realty Enterprises HK Ltd. There were two nominated sub-contractors. The main contract used was the Hong Kong Standard Form, similar to JCT 63. Clause 27(c) allowed direct payment to nominated sub-contractors where the main contractor failed to pay the nominated sub-contractor sums certified by the architect. Prior to the presentation of the petition to wind up Right Time Construction and the subsequent making of an order, the architect had issued an interim certificate which included sums due with regard to work by nominated sub-contractors. The employer, with the consent of the main contractor, paid sums outstanding to the nominated sub-contractors direct, but this was after the petition to wind up the main contractor had been presented. On an application by the liquidator, the court held that the direct payments were void under Hong Kong insolvency law as they favoured certain creditors of the company in liquidation above others.

3.11   In the second case, *Jo Yee Construction*, the courts in the Far East again took a restrictive approach. The main contractor went into liquidation, with all current interim certificates fully paid in his favour. However, the main contractor failed to discharge sums certified in favour of nominated sub-contractors. The employer, the Government of Singapore, proposed to pay the nominated sub-contractors direct and to deduct payment from sums due to the main contractor. The main contractor's liquidator argued that such payments would be in contravention of the Singapore Companies Act 1985. The payments would make the nominated sub-contractors preferential creditors in contravention of the *pari passu* principle. The Singapore High Court, which analysed relevant English case-law in great detail, found such payments irreconcilable with insolvency legislation. The judge was particularly influenced by the failure of the English cases generally, and with the notable exception of the non-construction *British Eagle* decision (discussed below) to attach any significance to insolvency legislation.

3.12   The construction industry, drafters of construction contracts and construction lawyers were hit by the perceived ramifications of the House of Lords' decision in *British Eagle International Airlines Ltd v Compagnie Nationale Air France.*[3] This case related to the IATA, a body established in Canada. This fulfilled the role, among others, of providing a clearing house to settle mutual rights and liabilities between airlines. The effect of the arrangement was, on the face of it, to allow for a distribution

---

1   (1990) 52 BLR 117.
2   (1991) 7 Const LJ 53.
3   [1975] 1 WLR 758.

of a company's assets in a manner different from that prescribed by what is now s 107 of the Insolvency Act 1986.

3.13   Both the trial judge and the Court of Appeal had concluded that, since monies in the common fund were not the property of British Eagle, there was no breach of the *pari passu* principle. British Eagle had the right, if in credit, to receive a payment from the clearing house. However, the decision was reversed by a 3:2 majority in the House of Lords. According to Lord Cross of Chelsea:

> 'The question is, in essence, whether what was called in argument the "mini liquidation", flowing from the clearing house arrangements is to yield or to prevail over the general liquidation. I cannot doubt that on principle the rules of the general liquidation should prevail.'[1]

The House of Lords' majority was encouraged by the reasoning in *Ex parte Mackay*,[2] and, again, in the words of Lord Cross:

> 'What the respondents are saying here is that the parties to the "clearing house" arrangements by agreeing that simple contract debts are to be satisfied in a particular way have succeeded in "contracting out" of the provisions contained in section 302 of the 1948 Act [the predecessor to s 107 of the Insolvency Act 1986] for the payment of unsecured debts "*pari passu*". In such a context it is to my mind irrelevant that the parties to the "clearing house" arrangements had good business reasons for entering into them and did not direct their minds to how the arrangements might be affected by the insolvency of one or more of the parties. Such a "contracting out" must, to my mind, be contrary to public policy.'[3]

3.14   In Ireland, Costello J considered direct payment clauses in the High Court in *Glow Heating Ltd v Eastern Health Board and Another*.[4] Here, Costello J was required to consider whether payments to nominated sub-contractors would contravene s 275 of the Irish Companies Act 1973 – legislation of similar scope and effect to that operating in England. The plaintiff was a nominated sub-contractor for the mechanical services installation in a health centre. The main contract, in a form approved by the Irish Department of Health, provided that sums certified as due to the sub-contractor should be included in certificates and payments issued to the main contractor; if they were not paid to the sub-contractor, the contract allowed the employer himself to pay such amounts upon the certificate of the architect and to deduct the amount so paid from any sums otherwise payable to the contractor. More precisely, clause 55(a) of the main contract stated:

> 'On application to the Architect, and within twenty-one days of the agreement by the Architect of the amount due, the Contractor shall be entitled to receive without undue delay a certificate from the Architect of the amount due to him from the Employer including sums due (if any) in respect of nominated sub-contractors (which sums shall be shown separately on each certificate) and before issuing any such certificate the Architect shall require the Contractor to furnish to him reasonable proof that all nominated sub-contractors' accounts included in previous certificates have been duly discharged (or, if not discharged, that the Contractor has reasonable cause for withholding payment) and

---

1   [1975] 1 WLR 758 at 780–781.
2   (1873) LR 8 Ch App 643.
3   [1975] 1 WLR 758 at 780.
4   (1992) 8 Const LJ 56.

in default of such proof, or satisfactory explanation of the cause of withholding payment, the Employer shall himself pay such accounts upon the certificate of the Architect and deduct the amount so paid from any sums otherwise payable to the Contractor.'

3.15   The sub-contract provided that monies received by the main contractor in respect of sub-contractor work should be held in trust by the main contractor for the benefit of the nominated sub-contractors, with the main contractor's interest in retention monies held by the employer being fiduciary as trustee for the nominated sub-contractors. If the main contractor failed to pay certified monies due to the nominated sub-contractors, clause 11(e) of the contract provided:

> '[The nominated sub-contractor] may (without prejudice to any other right or remedy) apply directly to the Employer for and the Employer may make payment of the amount certified to be due to the Sub-Contractor direct to the Sub-Contractor and the Employer may set-off the amount of any payment or payments by him to the Sub-Contractor against any monies due or to become due to the Contractor.
>
> Payment by the Employer to the Sub-Contractor direct shall be regarded as payment by the Contractor to the Sub-Contractor.'

Clause 12 of the sub-contract further provided that the main contractor would obtain for the nominated sub-contractor the rights and benefits of the main contract insofar as they were applicable to the sub-contract works.

3.16   Following the main contractor's liquidation, the liquidator decided to complete the main contract works. Prior to the date of the liquidation, the sum of £6,617 had been certified as due to the sub-contractor. It had been paid to the contractor but not passed to the sub-contractor. In addition, there was £12,148 outstanding in respect of:

– monies due for work carried out *after* the date of the liquidation;
– retention monies held by the employer.

3.17   The liquidator argued that to pay either of these sums direct would infringe the provisions of the Irish Companies Act 1963. Section 275 of the Companies Act 1963 provided that, subject to certain provisions with regard to preferential payments, the property of an insolvent company, on its winding-up, would be applied in satisfaction of its liabilities *pari passu*. The liquidator also relied on clause 22 of the sub-contract, which provided that if the provisions of the main contract were repugnant to or inconsistent with the sub-contract then the provisions of the sub-contract would prevail. He argued that since the direct payment provision of the main contract was expressed in a mandatory form it was inconsistent with a similar provision in the sub-contract which was expressed in a permissive form; therefore, the provision of the main contract was of no effect.

3.18   The judge chose to follow *Re Wilkinson ex parte Fowler*[1] and distinguish *British Eagle*.[2] The combined effect of the provisions of the main contract and sub-contracts was not to reduce the property of the insolvent contractor; the liquidator took the property of the contractor subject to the same equities as bound the

---

1   [1905] 2 KB 713; and see **3.4**.
2   [1975] 1 WLR 758; and see **3.12**.

contractor. The monies in question were not the property of the contractor because they were held in trust for the sub-contractor. In the words of his judgment:

'Prior to the *British Eagle* case, the validity of direct payment clauses was considered to be well established. As stated in *Hudson's Building and Engineering Contracts*, 1970 edition, at pages 791 and 792, a provision enabling the employer to effect direct payment of sub-contractors where the main contractor fails to make payment was in accordance with the general principle that the trustee or liquidator takes the bankrupt's property subject to liabilities which affected it in the bankrupt's hands and is binding on a trustee and liquidator. The authority for this proposition is in *Re Wilkinson ex parte Fowler* ... , a case which concerned the contract with a local authority for the construction of sewage works which contained a clause (cl. 54) which allowed the engineer named in the contract to order direct payment to firms providing machinery for the contract when he had reasonable cause to believe that the contractor was unduly delaying proper payment. In October 1904, the contractor was adjudicated bankrupt and there was then due to him under the contract £1,574 approximately made up of the sum of £1,349 approximately for retention money and £224 approximately payable on the next certificate. But there was due by him £836 in various amounts to specified firms for machinery supplied to him for the works. After adjudication, the engineer issued a certificate directing the payment of the £836 direct to the suppliers out of the retention money in the sum of £224. The court held that the authority given by the bankrupt to the engineer by the contract was not revoked by the bankruptcy, and that the engineer was entitled to order that the suppliers be paid direct out of the retention money.'[1]

3.19   Dealing with the *British Eagle* judgment, Costello J stated:

'The Court of Appeal held that the [IATA] arrangement did not contravene insolvency laws because "those laws require that the property of the insolvent company shall be distributed pro rata among its unsecured creditors, but the question here is whether the claim asserted against Air France is property of British Eagle. In our judgment it is not; British Eagle has long since deprived itself of any such property by agreeing to the clearing house scheme" ... This, too, was the view of the minority in the House of Lords; in their view, as stated by Lord Morris at p 768, the only property owned by British Eagle was the right, if on balance they proved to be in credit, to receive a payment from the clearing house. The majority took a different view of the clearing house scheme, holding that British Eagle had property at the commencement of the liquidation, taking the form of what was termed an innominate cause of action which had some but not all of the characteristics of a debt against Air France ... Having construed the agreement in this way, the majority then held that the effect of the scheme was to provide that this asset would be distributed in a manner other than that provided in section 302 of the Companies Act 1948 (which is in similar terms to s 275 of our Act) and that an agreement which had such an effect was contrary to public policy and therefore void. I respectfully agree with the analysis later made of these judgments by Peter Gibson J in *Carreras Rothmans Ltd v Freeman Mathews Treasure Ltd*[2] and his view that the principle established by the case was:

"where the effect of a contract is that an asset which is actually owned by a company at the commencement of its liquidation would be dealt with in a way other than in accordance with section 302, then, to that extent, the contract as a matter of public policy is avoided, whether or not the contract was entered into for consideration for

---

1   (1992) 8 Const LJ 56 at 59.
2   [1985] 1 All ER 155.

bona fide commercial reasons and whether or not the contractual provision affecting that asset is expressed to take effect only on insolvency" (p 168).'[1]

DIRECT PAYMENT PROVISIONS IN STANDARD FORM BUILDING CONTRACTS

3.20   The way in which the English standard form building contracts have dealt with direct payments are discussed below, together with the alterations made by the JCT to take on board the perceived effects of the *British Eagle* decision.

Clause 27(c) of JCT 63[2] provided:

'Before issuing any certificate under clause 30 of these Conditions the Architect/ Supervising Officer may request the Contractor to furnish him reasonable proof that all amounts included in the calculation of the amount stated as due on previous certificates in respect of the total value of work, materials or goods executed or supplied by the nominated sub-contractor have been duly discharged, and if the Contractor fails to comply with any such request the Architect/Supervising Officer shall issue a certificate to that effect and thereupon the Employer may himself pay such amounts to any nominated sub-contractor concerned ... and to deduct the same from any sums due or to become due to the Contractor.'

JCT 80 – direct payment provisions

3.21   Under JCT 80, the relevant direct payment provisions are found in clause 35.13.5 and can be either mandatory or discretionary. If the employer and nominated sub-contractor have executed what used to be Agreement NSC/2 or NSC/2a (now NSC/W), the employer is bound to operate clauses 35.13.5.3 and 35.13.5.4. However, the operation of the direct payment regime is conditional upon the architect having issued, under clause 35.13.3, a certificate to the effect that the main contractor has failed to provide evidence of discharge of the obligation to pay nominated sub-contractors following receipt by the contractor of interim certificates. Under clause 35.13.1, the architect is required on the issue of each interim certificate, to direct the contractor as to the amount included in each certificate which is due to the nominated sub-contractors, with the main contractor obliged under clause 35.13.2 to discharge those amounts in favour of the nominated sub-contractors. Once the main contractor has failed to provide evidence of discharge of obligations in favour of nominated sub-contractors, clause 35.13.5.2 provides:

'Provided that the Architect has issued the certificate under clause 35.13.5 subject to clause 35.13.5.3 the amount of any future payment otherwise due to the Contractor under this Contract (after deducting any monies due to the Employer from the Contractor under this Contract) shall be reduced by any amount due to Nominated Sub-Contractors which the Contractor has failed to discharge (together with the amount of any value added tax which would have been due to the Nominated Sub-Contractor) and the Employer shall himself pay the same to the Nominated Sub-Contractor concerned. Provided that the Employer shall in no circumstances be obliged to pay amounts to Nominated Sub-Contractors in excess of amounts available for reduction as aforesaid.'

---

1   (1992) 8 Const LJ 56 at 60.
2   (1977 Revision).

3.22   The important limitations on the right to make direct payments are found in clause 35.13.5. The current clauses are found in JCT Amendment 10 (1991) with the position now changed by JCT Amendment 18 (1998) and JCT 98. First, clause 35.13.5.3.1 requires that the direct payment and reduction against the contractor are made at the same time as any balance due under an interim certificate payable to the contractor, or in the absence of a balance due, within 14 days after the contractor would otherwise be entitled to payment. Clause 30.1.1.2 allows deductions for direct payments to be made from the retention fund, although clause 35.13.5.3.2 limits the amount which may be deducted to the contractor's retention, with clause 35.13.5.3.3 further requiring direct payments to be made on a pro rata basis if the amount due to the contractor and available for deduction is insufficient to cover the total balance due. However, perhaps most importantly, the *British Eagle* decision was taken seriously by the JCT, to the extent that the direct payment clause in JCT 80 was amended in clause 35.13.5.3.4 to state that the provisions relating to direct payment of nominated sub-contractors contained in clause 35.13.5.2 ceased to have any effect if, at the date when the payment would otherwise be made, there is in existence:

–   either a petition presented to the court for the winding-up of the contractor; or
–   a resolution properly passed for the winding-up of the contractor other than for the purposes of amalgamation or reconstruction.

If the formal winding-up of the contractor does not proceed, it would appear, on the face of it, that direct payments to nominated sub-contractors are not possible because the mere presentation of a petition suffices to freeze the direct payment mechanism in perpetuity.

NOMINATED SUB-CONTRACTOR AGREEMENTS

3.23   Given the potential uncertainty of direct payment clauses under the law and the abstruse wording in JCT contracts, many employers dislike nomination and will operate the direct payment clauses only in the event that there is an executed Employer/Nominated Sub-Contractor Agreement, whether it be NSC/2, NSC/2a or NSC/W. There are identical clauses in NSC/2, NSC/2a, and NSC/W with regard to the effect of the contractor's bankruptcy or liquidation to take on board the decision in *British Eagle*:

'7.1 The Architect/Supervising Officer and the Employer shall operate the provisions in regard to the payment of the Sub-Contractor in Clause 35.13 of the Main Contract Conditions.

7.2 If, after paying any amount to the Sub-Contractor under Clause 35.13.5.3 of the Main Contract Conditions, the Employer produces reasonable proof that there was in existence at the time of such a payment a petition or resolution to which Clause 35.13.5.4.4 [prior to amendment 10] of the Main Contract Conditions refers the Sub-Contractor shall repay on demand such amount.'

3.24   However, the key provision to which the employer should have regard is that contained in 7.1, making it obligatory that the supervising officer operates the direct payment provisions in clause 35.13. On occasions, supervising officers can be lax in doing this, to the extent that the employer finds himself in arbitration under the

Warranty Agreement. The supervising officer's failure to operate the direct payment provisions becomes a breach of contract for which the employer is liable. Sometimes contract administrators are not overly fastidious in ensuring that the clause 35.13.3 obligations are complied with: namely, that, prior to the issue of each interim certificate, the contractor provides the architect with proof that money certified in favour of nominated sub-contractors is being paid. Requirement of proof goes beyond a simple airy assurance from the contractor that payments are up to date. Provided the circumstances apply in which the direct payment provisions are to be operated, the architect is mandated to issue the requisite certificate under clause 35.13.5.2, and any failure to do so will be a breach of contract for which he (and, if the NSC/W Agreement has been executed, the employer) will be liable.

3.25   If nominated sub-contractors are successfully to assert rights, the existence of the NSC/W Agreement is essential. Simply because the main contract purports to provide the nominated sub-contractor with a benefit, this does not of itself create the requisite degree of privity between employer and nominated sub-contractor. Both JCT 80, and its predecessor, JCT 63, are clear on this point:

> 'Neither the existence nor the exercise of the powers in clause 35 nor anything else contained in the Conditions shall render the Employer in any way liable to any Nominated Sub-Contractor except by way and in the terms of the Agreement NSC/W.'

Otherwise, the nominated sub-contractor would have to establish the existence of a collateral contract in accordance with the principles set out in *Shanklin Pier Ltd v Detel Products Ltd*.[1]

3.26   The modern provisions in JCT 80 were considered by the High Court of Northern Ireland in *B Mullan & Sons (Contractors) Ltd v Ross*.[2] The plaintiff, Mullan, was a sub-contractor to McLaughlin & Harvey when the main contractor went into administrative receivership. Shortly afterwards, the main contractor was placed in liquidation, with the defendants appointed as liquidators. The contract contained, inter alia, the standard JCT clause:

> '... the Employer may pay any supplier or sub-contractor for any materials or goods delivered or works executed for the purposes of this Contract (whether before or after the date of determination) in so far as the price thereof has not already been paid by the Contractor (clause 27.4.3.2).'

The liquidators argued that this clause contravened the applicable Northern Irish insolvency legislation and the *pari passu* principle. Inspired by the decision in *British Eagle*, Kerr J held:

> 'My conclusion that the payments due for the work executed by the sub-contractor constituted property of McLaughlin & Harvey at the time of the winding-up renders those payments equally subject to the pari passu principle. The decision in *British Eagle* recognises the fundamental and predominant nature of the principle of pari passu in insolvency law. It appears to me that, to exclude from its ambit payments due for work carried out by a sub-contractor which, before winding-up, would be payable to the main contractor, would represent a considerable encroachment on, and compromise of, the efficacy of the principle. I must also reject the submission that *ex parte Mackay* and *ex*

---

1   [1951] 2 All ER 471.
2   (1996) CILL 1149.

parte Jay can be distinguished on the basis that in those cases a deliberate attempt was made by one party to secure for itself an advantage over unsecured creditors. The fact that the payment to the sub-contractor is at the instance of the employer rather than the sub-contractor does not create a distinction of any significance in my opinion.'[1]

3.27   The judge also placed reliance upon a New Zealand decision, *Attorney-General v McMillan and Lockwood*.[2] In that case, under a public works contract, clause 19.11 allowed sub-contractors, suppliers, employees and other persons to be paid direct 'as if such persons were a lawful assignee of the contractor in respect of such monies'. By a majority, the New Zealand Court of Appeal held that the contract wording presupposed that the contractor had property in those monies. Direct payments were to be made out of monies then due or to become due to the contractors. With the contractor still having an interest in the monies at the date of liquidation, subsequent payments needed to be made strictly in accordance with *pari passu* principles. The majority concluded that the *Re Tout and Finch*[3] line of authorities allowed direct payments to be made to sub-contractors precisely because payment was made out of monies which were neither due nor would become due to the main contractor.

APPOINTMENT OF ADMINISTRATIVE RECEIVER OR ADMINISTRATOR

3.28   Often, practitioners deal with the appointment of an administrative receiver or an administrator. An administrative receiver is one appointed within the meaning of s 29(2) of the Insolvency Act 1986, whose appointment derives from a debenture secured by a floating charge over the whole or a substantial part of the debtor's property. The existence of a floating charge, prior to its crystallisation into a fixed charge on the appointment of an administrative receiver, does not prevent the use of assets subject to the charge in the ordinary course of business. On appointment, an administrative receiver takes over, for all intents and purposes, the responsibilities of the directors for the management of companies. The directors remain in office subject to their statutory responsibilities, but their powers are suspended in relation to those assets passed to the control of the receiver. Pending liquidation of the company, the receiver is deemed to be the agent of the company (s 44(1)(a) of the Insolvency Act 1986). As far as administration orders are concerned, the procedure is set out in ss 8–27 of the Insolvency Act 1986, with the principal objective being that of corporate rescue rather than immediate liquidation. The court can make an administration order if it is satisfied that the company concerned is unable to pay its debts or is likely to become unable to do so. A petition for an administration order may be presented by all or any of the company's directors or creditors. In most instances, it will be at the behest of the directors. The court must be satisfied that the administration order is likely to achieve one or more of the following:

–   the survival of the company, and the whole or any part of its undertaking, as a going concern;

---

1   (1996) CILL 1149 at 1150.
2   [1991] 1 NZLR 53.
3   [1954] 1 WLR 178; and see **3.5**.

- the approval of a voluntary arrangement under the Insolvency Act 1986;
- the sanctioning of a scheme of arrangement under the Companies Act 1985;
- the more advantageous realisation of the company's assets than would be achieved on a winding up.

Administrator and administrative receiver

3.29   Once an administration order has been made, for its duration the company will be managed by the administrator who will discharge those duties ordinarily undertaken by the directors. The principal distinction between an administrator and an administrative receiver is that the former is appointed by the court to manage the affairs of the company in the interests of all the creditors, whereas the latter's primary duty is to the debenture holder. The administration order permits a company's affairs to be 'frozen', imposing a moratorium on the rights of creditors to claim payment of sums owed to them. By this means, a framework is provided for any corporate rescue to be undertaken. During the period of the administration order, the enforcement of any securities or the taking of any other proceedings cannot occur except with leave of the court.

3.30   Although an administrative receiver has a statutory obligation to pay certain preferential creditors out of the assets in priority to the floating charge holder (s 40 of the Insolvency Act 1986), sub-contractors, whether nominated or domestic, are not preferential creditors for the purposes of Sch 6 to the Insolvency Act 1986. For this reason, administrative receivers often write to employers, who have nominated sub-contractors, broadly along the lines of the draft letter set out in the Appendix to this chapter. However, it is arguable that the monies due to the main contractor do not constitute a debt to the extent that they include nominated sub-contractors' monies, because the employer has the right to pay the sub-contractor direct, with those monies never being the property of the main contractor. With those monies outside s 40 of the Insolvency Act 1986 and not subject to the floating charge, direct payment is not restricted by principles akin to the *pari passu* principle operating on liquidation.

Administration orders

3.31   The position on administration is more complex. In *Contemporary Issues in Construction Law, Volume One – Security for Payment*,[1] Gerard McCormack, in his chapter 'Pari passu distribution in Construction Contracts' puts the position in the following terms:

> 'It has been argued that the position with respect to administration orders is different. See the major loose-leaf publication *Insolvency* by Peter Totty and Michael Jordan at para H6.03 "[W]hilst not every administration order leads onto a liquidation, the aim of an administration order is to freeze the situation as far as possible in relation to creditors pending either liquidation or a scheme or a return to solvency and that a direct payment would be contrary to the spirit of the relevant statutory provisions". The persuasiveness of this argument turns on the breadth of the moratorium on the enforcement of claims against the company that applies after the presentation of a petition for the appointment of an administrator during the currency of an administration order. During this period [an administration order], except with the consent of the administrator or the court, no steps

---

1   Davis and Odams (eds) (Construction Law Press, 1996) pp 83–98.

may be taken to enforce any security over the company's property. [Sections 10 and 11 of the Insolvency Act 1986.] "Security" has been given a broad interpretation within this context. In *Exchange Travel Agency Ltd v Triton Property Trust plc*[1] it was held that the forfeiture of a lease by a landlord through the exercise of his right of peaceable re-entry constituted the enforcement of security for the purpose of the provision. Surely, however, it would be stretching things too far if the concept of "security" was held to embrace a contractual entitlement on the part of the employer to withhold payment from the main contractor in certain circumstances. This is what a direct payment clause entails. Administration must leave intact the contractual status quo between employer and main contractor. There may be an argument that direct payment clauses are rendered inoperative after an administration order has been made by section 239 of the Insolvency Act 1986. This section invalidates any act or thing done by a company in a certain time scale which has the effect of putting a person in a better position than he would otherwise occupy in the event of the company's insolvent liquidation. It is submitted that direct payment clauses are unlikely to be caught by this provision. Firstly, it is questionable whether the agreement by the contractor company to the insertion of a direct payment clause in the main contract constitutes an act or thing done by it. Secondly, for a payment to be caught by the section the contractor company must have been "influenced by a desire" to prefer. In *Re MC Bacon Ltd*[2] Millett J distinguished between desire and the intention. Desire was subjective while intention was objective. A person might have to choose between the lesser of two evils without desiring either.'

PREFERENTIAL PAYMENTS TO NOMINATED SUB-CONTRACTORS

3.32 It is sometimes overlooked that the employer has a right, concurrent with that provided by clause 35.13.5 of JCT 80, under clause 27.4.2.2 but subject to the revisions made by JCT Amendment 11 (1992) to make direct payments to:

'... any supplier or sub-contractor for any materials or goods delivered or works executed for the purposes of this Contract ... in so far as the price thereof has not already been paid by the Contractor. The Employer's rights and any payments under clause 27.4.2 may be deducted from any sum due or to become due to the Contractor or shall be recovered from the Contractor by the Employer as a debt.'

This was the clause considered in the Northern Irish case, *Mullan*.[3] Where this seems to fall foul of the insolvency legislation, is in the express recognition that the deduction is from 'any sum due or to become due to the Contractor'. This is enough to create the presumption that a preference is being created. However, the story does not stop there. Clause 27.6.2.2 of Amendment 11 (1992), although similar in some respects to the original clause 27.4.2 of JCT 80, precludes the making of direct payments if an insolvency event of the type specified in clause 27.3.1 of Amendment 11 (eg the making of a winding-up order or the appointment of an administrator or administrative receiver) has occurred. Surprisingly, the proviso both to the JCT 80 clause (27.4.2) and the Amendment 11 clause does not mirror clause 35.13.5 of JCT 80. There is no reference in clause 27.4.2 or in clause 27.6.2.2 of Amendment 11 to the

---

1   [1991] BCLC 396.
2   [1991] Ch 127.
3   (1996) CILL 1149; and see **3.26**.

presentation of a petition as opposed to the making of a winding-up order. However, it would be imprudent for the employer to pay the sub-contractor direct in circumstances where he knew that a petition had actually been presented.

3.33   Whether or not it is provable that any employer has made direct payments to nominated sub-contractors in breach of the insolvency legislation, it would be imprudent for any employer, regardless of what is stated in the contract documentation, to make a direct payment without ensuring that this is on the basis that if it is subsequently held to have been made invalidly, the sub-contractor (assuming its continued insolvency) will pay back any monies illegally advanced.

3.34   Other solutions have been sought to the problem of securing monies due and payable to sub-contractors. Following Sir Michael Latham's report, *Constructing the Team*, the Department of the Environment issued its consultation paper, *Fair Construction Contracts*, in May 1995. The solution did not lie in reversing the *British Eagle* decision:

> 'The Government does not think it necesary to amend the Insolvency Act 1986 to reverse the *British Eagle* judgment (as recommended in "Constructing the Team") since it is considered that a properly constituted trust containing appropriate terms would deal adequately with the problems that have been identified in this field. It is understood, however, that some sectors of the construction industry are still concerned about problems that may arise for sub-contractors or in cases where a trust fund has not in practice been established. Further thought is being given to this issue.'

The trust account provisions taken from the ECA and ECC standard documentation are appended to this chapter. However, neither major funders nor main contractors have shown the slightest enthusiasm for a mechanism which requires money to be tied up in this way.

JCT AMENDMENT 18 (1998) AND JCT 98

3.35   The Housing Grants, Construction and Regeneration Act 1996 has meant changes to standard form building contracts. The provisions relating to nominated sub-contractors have now been altered. To comply with the principle of the 'final date for payment' under the 1996 Act, clause 35.13.2 now reads:

> 'Each payment directed under clause 35.13.1.1 shall be paid by the Contractor by the final date for payment in accordance with Conditions NSC/C . . .'

This reflects the amendments made to Conditions NSC/C in Amendment 7, April 1998. Clause 35.13.3 has substituted the word 'payment' for 'discharge' and clause 35.13.16.2 has been modified to comply with s 111 of the 1996 Act. There are, in addition, several other minor alterations.

Appendix

DRAFT LETTER FROM ADMINISTRATIVE RECEIVER TO EMPLOYER – WHERE CONTRACT IS JCT 80/JCT 98 AND PETITION PRESERVED

Dear Sirs,

[contract reference] (**'the Contract'**)

We write to inform you that a petition was presented on *[date]* for the winding-up of *[name of company]* ('the Company').

[1]Accordingly, we must advise you that it has not since this date been open to you to make any direct payment to nominated sub-contractors under clause 35.13.5.3 of the Contract or to any sub-contractors under clause 27.4.2. Clause 35.13.5.3 of the Contract has ceased to have effect under the provision in clause 35.13.5.4.4 and the provisions of clause 27.4.2 cease to operate by virtue of the stated exception to that clause. We put you on notice that if you make or have made any direct payments and purport to deduct a corresponding sum from monies due to the Company, we will challenge such deduction and claim the full amount of the said sum as monies remaining due to the Company from you. In such circumstances, should you make any direct payment to nominated sub-contractors, you will be compelled, in effect, to pay twice and to look to the relevant sub-contractors for reimbursement of the sums paid to them.

In any event, no direct payments could properly be made following the appointment of Administrative Receivers on *[date]*. Under a debenture dated *[date]*, a fixed charge exists over the Company's book debts so that all monies becoming due under the Contract are or have been assigned to the debenture holder. The debenture holder's charge thus takes precedence over the provision in clause 35.13.5.3 for direct payment.

For the avoidance of doubt, the Administrative Receivers do not hereby adopt the Contract and contract at all times as agents of the Company without personal liability.

Yours faithfully

---

1   Delete second paragraph if no petition has been presented and re-phrase third paragraph as appropriate to reflect simple appointment of administrative receivers.

ECC – TRUST ACCOUNT PROVISIONS

OPTION V: TRUST FUND

Defined terms   VI

VI.1   (1)   The Trust Fund is a fund held and administered by the *Trustees*.

(2)   The Trust Deed is a deed between the *Employer* and the *Trustees* which contains the provisions for administering the Trust Fund. Terms defined in this contract have the same meaning in the Trust Deed.

(3)   The Initial Value of the Trust Fund is an amount which is the total of the Prices at the Contract Date multiplied by 1.5 and divided by the number of months in the period between the Contract Date and the Completion Date.

(4)   Insolvency of an individual occurs when that individual has

- presented his petition for bankruptcy,
- had a bankruptcy order made against him,
- had a receiver appointed over his assets,
- made an arrangement with his creditors.

(5)   Insolvency of a company occurs when it has:

- had a winding-up order made against it,
- had a provisional liquidator appointed to it,
- passed a resolution for winding-up (other than in order to amalgamate or reconstruct),
- had an administration order made against it,
- had a receiver, receiver and manager, or administrative receiver appointed over the whole or a substantial part of its undertaking or assets, or
- made an arrangement with its creditors.

(6)   The Beneficiaries are the *Contractor* and

- Subcontractors,
- suppliers of the *Contractor*,
- subcontractors of whatever tier of a Subcontractor and
- suppliers of whatever tier of a Subcontractor or of his subcontractors

who are employed to Provide the Works.

(7)   A Trust Payment is a payment made by the *Trustees* out of the Trust Fund.

Trust Fund   **V2**

                          V2.1 The *Employer* establishes the Trust Fund within one week of the Contract Date.

                          V2.2 The Trust Fund is established

- by the *Employer* making a payment to the *Trustees* equal to the Initial Value, or
- by the *Employer* providing the *Trustees* with a guarantee of the Initial Value, payable to the *Trustees* on their first written demand, given by a bank or other financial institution acceptable to the *Trustees*, or
- if the *Employer* is a Government department or other public authority in the United Kingdom, by the *Employer* entering into irrevocable undertakings with the *Contractor* and the *Trustees* to pay the *Trustees* promptly on demand such amounts as they request for
  - Trust Payments, and
  - their fees and expenses for administering the Trust Fund.

                          V2.3 The *Contractor* informs his suppliers and his Subcontractors of the terms of the Trust Deed and of the appointment of the *Trustees*. He arranges that Subcontractors ensure that their suppliers and subcontractors, of whatever tier, are also informed.

Trust Deed   **V3**

                          V3.1 The Trust Fund is administered by the *Trustees* in accordance with the Trust Deed. The Trust Deed includes the following provisions.

                          (1) If a Beneficiary satisfies the *Trustees*

- that he has received all or part of a payment properly due to him under his contract relating to the *works* which was unpaid at the time of the Insolvency, and
- that the reason for the failure to pay is the Insolvency of the party which should have made the payment,

                          the *Trustees* may at their discretion make a Trust Payment to the Beneficiary of an amount not exceeding the value of the payment which he has not received.

                          (2) If a Beneficiary subsequently receives a payment from another party, in respect of which a Trust payment has been made, the Beneficiary passes on that payment to the *Trustees* (up to the value of the Trust Payment). Before making a Trust Payment the *Trustees* may require from a Beneficiary either an assignment of rights or an undertaking with respect to that payment in a form acceptable to them.

(3)   The *Trustees* have discretion to decide the amount and timing of every Trust Payment. They may make a Trust Payment on account or withhold a Trust Payment until they have assessed the total amount of debts owing to a Beneficiary arising out of an Insolvency. They may take into account any claims (including claims by way of set-off) which the party suffering from Insolvency may have against the Beneficiary as well as the likely ability of the liquidator or other administrator of the insolvent party to meet the claims of unsecured creditors from funds in his hands.

(4)   If the Trust Fund was established by a payment, the *Employer* maintains the Trust Fund at the Initial Value. If the Trust Fund was established by a guarantor, the *Employer* ensures that the guarantor maintains the Trust Fund at the Initial Value. The *Trustees* notify the Employer or the guarantor within one week of making a Trust Payment and the *Employer* or the guarantor restores the Trust Fund to the Initial Value within two weeks of the notification.

(5)   After the *Trustees* have made all Trust Payments, any amount in the Trust Fund (including any accrued interest) is paid by the *Trustees* to the *Employer*. If a guarantee has been provided, it is returned to the guarantor. The *Trustees* do not pay claims from Beneficiaries which they receive after the Defects Certificate has been issued.

(6)   The *Employer* pays the *Trustees* their fees and expenses for administering the Trust Fund.

(7)   The *Trustees* may engage professional consultants to help them with the administration of the Trust Fund and may make Trust Payments for their fees and expenses.

(8)   The *Trustees* hold the Trust Fund on an interest-bearing bank account.

. . .

Trust Account   11.2   The Contractor will procure that the Customer complies with his obligations in relation to the Trust Account insofar as they relate to this Agreement. The procedures for establishing and operating the Trust Account shall be as follows:

(a)   the Customer shall prior to the first Transfer Date under the Principal Contract open and thereafter maintain the Trust Account with the Bank and shall be responsible for establishing procedures for making all payments from the Trust Account on each Settlement Date in accordance with the Principal Contract;

(b) the moneys paid into the Trust Account on each Transfer Date together with any further moneys lodged therein pursuant to Clause 11.4(c) or 11.6(c) but excluding any interest accruing from time to time shall be held on trust by the Customer for the benefit of the Contractor and each Specialist Contractor named in the Payment Summary relevant to that Transfer Date according to the amounts shown in that Payment Summary as payable to each of them on the relevant Settlement Date. The Customer shall have no obligation as trustee to invest such moneys;

(c) if the employment of the Contractor is terminated under Clause 20 of the Principal Contract or if the employment of the Specialist Contractor is terminated by the Contractor under Clause 20 of this Agreement between a Transfer Date and the Settlement Date relevant to that Transfer Date and if the Customer, as trustee, is aware of notice of such termination being given, then the moneys which would otherwise have been payable to the Contractor or that Specialist Contractor on the Settlement Date shall be retained in the Trust Account by the Customer, as trustee, to be dealt with in accordance with the provisions contained in the termination clause in the applicable conditions of contract;

(d) the Trust Account shall have the designation referred to in the Appendix (which shall include the word 'trustee') and the Customer shall, on opening the Trust Account, notify the Bank that the monies from time to time in the Trust Account are held by the Customer as trustee upon the terms of the Principal Contract;

(e) the Customer shall notify the Bank of the appointment of the Specialist Contractor for whom he shall hold monies on trust in accordance with Clause 11.2(b) as soon as he is advised by the Contractor of such appointment;

(f) the Customer shall within 7 days of a written request by the Contractor or any Specialist Contractor provide sufficient information to the Contractor or any Specialist Contractor to show that the Trust Account has been opened and is being maintained in accordance with Clause 11.2(a);

(g) the Customer shall be absolutely entitled to all interest from time to time accruing on moneys standing to the credit of the Trust Account and shall be allowed to use such interest until closure of the Trust Account;

(h) after the certification referred to in Clause 11.6(e) of the Principal Contract, the Customer shall be entitled to close the Trust Account; and

(i) in the event of court proceedings being commenced pursuant to Clause 19.8 of the Principal Contract or Clause 19.9 of this Agreement, the Customer and the

Contractor shall, nonetheless, certify to the Bank in the manner described in Clause 11.6(e) of the Principal Contract in order to allow the closure of the Trust Account. Any sum which the court thereafter determines is due from the Contractor to the Specialist Contractor or the Specialist Contractor to the Contractor shall be paid as the courts direct.

Transfer Dates   11.3   Transfer Dates and Settlement Dates shall be established as follows:

(a)   Under the Principal Contract:

  –   where there are no advance payments in accordance with Clause 11.5 of the Principal Contract the first Transfer Date will be 3 days before the commencement date under the Principal Contract as set out in the Appendix and subsequent Transfer Dates shall be at intervals of one month calculated from the date of the first Transfer Date until the final payment has been made;

  –   where advance payment(s) are required in accordance with Clause 11.5 of the Principal Contract the first Transfer Date will be one month and 3 days prior to the first advance payment date;

  –   the first Settlement Date under the Principal Contract will be one month and 3 days after the first Transfer Date under the Principal Contract and subsequent Settlement Dates shall be at intervals of one month calculated from the date of the first Settlement Date until the final payment has been made.

(b)   Under the Agreement the first Settlement Date will be as set out in Tender (SC) and the first Transfer Date will be one month and 3 days before that Settlement Date.

Interim Payments   11.4   The procedure for making interim payments to the Specialist Contractor shall be as follows:

(a)   8 days before each Transfer Date the Specialist Contractor shall submit to the Contractor a copy of the then current Payment Schedule showing the VAT exclusive amount due to the Specialist Contractor on the relevant Settlement Date. The Contractor will then consolidate the Payment Schedule from the Specialist Contractor into the Payment Summary which he will then submit to the Customer together with the then current Payment Schedule under the Principal Contract;

(b)   on each Transfer Date the Customer shall transfer to the Trust Account an amount equal to the aggregate of (i) the amount shown in the Contractor's Payment Schedule referred to in Clause 11.4(a) of the Principal Contract as due on the relevant Settlement Date and (ii) any VAT subsequently due on such amount at the tax point relevant to that Settlement Date;

(c)   the Contractor shall 4 days before the relevant Transfer
Date transfer to the Trust Account an amount equal to
the aggregate of:

–   any VAT in relation to the amount shown in the
Payment Summary as being subsequently due to
Specialist Contractors at the relevant tax point
where the Works under the Principal Contract are
zero-rated and Works carried out by Specialist
Contractors are standard rated;

–   any shortfall between the total amount shown in
the Payment Summary as being due to Specialist
Contractors and the amount shown in the payment
schedule referred to in Clause 11.4(a) of the
Principal Contract as being due from the Customer on the relevant Transfer Date together with
any VAT subsequently due on such shortfall at
the relevant tax point;

(d)   on each Transfer Date the Customer, as trustee, shall
give the Specialist Contractor notice of the total amount
which is payable to him on the relevant Settlement Date
and confirm that the relevant funds have been transferred to the Trust Account;

(e)   on each Settlement Date the Customer, as trustee, shall
out of the moneys in the Trust Account effect payment
to the Specialist Contractor of the amount shown as due
to the Specialist Contractor in the Payment Summary
referred to in Clause 11.4(a) save where the Specialist
Contractor has failed to provide a Retention Bond and
the Contractor has advised the Customer accordingly;

(f)   if the Trust Account has insufficient funds to meet all
moneys due on the Settlement Date, the Customer, as
trustee, shall make payment to the Contractor and to
each Specialist Contractor on a pro rata basis according
to the amounts shown as due to the Contractor and to
each Specialist Contractor in the Payment Summary
referred to in clause 11.4(a).

Payment for Work in   11.5   Where in tender (SC) or prior to the date of this Agreement,
Advance of   the Contractor had agreed with the Specialist Contractor's
Commencement Date   proposal for advanced payments then the provisions of
Clause 11.3(b) shall apply.

Final Payment   11.6   The procedure for making final payment to the Specialist
Contractor shall be as follows:

(a)   not later than 60 days following the date of Acceptance
the Specialist Contractor shall submit to the Contractor
the finally adjusted Payment Schedule showing the
amount due to him. The finally adjusted Payment
Schedule shall show the final amount due to the
Specialist Contractor except where notice has been

given under Clause 19.9 of this Agreement. The Contractor will then consolidate the Payment Schedule from the Specialist Contractor into the next Payment Summary;

(b)   the Contractor shall submit to the Customer the Payment Summary incorporating the final amount due to the Specialist Contractor 4 days before the Transfer Date following settlement of the then current Payment Schedule of the Principal Contract in accordance with Clause 11.6(a) of this Agreement;

(c)   on the relevant Transfer Date the Customer shall transfer to the Trust Account an amount equal to the aggregate of (i) the amount shown in the Contractor's Payment Schedule as due on the relevant Settlement Date and (ii) any VAT subsequently due on such amount at the tax point relevant to that Settlement Date;

(d)   the Contractor shall 4 days before the relevant Transfer Date transfer to the Trust Account an amount equal to:

–   any VAT in relation to the amount shown in the Payment Summary as being subsequently due to Specialist Contractors at the relevant tax point or an adjustment to the Payment Schedule the matter may be referred by either party to the Referee for a decision.

ECA – MAIN CONTRACT CONDITIONS

11.   PAYMENT PROVISIONS

Payment Schedule and   11.1   Payments shall be made in accordance with the Payment
Adjustments   Schedule and the provisions of this Clause:

    (a)   the Payment Schedule shall be adjusted from time to
time to take account of:

-     adjustments agreed by the parties pursuant to
Clause 3.5;
-     adjustments arising from instructions pursuant to
the provisions of Clause 8;
-     adjustments made to reflect extensions of time
granted under Clause 10;
-     adjustments to take account of fluctuations pursuant to Clause 12;
-     loss and/or expense becoming due to the Contractor under Clause 13;
-     decisions of the Referee causing a change in the
Contract Sum and/or Payment Schedule;

    (b)   where the Payment Schedule is to be adjusted pursuant
to Clause 11.1(a) only adjustments made to the Payment Schedule at least 10 days before a Transfer Date
shall be taken into account in calculating the amount
payable;

    (c)   any dispute concerning any adjustment to the Payment
Schedule and/or Contract Sum may be referred by
either party to the Referee for a decision.

Trust Account   11.2   The procedures for establishing and operating the Trust
Account shall be as follows:

    (a)   the Customer shall prior to the first Transfer Date open
and thereafter maintain the Trust Account with the
Bank and shall be responsible, as trustee, for establishing procedures for making all payments from the
Trust Account on each Settlement Date in accordance
with this Agreement;

    (b)   the moneys paid into the Trust Account on each
Transfer Date together with any further moneys lodged
therein pursuant to Clause 11.4(c) or 11.6(c) but
excluding any interest accruing from time to time shall
be held on trust by the Customer for the benefit of the
Contractor and each Specialist Contractor named in the
Payment Summary relevant to that Transfer Date
according to the amounts shown in that Payment
Summary as payable to each of them on the relevant

Settlement Date. The Customer shall have no obligation as trustee to invest such moneys;

(c) if the employment of the Contractor is terminated under Clause 20 of this Agreement or the employment of any Specialist Contractor is terminated by the Contractor under Clause 20 of the sub-contract conditions for use with these conditions between a Transfer Date and the Settlement Date relevant to that Transfer Date and if the Customer, as trustee, is aware of notice of such termination being given, then the moneys which would otherwise have been payable to the Contractor or that Specialist Contractor on the Settlement Date shall be retained in the Trust Account by the Customer, as trustee, to be dealt with in accordance with the provisions contained in the termination clause in the applicable conditions of contract;

(d) if a Specialist Contractor gives notice to terminate or has his employment automatically terminated under Clause 20 of the sub-contract conditions for use with these Conditions, then the Contractor shall notify the Customer, as trustee, as to the amount ascertained as due to that Specialist Contractor up to the date of termination and such amount shall be deemed to be an amount contained in the next Payment Summary submitted by the Contractor to the Customer and payable to that Specialist Contractor in accordance with the provisions of this Clause 11. If the Customer receives notice from the Specialist Contractor to the effect that the Contractor has failed to notify the Customer within 7 days of the amount due to the Specialist Contractor being ascertained, the Customer shall accept the Specialist Contractor's notice as to the amount ascertained as due to it and, for this purpose, deal with the Specialist Contractor as attorney for the Contractor;

(e) the Trust Account shall have the designation referred to in the Appendix (which shall include the word 'trustee') and the Customer shall, on opening the Trust Account, give notice to the Bank in the form set out in Schedule 2 notifying the Bank that the moneys from time to time in the Trust Account are held by the Customer as trustee upon the terms of this Agreement;

(f) the Customer shall notify the Bank of the appointment of each Specialist Contractor for whom he shall hold moneys on trust in accordance with Clause 11.2(b) as soon as he is advised by the Contractor of such appointment;

(g) the Customer shall within 7 days of a written request by the Contractor or any Specialist Contractor provide sufficient information to the Contractor or any Specialist Contractor to show that the Trust Account has been opened and is being maintained in accordance with Clause 11.2(a);

(h) the Customer shall be absolutely entitled to all interest from time to time accruing on moneys standing to the credit of the Trust Account and shall be allowed to use such interest until closure of the Trust Account;

(i) after the certification referred to in Clause 11.6(e) the Customer shall be entitled to close the Trust Account; and

(j) in the event of court proceedings being commenced pursuant to Clause 19.8, the Customer and the Contractor shall, nonetheless, certify to the bank in the manner described in Clause 11.6(e) in order to allow the closure of the Trust Account. Any sum which the court thereafter determines is due from the Customer to the Contractor or the Contractor to the Customer shall be paid as the court directs.

Transfer Dates and Settlement Dates
11.3 Transfer Dates and Settlement Dates shall be established as follows:

(a) where there are no advance payments in accordance with Clause 11.5 the first Transfer Date will be 3 days before the Commencement Date and subsequent Transfer Dates shall be at intervals of one month calculated from the date of the first Transfer Date until the final payment has been made;

(b) where advance payment(s) are required in accordance with Clause 11.5 the first Transfer Date will be one month and 3 days prior to the first advance payment date;

(c) the first Settlement Date will be one month and 3 days after the first Transfer Date and subsequent Settlement Dates shall be at intervals of one month calculated from the date of the first Settlement Date until the final payment has been made.

Interim Payments
11.4 The procedure for making interim payments shall be as follows:

(a) 4 days before each Transfer Date the Contractor shall submit to the Customer a copy of the then current Payment Schedule and Payment Summary;

(b) on each Transfer Date the Customer shall transfer to the Trust Account an amount equal to the aggregate of (i) the amount shown in the Payment Schedule referred to in Clause 11.4(a) as due on the relevant Settlement Date and (ii) any VAT subsequently due on such amount at the tax point relevant to that Settlement Date;

(c) the Contractor shall 4 days before the relevant Transfer Date transfer to the Trust Account an amount equal to the aggregate of:

> – any VAT in relation to the amount shown in the Payment Summary as being subsequently due to Specialist Contractors at the relevant tax point where the Works under this Agreement are zero-rated and works carried out by Specialist Contractors are standard rated;
>
> – any shortfall between the total amount shown in the Payment Summary as being due to Specialist Contractors and the amount shown in the Payment Schedule referred to in Clause 11.4(a) as being due from the Customer on the relevant Transfer Date together with any VAT subsequently due on such shortfall at the relevant tax point;

(d) on each Transfer Date the Customer, as trustee, shall give the Contractor and every Specialist Contractor notice of the total amount which is payable to each of them on the relevant Settlement Date and confirm that the relevant funds have been transferred to the Trust Account;

(e) on each Settlement Date the Customer, as trustee, shall out of the moneys in the Trust Account effect payment to the Contractor and each Specialist Contractor of the amount shown as due to each of them in the Payment Summary referred to in Clause 11.4(a) save that the Customer may, in his capacity as trustee, withhold payment to the Contractor if he has failed to provide a Retention Bond and that the Customer, as trustee, shall not effect payment to any Specialist Contractor in respect of whom the Contractor has given notice to the Customer that the Specialist Contractor has failed to provide a Retention Bond;

(f) if the Trust Account has insufficient funds to meet all moneys due on the Settlement Date, the Customer as trustee, shall make payment to the Contractor and to each Specialist Contractor on a pro rata basis according to the amounts shown as due to the Contractor and to each Specialist Contractor in the Payment Summary referred to in clause 11.4(a).

Payment for Work in Advance of Commencement Date

11.5 Where, in Tender PC or prior to the date of this Agreement, the Customer had agreed with the Contractor's proposal for advanced payment(s) then the provisions of Clause 11.3(b) shall apply.

Final Payment

11.6 The procedure for making final payment shall be as follows:

(a) not later than 70 days following the date of Acceptance the Contractor shall submit to the Customer the finally adjusted Payment Schedule together with a final Payment Summary showing the amounts outstanding to the Contractor and to any Specialist Contractor. The amounts shown in the Final Payment Summary shall represent the final amounts due to the respective parties except where notice has been given under Clause 19.8;

(b) on the next Transfer Date following receipt of the finally adjusted Payment Schedule and the final Payment Summary the Customer shall transfer to the Trust Account an amount equal to the aggregate of (i) the amount shown in the finally adjusted Payment Schedule as due on the final Settlement Date and (ii) any VAT subsequently due on such amount at the tax point relevant to that final Settlement Date;

(c) the Contractor shall 4 days before the relevant Transfer Date transfer to the Trust Account an amount equal to:

- any VAT in relation to the amount shown in the final Payment Summary as being subsequently due to Specialist Contractors at the relevant tax point where the Works under this Agreement are zero-rated and works carried out by Specialist Contractors are standard rated;

- any shortfall between the total amount shown in the final Payment Summary as being due to Specialist Contractors and the amount shown in the finally adjusted Payment Schedule referred to in Clause 11.6(a) as being due from the Customer on the relevant Transfer Date together with any VAT subsequently due on such shortfall at the relevant tax point;

(d) when the funds have been transferred into the Trust Account by the Customer and/or the Contractor the Customer, as trustee, shall give the Contractor and any Specialist Contractor notice of the amount of final payment due to each of them and confirm that the relevant funds have been transferred to the Trust Account;

(e) payment of the final amounts due to the Contractor and any Specialist Contractor shall be effected by the Customer, as trustee, out of the Trust Account on the final Settlement Date. Following such payment the Customer, as trustee, and the Contractor shall together certify in writing to the bank that the obligations of the trustee have been completed and that any residual funds shall revert to the Customer;

(f) if the Trust Account has insufficient funds to meet all moneys due on the final Settlement Date, the Customer, as trustee, shall make payment to the Contractor and to any Specialist Contractor on a pro rata basis according to the amounts shown as due to the Contractor in the final Payment Schedule and to any Specialist Contractor in the final Payment Summary.

Chapter 4

RETENTION OF TITLE, PLANT SECURITY AND LIENS

Introduction – The Romalpa principle and retention of title clauses – Goods or materials fixed to the land – Sale of Goods Act 1979, section 25 – Standard form contracts – Use of contractor's equipment – Appendix

INTRODUCTION

4.1   Many textbooks on retention of title law fail to give any serious consideration to the problem of retention of title or *Romalpa* clauses in the context of the construction industry. Here, retention of title provisions may come into conflict with goods and materials vesting clauses under standard form contracts. Traditionally, the practice developed of employers paying for certain materials or goods before incorporation in the works, thereby placing employers (subject to adequate provisions applying under the building contract) in a position where the contractor may have received payment for goods or materials to which he does not have good title to pass on. Whatever the legal problems, commercially clauses allowing for payment of goods or materials off site may be attractive to both contractor and supplier. For contractors, payment for off-site goods and materials aids cash flow and may lead to more attractive tender prices being achievable. For employers, particularly those in the public sector, it may be attractive to adjust the times when monies are passed to the contractor in order better to regulate the expenditure of public funds in different financial years. Because of the apparent clash between retention of title provisions and vesting clauses, many lawyers have advised over the years that employers should not make financial provision for goods and materials prior to their incorporation in the works, and have criticised clauses in the standard form contracts which purport to overcome the problems as being unsatisfactory.

THE *ROMALPA* PRINCIPLE AND RETENTION OF TITLE CLAUSES

4.2   Before examining in detail the vesting provisions in the standard form contracts, it is beneficial to review the *Romalpa* principle. The basic rule is that title to goods passes when the parties to the contract intend it to pass, both in regard to the time at which and the conditions under which property is to pass to the buyer (Sale of Goods Act 1979, ss 17 and 19). According to s 19(1) of the Sale of Goods Act 1979:

> 'Where there is a contract for the sale of specific goods or where goods are subsequently appropriated to the contract, the seller may, by the terms of the contract or appropriation,

reserve the right of disposal of the goods until certain conditons are fulfilled; and in such a case, notwithstanding the delivery of the goods to the buyer, or to a carrier or other bailee or custodian for the purpose of transmission to the buyer, the property in the goods does not pass to the buyer until the conditions imposed by the seller are fulfilled.'

Parties' intentions (as to when title is to pass)

4.3   The intention of the parties (as to when title is to pass) is to be ascertained by reference to the express and/or implied terms of the contract, the conduct of the parties and the particular facts of the case. If the parties' intentions cannot otherwise be ascertained, s 18 of the Sale of Goods Act 1979 applies. The property then passes at the time the contract was made, provided the goods are specific and in a deliverable state, irrespective of whether payment for delivery is to take place at a later date. If the goods are unascertained property, the title cannot pass (s 16 of the Sale of Goods Act 1979). Once goods or materials are fixed to the land of another, title passes to the owner of that land in accordance with the maxim *quicquid plantatur solo, solo cedit*.[1] The seller's title in goods may also be lost if the seller's goods are mixed with those of the purchaser or of a third party in circumstances where the goods supplied cannot be separated out and lose their distinctive and identifiable quality.[2] Annexation to land or mixing with other goods is sufficient to defeat even the most sophisticated of clauses which aim to protect the seller out of proceeds of sale, proceeds of manufacture etc, particularly in insolvency situations.

Goods used in manufacturing

4.4   The *Romalpa* clause developed in response to the unsecured creditor's inability in most insolvency situations to recover monies outstanding. The principle owes its name to the important decision in *Aluminium Industrie Vaassen BV v Romalpa Aluminium Ltd*.[3] Although the *Romalpa* case set the benchmark, a string of later cases developed and refined the principle. It is relatively straightforward to retain title to goods which may be in the purchaser's possession and which retain an identifiable character and which can be repossessed if necessary. However, the position is different if goods sold and delivered have been used in a manufacturing process or passed on to a subsequent buyer. In *Re Bond Worth*,[4] a particular type of yarn was sold to a company to be used in the manufacture of carpets. The sale of the yarn was subject to a clause which retained the seller's 'equitable and beneficial ownership' of the yarn and of the proceeds of sale of any goods made out of the yarn. Here, the clause was held to constitute a registrable charge and, through lack of registration under the relevant companies legislation, was void as against third parties. The question of a product having lost its distinctive identity was considered in *Borden (UK) Ltd v Scottish Timber Products*.[5] The plaintiff supplied resin for the defendant to use in the manufacture of chipboard. On the purchaser's insolvency, the seller attempted to recover both the unused resin and to establish rights over the fabricated

---

1   *Appleby v Myers* (1867) LR 2 CP 651.
2   *Hendy Lennox (Industrial Engines) Ltd v Grahame Puttick Ltd* [1984] 1 WLR 485.
3   [1976] 1 WLR 676.
4   [1980] Ch 228.
5   [1981] Ch 25.

chipboard. According to the Court of Appeal, once the resin had been used in the manufacture of chipboard it ceased to exist as a distinct entity.

4.5 The next major development arose in *Re Peachdart Ltd*,[1] where leather had been sold and delivered for use in the manufacture of handbags. The seller purported to retain the property in the leather as well as in the handbags made out of the leather supplied. The court refused to accept that the apparent wording of the contract was such as to call into question the inference that the property in the leather passed to the purchaser when the leather was worked.

Drafting of clauses

4.6 The principle of *Romalpa* clauses was confirmed by the Court of Appeal in *Clough Mill Ltd v Martin*.[2] While approving the use of such clauses, the Court of Appeal stressed that such clauses needed to be carefully drafted to be effective. A reasonable summation of the Court of Appeal's views can be gleaned from the headnote to the case which states:

> 'If a seller in the exercise of his rights under a retention of title clause repossesses goods and resells them while the contract still subsists, he is only entitled to resell that amount needed to discharge the balance of the outstanding purchase price and if he sells more he is accountable to the buyer for the surplus. However, if the contract has been terminated, eg by an accepted repudiation, the seller can resell the goods as the owner uninhibited by any contractual restrictions and therefore while he would have to refund any part of the purchase price paid by the buyer, which would be recoverable on the ground of failure of consideration, he is entitled to retain any profit on the resale.
>
> If goods which are subject to a retention of title clause have been incorporated in, or used as material for, other goods, it is to be assumed that the newly manufactured goods are owned by the buyer of the original goods, subject to a charge created in favour of the seller by the retention of title clause, unless (per Sir John Donaldson MR) the use of the original goods leaves them in a separate and identifiable state, in which case it is possible for the seller to retain ownership of them.'

Floating charges

4.7 In the construction context, the Official Referee, His Honour Judge Newey QC considered retention of title clauses in *Stroud Architectural Systems Ltd v John Laing Construction Ltd*.[3] Stroud, which manufactured and supplied glazing units, sued Laing in conversion relating to the supply of certain glazing units.

4.8 Stroud had supplied the units to a Laing sub-contractor, TCCI, which became insolvent before paying for the units. TCCI had supplied in accordance with a widely drafted retention of title clause which had not been registered as a charge under s 395 of the Companies Act 1985. There was a power to repossess units in the event of buyer insolvency.

The issues were:

---

1   [1983] 3 All ER 204.
2   [1984] 3 All ER 982.
3   [1993] 35 Conv LR 135.

- whether Stroud retained title;
- whether Stroud had a sufficient interest in the glazing and a right to possession to claim its return or value from Laing.

The Official Referee held that Stroud's interest in the glazing units amounted only to a floating charge which, through lack of registration under s 395 of the Companies Act 1985, was 'void against the liquidator and Administrator and any creditor of the company'. With Laing as possibly debtors of TCCI and not necessarily creditors, the unregistered floating charge was presumably valid against Laing. However, there was a subsidiary issue. Unless the charge had ceased to float and become specific, Stroud had no right to possession, thereby establishing a claim in conversion.

4.9   In the particular case, no termination notice had been served on TCCI's insolvency. In that event, Stroud could have recovered damages and/or entered on the site to recover the glazing units. This had not occurred. A floating charge had been created which, through lack of registration, failed.

Insolvency Act 1986

4.10   The status of the *Romalpa* clause has now been recognised by s 251 of the Insolvency Act 1986. This defines a 'retention of title agreement' as:

> 'Agreement for the sale of goods to a company, being an agreement – which does not constitute a charge on the goods, but under which, if the seller is not paid and the company is wound up, the seller will have priority over all other creditors of the company as respects the goods or any property representing the goods.'

Contracts

4.11   It may appear a trite proposition, but, to have any relevance, a *Romalpa* clause must form part of the contract between the supplier and the purchaser. On many occasions, a supplier relies on a worthless retention of title provision in a document, usually an invoice, produced long after the contract was made. The validity of a retention of title clause will often become a matter to be resolved as part of the 'battle of the forms' exercise. The importance of this is demonstrated by *Sauter Automation Ltd v Goodman (Mechanical Services) Ltd (in Liquidation) and Another.*[1] A control panel and ancillary equipment were supplied to a contractor for incorporation in certain works. The supply contract was preceded by a quotation which included a retention of title clause. The contractor 'accepted' the quotation on the basis that the terms and conditions of the main contract, GC/Works/1 Edition 2, would apply. The contractor's order was construed as a counter-offer. It contained specific provisions transferring ownership of materials brought on to site to the contractor. These excluded previous conflicting terms and ancillary conditions.

GOODS OR MATERIALS FIXED TO THE LAND

4.12   Once goods or materials are fixed to the land, they conventionally become part of the land, and any retention of title clause is defeated. It is easy to see

---

1   [1986] 34 BLR 81.

construction materials as being ordinarily fixed to the land, although DE Ballard, in his paper *Payment for Materials or Goods Not Yet Incorporated in the Works*,[1] gives some interesting examples of particular items, the status of which might be open to some doubt. With mechanical and electrical plant, individual items and component parts supplied can be identified and, if necessary, physically removed from the plant in which they have been placed without any damage occurring to the latter. Ballard refers to *Jordan v May*,[2] and, by way of illustration, *Hendy Lennox (Industrial Engines) Ltd v Grahame Puttick Ltd*.[3] In the first case, the dispute related to batteries for a power generator. The generator itself was attached to a concrete bed and held to be a fixture, whereas the batteries, although wired into the generator, were held not to be fixtures. In the second case, Staughton J considered the right of the plaintiff, a supplier of diesel engines to the defendant, under terms which included a retention of title provision. The engines were linked to other equipment. After the defendant's insolvency, the plaintiff sought to rely upon its retention of title clause. Staughton J held that the engines never lost their identifiable quality when incorporated into other plant and equipment and, unlike resin used in the fabrication of chipboard or fibres used to manufacture yarn, they remained identifiable.

4.13   Anthony Thompson QC considered when a chattel becomes a fixture in *Potton Developments v Thompson and Another*,[4] which is of significance with retention of title arguments. In the particular case, the plaintiff manufactured and hired out portable, pre-assembled bedroom accommodation. The defendants owned and operated a pub to which the plaintiff supplied nine units. The plaintiff retained its title in the units and the parties agreed that they would not be considered as fixtures. The units were placed on a concrete slab and were attached to a bracket embedded in the slab. The units were transported by lorry and put in place by crane. Did the units become part of the freehold? It was held that they did not. Evidence before the court was that the units would not be difficult to remove undamaged.

4.14   Following *Holland v Hodgson*,[5] the agreement, the mode of installation and removal, and the fact that they were fixed largely by their own weight, favoured chattel status in *Potton*. Fixing to the brackets suggested they were part of the land. Modern cases suggest that bolting is not conclusive to connote permanence: *Billing v Pill*.[6] The defendant relied on *Mellhuish v BMI*[7] and *Elitestone v Morris*.[8] The latter case suggested that a house might remain a chattel if constructed in such a way that it could be removed.

4.15   On the facts in *Potton*, units were not built on site; although they were nailed down, only 30 mm nails had been used. The units were essentially there by virtue of their weight. The uniform appearance of the units was intended to give an appearance

---

1   (Alfred Hudson Prize, 1992) pp 23–24.
2   [1947] 1 KB 427.
3   [1984] 1 WLR 485.
4   [1998] NPC 49.
5   (1872) LR CP 328.
6   [1954] 1 QB 70.
7   [1996] AC 454.
8   [1997] NPC 66.

of permanence but what mattered was that they were built off site and could be removed.

SALE OF GOODS ACT 1979, SECTION 25

4.16   On occasions, s 25 of the Sale of Goods Act 1979 will defeat retention of title clauses. However, the Sale of Goods Act 1979 is applicable only to pure sale of goods transactions and not to supply and fix arrangements which are prevalent in the construction industry. In *Dawber Williamson Roofing Ltd v Humberside County Council*,[1] the employer had paid the insolvent contractor for slates brought to site by Dawber as part of a 'supply and fix' sub-contract. At the date of the contractor's liquidation, no monies had passed to Dawber. The Court of Appeal, apart from considering the standard provisions under the then relevant building contract, JCT 63, held that s 25 of the Sale of Goods Act 1979 was inapplicable. The main contractor was not in possession of the goods with the permission of the seller, as title had never passed from the supplier to the sub-contractor, let alone to the main contractor. The contrast can be demonstrated by looking at *Archivent Sales and Developments Ltd v Strathclyde Regional Council*.[2] Here, the contract for the sale and purchase of ventilators contained a retention of title clause. The contractor, who was supplying the ventilators without any fixing obligations to the employer was paid by the employer for the ventilators (the employer having no knowledge of the existence of the retention of title clause). Unlike *Dawber Williamson*, the case fell within s 25 of the Sale of Goods Act 1979, with the employer acquiring title. Another illustrative example of the s 25 argument is found in *W Hanson (Harrow) Ltd v Rapid Civil Engineering Ltd*.[3] Hanson supplied timber to Rapid on terms which included the following:

> '10. Transfer of Property
> The property in the goods shall not pass to you until payment in full of the contract price to us. The above condition may be waived at our discretion, where goods or any part of them have been incorporated in building or constructional works.'

Hanson delivered timber to three sites in London where Rapid was working for the same employer. Rapid had the benefit of payments, including monies from materials. Following Rapid's insolvency, Hanson sought the recovery of materials still on site. The employer retaliated by relying upon s 25 of the Sale of Goods Act 1979, suggesting that the employer had received them 'in good faith and without notice of any right of the original seller of the goods'. The Official Referee, Judge John Davies QC, found for the supplier.

4.17   A retention of title clause may be defeated in particular insolvency situations. A supplier cannot repossess goods and materials or take proceedings without permission from the administrator or by leave of the court. The court can empower the administrator to sell goods and materials delivered to site (ss 10, 11 and 15 of the Insolvency Act 1986). Further, an administrator, administrative receiver, liquidator or trustee in bankruptcy (but not a supervisor under an individual or

---

1   (1979) 14 BLR 70.
2   (1984) 27 BLR 98.
3   (1987) 11 Conv LR 119.

corporate voluntary arrangement) may have a defence to any claims from suppliers if he disposes of or uses goods or materials subject to a valid retention of title provision, believing, on reasonable grounds, that he is entitled to do so (ss 234, 287 and 304 of the Insolvency Act 1986).

STANDARD FORM CONTRACTS

4.18   The provisions in the standard form building contracts have undergone some changes with the coming into operation of the 1998 contract versions. The provisions in clauses 16 and 30 of JCT 80 (clauses 14 and 30 of JCT 63), in clauses 1.10 and 1.11 of the Intermediate Form of Contract (IFC 84) allow specifically for the transfer of ownership in unfixed materials and goods on and off site to the employer when paid for in a certificate. Clause 15 of JCT 81 (With Contractor's Design) extends only to on-site materials and goods. Such provisions must be read in the context of the general law of retention of title and will be effective only to the extent that the contractor has adequate title to pass to the employer. Clause 16.1 of JCT 80, concerned with unfixed materials and goods on site, provides that, when the contractor has been paid under an interim certificate, the value of such materials and goods fall under clause 30.2.1.2 such that 'the materials and goods comprised within the certificate become the property of the employer'. If the employer fails to pay part of an 'amount properly due', the property in materials and goods included in the unpaid interim certificate cannot pass to him. The clause also provides that unfixed materials and goods cannot be removed from site without the architect's consent. Clause 16.2 deals with unfixed materials or goods off site. Where the architect has exercised his optional powers under clause 30.3 (clause 30.2A of JCT 63), if certain criteria have been met and the contractor has been paid for such materials or goods, the materials or goods become the property of the employer. However, Ballard, in his paper, *Payment for Materials or Goods Not Yet Incorporated in the Works*,[1] is unhappy with the standard contract wording, and suggests that clause 16.1 of JCT 80 should be amended in the following way to protect employers in situations where the value of a sub-contractor's goods and materials have been included in a main contractor application:

> 'The property in any materials or goods shall not pass to the Employer until the Employer shall have made payment for them or until they have been incorporated into the Works. Incorporation into the Works shall not be deemed to have taken place until the materials or goods have become affixed to the land in such a way that they cannot be removed without significant damage occurring either to them or to other materials and goods which are the subject of this Contract.'

It is Ballard's view that an amendment to clause 16.1 in these terms will then allow clauses 16.2, 30.2.1.3 and 30.3 of JCT 80 to be discarded.

4.19   There is a distinction between clauses 30.2.1.2 and 30.3.2 of JCT 80. Under the first, payment for materials or goods delivered to or adjacent to the works and intended for incorporation therein is mandatory. More difficult is the architect's discretion under clause 30.3.2 to pay for materials or goods off site. Clause 30.3.4 appears to be in direct contravention of the basic principles of retention of title. The

---

1   (Alfred Hudson Prize, 1992), pp 23–24; see also **4.12**.

clause states that the contract for the supply of materials shall expressly provide for property in those materials to pass unconditionally upon the happening of specified events.

JCT 80

4.20   Where the standard form main contracts are singularly unsuccessful is in provisions such as those found in clause 30.3.5 of JCT 80. It is wholly unrealistic to suggest that a contractual framework can permeate out from JCT 80 to govern relationships between suppliers and sub-contractors where retention of title clauses will be used.

4.21   The decision in *Dawber Williamson Roofing Ltd v Humberside County Council*[1] was an object lesson in the problems that can arise. In that case, the employer had paid the insolvent contractor for slates brought to site by Dawber as part of a 'supply and fix' sub-contract. At the date of the contractor's liquidation, no monies had been passed to Dawber. The employer sought to rely on clause 14 of JCT 63 to defend Dawber's retention of title claim. The court held that property in a sub-contractor's materials could not pass to the employer in circumstances where title had not passed from the sub-contractor to the contractor. JCT 80 has been amended (Amendment 1: 1984) to avoid the *Dawber Williamson* situation. Clause 19.4.2 of JCT 80 (reflected in clause 18.3.2 of JCT CD 81 and clause 3.2.2 of IFC 84) obliges the contractor to ensure that a sub-contract contains an undertaking by the sub-contractor that:

> 'He will not, without the Contractor's consent, remove from the site materials and goods delivered thereto for use in the Works; ...
>
> Materials and goods delivered to the site and included in an Architect's Interim Certificate paid by the Employer to the Contractor will become the Employer's property and the Sub-Contractor will not deny the Employer's property in such materials and goods; ...
>
> Materials and goods paid for by the Contractor before inclusion in an Interim Certificate become the property of the Contractor.'

4.22   The amendment is not wholly satisfactory. Even if the contractor obtains a requisite undertaking from the sub-contractor, the sub-contractor cannot automatically provide the contractor with good title to pass to the employer where the sub-contractor is subject to a retention of title clause with his own supplier and the provisions in s 25 of the Sale of Goods Act 1979 do not apply. The DOM/1 sub-contract ordinarily used with JCT 80 states, in clause 21.4.5.2, that on-site materials or goods may be included in a gross valuation. The property in such materials or goods is set to pass to the employer on payment by the employer to the contractor or on payment by the contractor to the sub-contractor: clauses 21.4.5.2 and 21.4.5.3. Clauses 4.15.4.2 and 4.15.4.3 of NSC/C, the nominated sub-contract, are expressed in similar terms. Payment can also extend to off-site materials and goods under DOM/1, clause 21.4.1.3 and NSC/C, clause 4.15.4.4. A sub-contractor cannot remove unfixed materials or goods from site without the contractor's consent: clause 21.4.5.1 of DOM/1 and clause 4.15.4.1 of NSC/C. Finally, and not to be overlooked,

---

1   (1979) 14 BLR 70; see also **4.16**.

clause 27.4.1 of JCT 80, clause 27.6.1 of JCT Amendment 11: 1992, clause 27.1.4.2 of JCT CD 81 and clause 7.4 of IFC 84 permit the employer (subject to any contrary legal rights) to use any goods and materials on site in the completion of works following determination of the contractor's employment on insolvency.

4.23   The JCT scheme for off-site goods and materials relates to the value of any materials or goods which have 'in the discretion of the Architect' been included in an interim certificate. This requires the architect to operate in a bona fide way and not capriciously. What this means in practical terms is harder to establish. The architect must look at each situation on its merits and must avoid having a general policy of never certifying the value of off-site materials. Does this mean having to suggest to architects that they engage in a paper chase and, in trying to trace through title in goods and materials, perhaps analysing complex 'battle of the forms' arguments? Ballard[1] refers to the *dicta* of His Honour Judge John Davies QC in *Partington & Son (Builders) Ltd v Tameside Metropolitan Borough Council,*[2] a case on the equivalent clause on off-site materials found in JCT 63. According to the judge, as quoted by Ballard:

> 'The exercise of that discretion [with regard to off-site materials] is so circumscribed by the terms of that provision of the contract as to emasculate the element of discretion virtually to the point of extinction.'

4.24   There are major revisions in the standard form building contracts relating to unfixed materials. These were originally introduced via Amendment 18 to JCT 80, Amendment 12 to IFC 84 and Amendment 12 to JCT CD 81. The amendments are now found in the reissued forms, JCT CD 98 and IFC 98. The relevant clauses are clause 30.3 of JCT 98, clause 4.2.1(c)–4.2.5 and clause 15.2 of JCT CD 98. The clauses are set out in broadly similar terms. The purpose is to provide protection for the employer in circumstances where he wishes to pay for off-site goods and materials.

4.25   If the employer wishes to pay for off-site materials or prefabricated items before delivery to, or adjacent to, the works (clause 30.3.1 of JCT 98 and clause 1.11 of IFC 98), the employer must set them out in a list attached to the contract bills, the specification, and the schedules of work or list them in the employer's requirements. The contractor can therefore take the supply of these items into account at tender stage and will receive accelerated payment for such items. The conditions, with which compliance is necessary, are set out in the different contracts. Under JCT 98, there is a distinction between 'uniquely identified listed items' and listed items which are not 'uniquely identified'. In both instances, the contractor must show he has good title to pass to the employer, so-called 'reasonable proof'. For items which are not uniquely identified, the contractor must offer a bond in a prescribed form; the form being set out in the Appendix to this chapter, or such other form as the employer may require. For uniquely identified items, the bond is required only if the employer specifically requires it. Reasonable proof includes ensuring that the items have been set aside at the place of fabrication and/or clearly marked as belonging to the employer and the

---

1   (Alfred Hudson Prize, 1992), p 14.
2   (1985) 32 BLR 150.

destination of the works. The contractor is further duty bound to maintain appropriate insurances.

4.26   The new provisions are helpful but should not be seen as foolproof. Retention of title arguments are complex and the contractor cannot provide better title than he himself enjoys. The contractor is to provide only reasonable proof; not a cast-iron guarantee. The employer will remain cautious about paying, even with the benefit of a bond, to provide reimbursement on the contractor's breach, if the contractor is insolvent. It is still incumbent on a contractor to ensure that his sub-contracts are back to back with his own obligations and that he receives copies of all purchase orders and other relevant documents. If in doubt, the architect should obtain specialist assistance on any terms in a supply order which he does not understand. Employers must understand that payment in advance does constitute a risk.

4.27   There is also provision in the new contract forms for the contractor to benefit from an advance payment, supported by an advance payment bond, as set out in clause 30.1.1.6 of JCT 98, clause 4.2(b) of IFC 98 and clause 30.1.1.2 of JCT CD 98. These forms of security are particularly useful where the contractor will incur substantial up-front costs which it is beneficial for the employer to meet, sometimes for tax and sometimes for expenditure reasons and which are vital for the contractor to fund the project.

ICE 6th Edition

4.28   Although some of the conceptual problems are not resolved, the principal engineering contract, ICE 6th Edition, is clearer and more crisp on the question of materials in clause 54 than are the JCT contracts. First, the clause relates to off-site goods and materials, which are listed in the Appendix to the Form of Tender and comply with the following:

> 'Have been manufactured or prepared and are substantially ready for incorporation in the Works, and are the property of the Contractor or the contract for the supply of the same expressly provides that the property therein shall pass unconditionally to the Contractor upon the Contractor taking the action referred to in sub-clause (2) of this Clause.'

Sub-paragraphs (a)–(d) inclusive of clause 54(2) represent useful advice to the engineer. A similar checklist would be useful in JCT 80 to assist the architect in the exercise of his discretion. The four requirements are that:

(i)   documentary evidence is available that the property in the goods and materials is vested in the contractor;
(ii)   the goods are suitably marked and identified prior to delivery;
(iii) separate storage of the goods and materials is maintained;
(iv)   provision is made for the engineer to be sent a schedule listing and giving the value of every item of the goods and materials set aside and stored, and inviting inspection.

4.29   Of course, clause 54 is not entirely satisfactory. Sub-clause (6) requires the contractor to include 'back-to-back' provisions in his own sub-contracts. That is not to say that particular sub-contractors will necessarily organise suitable arrangements with their own suppliers to overcome the standard difficulties with retention of title clauses referred to above.

USE OF CONTRACTOR'S EQUIPMENT

4.30 Alongside clauses in standard form building contracts which suggest that ownership in goods and materials on and off site may pass to the employer in particular circumstances, certain contracts permit the employer to use contractor's equipment on site for completion of the works following contractor insolvency. The purpose of such clauses is obvious. They are to permit the employer to reduce the inconvenience he might otherwise have in completing the works, particularly when certain items of plant and equipment may be difficult to obtain, and delay in obtaining them might lead to the project being severely disrupted with substantial additional costs. The civil engineering contracts, now the ICE Conditions of Contract 6th Edition, have long made provision for this occurrence. According to clause 53(1):

> 'All Contractor's Equipment, Temporary Works, materials for Temporary Works or other goods or materials owned by the Contractor shall when on Site be deemed to be the property of the Employer and shall not be removed therefrom without the written consent of the Engineer, which consent shall not unreasonably be withheld where the items in question are no longer immediately required for the purposes of the completion of the Works.

> The Employer shall not at any time be liable save as mentioned in Clauses 22 and 65 for the loss of or damage to any Contractor's Equipment, Temporary Works, goods or materials.

> If the Contractor fails to remove any of the said Contractor's Equipment, Temporary Works, goods or materials as required by clause 33 within such reasonable time after completion of the Works as the Engineer may allow then the Employer may sell or otherwise dispose of such items. From the proceeds of the sale of any such items the Employer should be entitled to retain any costs or expenses incurred in connection with their sale and disposal before paying the balance (if any) to the Contractor.'

Determination

4.31 Alongside the clause 53 powers must be read the provisions of clause 63, the determination clause. Provided the employer is permitted to determine under the two-stage process set out in clause 63(1), on the face of it the employer has the twin powers provided by sub-clauses (2) and (3). According to sub-clause (2):

> 'Where the Employer has entered upon the Site and the Works as hereinbefore provided he may himself complete the Works or may employ any other contractor to complete the Works and the Employer or such other contractor may use for such completion so much of the Contractor's Equipment, Temporary Works, goods and materials which have been deemed to become the property of the Employer under clauses 53 and 54 as he or they may think proper and the Employer may at any time sell any of the said Contractor's Equipment, Temporary Works and unused goods and materials and apply the proceeds of sale in or towards the satisfaction of any sums due or which may become due to him from the Contractor under the Contract.'

Sub-clause (3) states:

'By the said notice or by further notice in writing within 7 days of the date of expiry thereof the Engineer may require the Contractor to assign to the Employer and if so required the Contractor shall forthwith assign to the Employer the benefit of any agreement for the supply of any goods or materials and/or for the execution of any work for the purposes of this Contract which the Contractor may have entered into.'

Vesting clauses

4.32   Until the Court of Appeal decision in *Ian Clark Administrator of Cosslett (Contractors) Ltd v Mid Glamorgan County Council*,[1] case-law had not considered for many years the status of so-called vesting clauses, the purpose of which is to safeguard the employer's uninterrupted use of contractor's plant for the benefit of the works. Admittedly, the case related to an amended 5th Edition but the distinctions between it and the 6th Edition are not material. The lesson of *Cosslett* is that clause 53 of the ICE Conditions of Contract 6th Edition does not mean an outright transfer of property as between contractor and employer. It contains the unfortunate words 'be deemed to be the property of …'. The argument adopted by insolvency practitioners has been that, with an absence of actual transfer of title, vesting clauses may impose a mortgage or charge which may be void as against an administrator or liquidator for lack of registration under s 398 of the Companies Act 1985.

4.33   Prior to the *Coslett* decision, the question of vesting clauses had been considered in a number of decisions. For instance, at the beginning of the 20th century, Farwell J considered the question in *Hart v Porthgain Harbour Company*.[2] The contractor had entered into a contract for tidal works. These included the construction of a temporary dam which, at the date of the contractor's insolvency, had been constructed with plant and tools brought to site. The contractor had mortgaged the materials used in the temporary dam as well as his plant and materials and had registered the relevant bill of sale. According to the contract, the plant and materials:

'… shall be considered the property of the Company until the Engineers shall have certified the completion of the Contract, and no plant and materials shall be removed or taken away without the consent or order in writing of the Engineers.'

4.34   Disputes arose between the mortgagee and the employer regarding priority. According to Farwell J, the clause referred to above vested property in the employer, leaving him with title to the plant and materials in priority to the mortgagee. There are certainly similarities between *Hart* and the modern provisions; there appears to be no essential distinction between the word 'deemed' in present day contracts and the use of 'considered' at the beginning of the 20th century.

4.35   However, the simple clarity of *Hart* was placed in some doubt by a more recent Privy Council decision, *Bennett & White (Calgary) Ltd v Municipal District of Sugar City*.[3] The construction contract related to an irrigation scheme, with the relevant part of the contract conditions providing:

'All machinery, tools, plant, materials, equipment, articles and things whatsoever, provided by the Contractor … for the works … shall from the time of their being so

---

1   [1998] 2 WLR 131.
2   [1903] Ch 690.
3   [1951] AC 786.

provided become and until the final completion of the said works shall be the property of His Majesty for the purposes of the said works . . .'

Here, there is an obvious and immediate distinction between the contract conditions in question and the standard form building contracts. The contract expressly called for the transfer of property. Lord Reid carried out a general review of the law and considered the status of a number of 19th century decisions, not necessarily consistent with *Hart*. These were subsequently reviewed in the Companies Court and the Court of Appeal in *Cosslett*. According to Lord Reid in *Bennett & White*:

> 'In some of the cases a distinction has been drawn between clauses which provide that as and when plant and materials are brought to the site they shall be "considered" or "deemed" to become the property of the building owner; and, on the other hand, clauses which provide that they are to "be and become" his property. In the former case it has sometimes been held that the clause was ineffective to achieve its aim and that the property remained in the builder, at the mercy of his creditors and trustee in bankruptcy; see *In re Keen & Keen*.[1] Where as in *Reeves v Barlow*,[2] a decision of the Court of Appeal and, perhaps the leading decision in the field, the formula is "be and become" or its equivalent, that case decides that the clause means what it says, operates according to its tenor, and effectively transfers the title. In *Hart v Porthgain Harbour Co Ltd*[3] Farwell J. seems to have thought it immaterial which formula was used; but on any view "be and become" is effective and the same must hold good of "become and be" – the wording employed in this case.'[4]

Although Lord Reid did not expressly disapprove of *Hart*, nevertheless he left matters sufficiently open for their subsequent discussion by the Court of Appeal in *Cosslett*.

Power of sale

4.36   Even if the provisions in standard form construction contracts did not operate to transfer ownership in property to the employer, lawyers traditionally advised clients that there was little doubt that such clauses would operate as a contractual licence to use contractor's plant and equipment. The final question, and one which was considered at some length in *Cosslett*, was whether the effect of the civil engineering contracts was to create a security interest such as a mortgage or charge. The power of sale set out in clause 63(1) of the ICE Conditions of Contract 6th Edition may be indicative of such an intention.

4.37   *Cosslett*, the key modern decision on the interpretation of clauses 53 and 63 of the ICE Conditions of Contract (albeit in the context of an amended 5th Edition), has established the modern legal position in the light of an administrator/appointment. In the first instance judgment in *Re Cosslett (Contractors) Ltd*,[5] Jonathan Parker J held that the 'deeming' provision did not have the effect of passing general property in the coal washing plants (the equipment in question) to the county council. The rights given to the county council by clause 63 provided an equitable proprietary interest which could be enforced by specific performance. Since the county council's

1   [1902] 1 KB 555.
2   (1884) 12 QBD 436.
3   [1903] 1 Ch 690.
4   [1951] AC 786 at 813.
5   [1996] 3 WLR 299.

contractual rights allowed for the sale of plant on the site at the date of forfeiture and gave the county council the right to refuse to permit removal, even when plant was not immediately required to complete the works, the equitable proprietary interest was in the nature of a specific charge over the plant when on site. It was not a floating charge and therefore not registerable under s 395 of the Companies Act 1985. The administrator appealed to the Court of Appeal, which considered the county council's right to retain possession of the plant, and the alleged right to sell the plant in accordance with clause 63 of the contract.

4.38   The administrator contended that the county council's right constituted a floating charge which was void for lack of registration under s 398 of the Companies Act 1985. In the Court of Appeal,[1] Millett LJ formulated the questions in the following way:

> 'Whether clause 53(2) of the contract has the effect of transferring the legal property and the plant to the council. If it does then (i.) it was still the property of the council when delivery up was demanded; and (ii.) there can be no question of the council's rights in respect of the plant constituting a charge on its own property.
>
> If it does not, whether the council's right to retain possession of the plant and use it to complete the works constitutes an equitable charge.
>
> Whether the council's power of sale arises by way of an equitable charge or possessory lien.
>
> If either right arises by way of charge, whether the charge is a fixed or floating charge.
>
> If so, what are the consequences of the company's failing to register it?'

The two leading judgments, those of Evans LJ and Millett LJ, clearly establish that 'the deeming provision' did not transfer legal property in the plant to the council. A number of cases were considered; with Millet LJ conceding that not all the cases were consistent. According to Millett LJ:

> 'In the present case there are several indicia that the legal ownership of plant and materials brought onto the site does not pass to the council. Such plant and materials are described throughout as "plant and materials which have been deemed to become the property" of the council, a circumlocution which might well have been dispensed with if they had become the actual property of the council. The company is prohibited by clause 53(6) from removing the plant and materials from the site without the consent of the engineer (a similar clause was said in *In re Keen & Keen* to be unnecessary if the plant and materials belonged to the Council). Finally, Clause 53(9) exempts the Council from liability for loss of or injury to plant and materials brought onto the site (a provision which was also said in *In re Keen & Keen* to be inconsistent with the property having passed to the Council).'[2]

4.39   Millett LJ was not persuaded that clauses 53(6) and (7), which allowed use and re-vesting of plant and materials in favour of the company, supported a transfer of legal ownership under clause 53(2).

On the question whether or not the council's right to retain possession of the plant under clause 63(1) and use it to complete the works constituted an equitable charge, it was not an equitable charge because:

---

1   [1998] 2 WLR 131 at 139–140.
2   Ibid, at 140–141.

–   it did not give the council a proprietary interest in the plant but only rights of
    possession and use; and
–   it was not by way of a security.

4.40   Where the Court of Appeal judgment was even more significant was in its
consideration of the power of sale under clause 63 of the Conditions of Contract, a
matter which had not been brought before Jonathan Parker J at first instance (the
administrator's application was for an order to deliver up the plant under s 234 of the
Insolvency Act 1986). The Court of Appeal was asked to review this question on an
obiter basis. The Court of Appeal was satisfied that the power of sale and application
of the proceeds of sale was a security interest. It constituted an equitable charge which
crystallised on notice of expulsion and was a floating charge registrable under s 395 of
the Companies Act 1985. The failure to register the charge rendered the security
created by the power of sale void as against the administrator. The council argued that
its rights constituted a possessory lien with a power of sale, such rights not being an
equitable charge. This proposition was roundly rejected by the Court of Appeal. The
council's rights in relation to the plant and materials were exclusively contractual and,
insofar as they were by way of security, constituted an equitable charge. The Court of
Appeal dealt with the question of whether such a charge was fixed or floating by
reference to the three characteristics of a floating charge identified by Romer LJ in *Re
Yorkshire Woolcombers Association Ltd.*[1] There was no difficulty with the first two
features of such a charge. Plant and materials became subject to the charge as they
were brought on to the site, and ceased to be subject to it as they were removed from
the site. Therefore, the charge was one on present and future assets of the company.
Disputed was the third characteristic. The administrator contended that, until the
council exercised its rights under clause 53(1), the company was free to carry on its
business in the ordinary way with the plant and materials on the site. At first instance,
Jonathan Parker J accepted the council's submission that the council had an absolute
right under clause 53(6) to refuse to permit the company to remove from the site plant
and materials immediately required to complete the works. There was also a qualified
right to refuse permission for the removal of plant and materials not immediately
required for this purpose, provided the council acted reasonably. Here, the Court of
Appeal differed in its judgment from Jonathan Parker J. The restriction on the removal
of plant from site was not to protect the council's security but to ensure that the
company would give proper priority to the completion of the works. Therefore, the
charge was a floating rather than a fixed charge. In dealing with the consequences of
non-registration, it was only the power of sale which constituted a charge which was
registrable under s 395 of the Companies Act 1985. Section 399 of the 1985 Act meant
the failure to register a charge rendered that charge void as a security against a
liquidator or administrator. The right of use was not affected, not being a security
which required registration. The council's contractual rights to retain possession of
plant and materials and use them to complete the works was unaffected by the failure
to register the clause 63(1) security.

4.41   The consequences of the *Cosslett* decision might have sent a ripple through
the civil engineering industry. However, the Conditions of Contract Standing Joint
Committee (CCSJC), the committee responsible for drafting civil engineering

---

1   [1903] 2 Ch 284.

contracts, viewed *Cosslett* as a 'one-off'. The reality is that most plant brought to site is not, as in the *Cosslett* case, owned by the contractor, but is plant in which third parties have an interest and over which rights cannot be taken without the consent of the relevant third parties. It is understood, however, that the CCSJC, in the process of revising the civil engineering contracts, will make fundamental alterations in the 7th Edition of the Conditions of Contract.

4.42   The provisions to be found in the JCT contracts relating to use of a contractor's materials, plant or equipment, post-insolvency, are fundamentally different. There is nothing akin to the purported power of sale of contractor's plant and equipment allied to the use of the proceeds of sale to set off against employer claims. Under JCT Amendment 11: 1992, clause 27.6.1 provides:

> 'The Employer may employ and pay other persons to carry out and complete the Works to make good defects of the kind referred to in Clause 17 and he or they may enter upon the site and the Works and use all temporary buildings, plant, tools, equipment and Site Materials, and may purchase all materials and goods necessary for the carrying out and completion of the Works and for the making good of defects as aforesaid; provided that where the aforesaid temporary buildings, plant, tools, equipment and Site Materials are not owned by the Contractor the consent of the owner thereof to such use is obtained by the Employer.'

The contractual right to use should not cause any operational problems.

4.43   The standard form construction contracts have attempted to provide a contractual mechanism which protects an employer's position and allows that employer to take comfort in the event that there is a delay to the completion of the works by the insolvency of a contractor. The contracts attempt to secure the employer's access to plant and materials, but at times this exercise appears to be carried out with little heed to the general provisions of insolvency legislation or the reality that most suppliers of plant and materials will have secured their interests in those items and the actual user on site will not be in a position to provide the employer with rights which override those of the original supplier. This means that contract administrators, and the lawyers who advise them, must view with caution the contractual mechanisms which often offer greater prospects of security than they can deliver.

Appendix

JCT 80: AMENDMENT 18 (1998) BOND: IN RESPECT OF PAYMENT FOR OFF-SITE MATERIALS AND/OR GOODS

1   THE parties to this Bond are:

whose registered office is at _____

_____ ('the Surety'), and

(2) _____

of _____

_____ ('the Employer').

2   The Employer and _____ ('the Contractor')

have agreed to enter into a building contract for building works ('the Works')

at _____ ('the Contract').

3   Subject to the relevant provisions of the Contract as summarised below but with which the Surety shall not at all be concerned:

   (a)   The Employer has agreed to include in the amount stated as due in Interim Certificates (as defined in the Contract) for payment by the Employer the value of those materials or goods or items pre-fabricated for inclusion in the Work which have been isted by the Employer ('the listed items'), which list has been included as part of the Contract, before their delivery to or adjacent to the Works; and

   (b)   the Contractor has agreed to insure the listed items against loss or damage for their full value under a policy of insurance protecting the interests of the Employer and the Contractor during the period commencing with the transfer of the property in the items to the Contractor until they are delivered to, or adjacent to, the Works; and

   (c)   this Bond shall exclusively relate to the amount paid to the Contractor in respect of the listed items which have not been delivered to or adjacent to the Works.

4   The Employer shall in making any demand provide to the Surety a Notice of Demand in the form of the **Schedule** attached hereto which shall be accepted as conclusive evidence for all purposes under this Bond. The signatures on any such demand must be authenticated by the Employer's bankers.

5   The Surety shall within 5 Business Days after receiving the demand pay to the Employer the sum so demanded. 'Business Day' means the day (other than a Saturday or a Sunday) on which commercial banks are open for business in London.

6   Payments due under this Bond shall be made notwithstanding any dispute between the Employer and the Contractor and whether or not the Employer and the Contractor are or might be under any liability one to the other. Payments by the Surety under this Bond shall be deemed a valid payment for all purposes of this Bond and shall discharge the Surety from liability to the extent of such payment.

7   The Surety consents and agrees that the following actions by the Employer may be made and done without notice to or consent of the Surety and without in any way affecting changing or releasing the Surety from its obligations under this Bond and the liability of the Surety hereunder shall not in any way be affected hereby. The actions are:

    (a)   waiver by the Employer of any of the terms, provisions, conditions, obligations and agreements of the Contractor or any failure to make demand upon to take action against the Contractor;

    (b)   any modification or changes to the Contract; and/or

    (c)   the granting of an extension of time to the Contractor without affecting the terms of clause 9(b) below.

8   The Surety's maximum liability under this Bond shall be *[_____].

9   The obligations of the Surety and under this Bond shall cease upon whichever is the earlier of

    (a)   the date on which all the listed items have been delivered to or adjacent to the Works as certified in writing to the Surety by the Employer; and

    (b)   [longstop date to be given],

and any claims hereunder must be received by the Surety in writing on or before such earlier date.

10   The Bond is not transferable or assignable without the prior written consent of the Surety. Such written consent will not be unreasonably withheld.

11   This Bond shall be governed and construed in accordance with the laws of England and Wales.

*The value stated in the Contract which the Employer considers will be sufficient to cover him for maximum payments to the Contractor for the listed items that will have been made and not delivered to the site at any one time.

IN WITNESS hereof this Bond has been executed as a Deed by the Surety and delivered on the date below:

EXECUTED as a Deed by: _____

    for and on behalf of the Surety: _____

EXECUTED as a Deed by: _____

    for and on behalf of the Employer: _____

Date: _____

SCHEDULE TO BOND

(clause 4 of the Bond)

Notice of Demand

Date of Notice: _____

Date of Bond: _____

Employer: _____

Surety: _____

We hereby demand payment of the sum of _____
being the amount stated as due in respect of listed items included in the amount stated as due in an Interim Certificate(s) for payment which has been duly made to the Contractor by the Employer but such listed items have not been delivered to, or adjacent to the Works.

Address for payment: _____

_____

This Notice is signed by the following persons who are authorised by the Employer to act for and on his behalf:

Signed by _____

    Name: _____

    Official Position: _____

Signed by _____

    Name: _____

    Official Position: _____

The above signatures to be authenticated by the Employer's bankers.

[Reproduced by kind permission of the Joint Contracts Tribunal.]

Chapter 5

BONDS AND GUARANTEES[1]

Protections from main contractor insolvency – Performance bonds – What is a default? – Disputing liability to pay under bonds – Procedural requirements – Resisting the call: conditional bonds – Is it always a bleak outlook with on-demand bonds? – Preventing payment under an on-demand bond – General considerations relating to bonds – Looking to the future – ABI model form of guarantee bond – Other forms of bond – Appendix

PROTECTIONS FROM MAIN CONTRACTOR INSOLVENCY

5.1   With the frequently cyclical nature of activity in the construction industry, employers want, to the maximum extent possible, to protect themselves from the consequences of main contractor insolvency. To ease the pain of main contractor insolvency, the principal protections are set out below.

Retention

5.2   Increasing the retention percentage deducted from the interim payments (usually 5 per cent reducing to 2.5 per cent on practical/substantial completion) strengthens the employer's position. Postponing the date of release of the second one-half retention until perhaps the resolution of the contractor's final account further increases the employer's security.

Milestone schedules

5.3   These are a major departure from JCT and ICE practice, although very common in bespoke contract arrangements. Instalment payments are made from the contract sum at completed stages of the works. Money only passes to the contractor from the employer when an element of work is properly completed. This can, of course, lead to arguments. For the employer, it has the obvious advantage that the contractor bears more of the risk, in that he may have substantial sums of money tied up in a particular section of the works. In order to sweeten the pill for the contractor, the milestone system can be linked to an advance payment to assist the contractor's cash flow.

Parent company guarantees

5.4   These are a useful form of security whenever the contractor is a subsidiary of a large group of companies and there is confidence in the financial viability of the parent. An obvious example of where a parent company guarantee would be suitable

---

1   This chapter was originally presented as 'A Practical High-Level Guide to Construction Insolvency', 23 February 1999, The Berners Hotel, London W1.

is where a holding company has formed a specific subsidiary to carry out a particular project. However, many parent companies are themselves intermediate shells in the corporate pattern and are of little substance. It is essential to check the following details of any parent company guarantee carefully, since it may be that the protection it provides to the employer is not as all-embracing as appears at first sight or even that the protection is illusory:

–   some parent company guarantees cannot be activated until such time as all potential remedies against the defaulting contractor have been tested and exhausted. From the employer's point of view, it is preferable that a parent company guarantee operates on an on-demand basis rather than on a proof of default basis;

–   it is essential to check the place of business of the parent company providing the guarantee. The parent company may be based overseas, and, although not in itself an insurmountable difficulty if money has to be pursued in litigation, the intervention of overseas companies can lead to additional cost and complications;

–   ensure, if the employer, that the parent company guarantee is given in regard to the contractor actually carrying out the work;

–   some guarantees have unduly restrictive cut-off dates for bringing claims, cap the level of recoverable losses and seek to restrict liability until practical/ substantial completion rather than up to making good of defects/end of the maintenance period.

5.5   On their wording, some parent company guarantees are not what they seem but contracts of indemnity. The decision of the Court of Appeal in *Alfred McAlpine Construction Limited v Unex Corporation Limited*[1] was an object lesson to those who think they have the benefit of a parent company guarantee if the courts are asked to construe a particular document. McAlpine was main contractor under a design-and-build contract with Panatown Limited, which was subject to the usual JCT arbitration clause. Following determination of McAlpine's employment, disputes between McAlpine and Panatown were referred to arbitration. Unex had provided a parent company guarantee for Panatown in the following terms:

'If Panatown (unless relieved from the performance by any clause of the contract or by statute or by the decision of a tribunal of competent jurisdiction) shall in any respect fail to execute the contract or commits any breach of its obligations thereunder then Unex will indemnify McAlpine against all losses, damages, costs and expenses which may be incurred by McAlpine by reason of any default on the part of Panatown in performing and observing the agreements and provisions on its part contained in the contract provided always that Unex shall not be under any greater liability to McAlpine than Panatown would have been liable in contract pursuant to the express terms of the contract.'

McAlpine commenced High Court proceedings against Unex to enforce the parent company guarantee. Unex unsuccessfully applied to the Official Referee, His Honour Judge Esyr Lewis QC, for a stay of those proceedings both under the inherent jurisdiction of the court, and, in the alternative, under s 4 of the Arbitration Act 1950. The matter then came before the Court of Appeal with the following findings:

–   the parent company guarantee was not a guarantee but a contract of indemnity;

---

1   (1994) CILL 952.

– Unex was not bound by the result of the arbitration; the principle in *Re Kitchen*[1] applied. In the absence of explicit words, a guarantor is not bound by a finding against the principal;

– Unex could not achieve a stay of proceedings under s 4 of the Arbitration Act 1950, since it was not a *person claiming through or under* Panatown. A surety was outside s 4 of the Arbitration Act 1950;

– the Court of Appeal was divided on whether the arbitrator's award would set a maximum on the liability of Unex.

At p 953, Evans LJ stated:

'The form used in the present case, although described as a "Guarantee", was held to be a contract of indemnity in *The London Line (Anglomar) Shipping Co Limited v Swan Hunter Shipbuilders Limited* [1980] 2 Lloyd's Rep 456, which will be referred to below. The form there used was said to have been "lifted" from the *Encyclopaedia of Forms and Precedents* (per Stephenson LJ at 468) and the "Parent Company Guarantee" in the present case may have had the same origins . . .

. . . the learned Judge referred to the well established general principle apparent from *In Re Kitchen* (1881) 17 Ch 668 that the amount of any debt or damages "must, if the surety insists, be proved as against him, just as it would have to be proved if the actions were against the principal" (per Lush LJ at 674), the reason being that "You must find explicit words to make a person liable to pay any amount which may be awarded against a third person, whether it be by jury, or a Judge, or an arbitrator" (ibid). He held that Unex's undertaking in the present case contains no such clear wording, and he was unable to accept Mr Thomas' submission that the wording does have the effect of defining the extent of Unex's obligations to McAlpine by reference to what is determined in arbitration proceedings between McAlpine and Panatown.[2]

. . . To hold that the reference to a "Tribunal of competent jurisdiction", even in the context of the employer's liability under the building contract, meant that the guarantor was undertaking to pay, not an amount properly due under the building contract, but whatever amount might be awarded against the employer by an arbitrator, would seem to me to be inconsistent with the reasoning of the judgements *In Re Kitchen* and with the requirement of "explicit words" for that result to be achieved. The surety would be "bound by any admissions or statements of the principal as to what amount is due", which in law he is not (per Lush LJ at 673).'

5.6 There is a frequent tendency, as part of project documentation, to require the provision of a parent company guarantee without any thought being given to the legal capacity of the guarantor to provide the guarantee. If the guarantor lacks the capacity, however finely drafted the obligation, it will be unenforceable and void. Again, another formality, with which compliance is necessary, is the Statute of Frauds 1677, which requires guarantees to be in writing and signed by the guarantor to be enforceable.

The powers of a company and how they are to be exercised are set out in the memorandum and articles of association. The memorandum of association must contain an express provision authorising the company to give guarantees of the type anticipated. In company law, there is a distinction between a provision which constitutes a substantive object of the company and one which constitutes an ancillary

---

1   (1881) 17 Ch 668.
2   *Alfred McAlpine Construction Ltd v Panatown Ltd* 88 BLR 67.

power of the company. Here, the key case is *Rolled Steel Products (Holdings) Ltd v British Steel Corporation.*[1]

For many companies, it is likely that the granting of guarantees would be ancillary to their core business and, therefore, a power in the sense established in the *Rolled Steel* case. It is better for companies that an act falls within its objects for which it has an implied power. If the company is merely relying on a power to do an act, entering into a guarantee must further the implied or express objects of the company, ie be in its interests and be of commercial benefit. This will depend on the facts of a particular case, but include the following considerations:

- is the trading relationship between the two companies sufficiently close to justify the guarantee?;
- what is the actual and projected strength of the group as a whole and the company being guaranteed?;
- are there any co-sureties who will be liable if the guarantee is called?;
- what is the risk in the guarantee being called?;
- what effect will the guarantee being called have on the guarantor's solvency?

A breach by a company's directors regarding the above would have an impact on them, leading to possible breaches of their fiduciary duty and allegations of misfeasance and personal liability.

However, beneficiaries of guarantees can derive comfort from ss 35, 35A and 35B of the Companies Act 1985:

- the validity of a company's acts cannot be questioned on the ground of lack of capacity because of anything in the memorandum;
- a beneficiary, acting in good faith, has the advantage that the company is bound regardless of any limitation to which it is subject;
- a party to a transaction has no duty to enquire as to any limitations that may affect the other company's ability to enter into the particular transaction.

Although care must be taken with parent company guarantees, as with any other legal documentation, they continue to be an intrinsic and important adjunct to construction industry documentation. On occasions, a potential guarantor may offer in place of a guarantee a so-called comfort letter. Usually, these are not meant to be legally binding and are meant to signify that the subsidiary has the capacity to fulfil a particular contract. They can be sufficiently ambiguous to give rise to litigation as to their interpretation and should, if at all possible, be avoided by potential beneficiaries as being second best to a parent company guarantee.

PERFORMANCE BONDS

5.7   The principal purpose of this chapter is to consider conditional and unconditional bonds which are often known, semi-colloquially, as performance bonds, which fall into two types. The on-demand bond is obviously popular with certain clients and has its origins in international contracting, particularly in the Middle East. Subsequently, it has been used on a number of UK projects. The

---

1   [1986] 1 Ch 246.

principle underlying the on-demand bond is that it can be called without the beneficiary having suffered loss, although the courts will, to temper the effect, pay close regard to any conditions relating to a call which is made. The second type of bond, the conditional or default bond, is more akin to a guarantee and has been regularly used in the UK, particularly by local authorities on civil engineering schemes, for a great number of years. Traditionally, the conditional bond has been for 10 per cent of the contract value. The conditional bond differs from the on-demand bond in one critical respect. It requires a fault to be proved on the part of the contractor before the value of the bond is paid out to the employer. The use of the words 'now the condition of the above-written Bond is such that if the Contractor shall duly perform and observe all the terms of the said Contract ... then this obligation shall be null and void' has been common for a very long time. That said, case-law has developed, discussed below, on what constitutes a default for the purposes of a bond being called. Frequently, insolvency is the cause of the contractor's default rather than necessarily the default itself. Again, a contractor may argue, when a bond is called, that there has been no default under the principal building contract. On occasions, it may be difficult to decide whether a bond is a conditional or an on-demand one. In *Esal (Commodities) Limited and Another v Oriental Credit Limited and Another*,[1] the bank agreed (per Ackner LJ):

> 'We undertake to pay the said amount on your written demand in the event that the supplier fails to execute the contract in perfect performance ...'

5.8   Although apparently a conditional bond, the Court of Appeal decided the bond was in fact unconditional because the trigger event under the bond was the demand. Commercially, it could not have been intended that the bank should be concerned with establishing whether or not there had been perfect performance of the contract.

5.9   For many years, the leading case on conditional bonds has been *Trade Indemnity Company Limited v Workington Harbour and Dock Board*.[2] The contractor was engaged for the construction of the dock and, following adverse ground conditions, the contractor went into liquidation. When the employer called in the bond, the bondsman refused to pay. The latter argued that the bond was a contract of insurance which had been voided through the non-disclosure of material facts. Lord Atkin stated:

> 'The first question that arises in regard to the plea of non-disclosure is whether the contract is one of insurance or of guarantee. The form of the contract is a money bond for £50,000 conditional upon the performance by the contractors of the contract in all things whatsoever. The defendants are described in the bond as the "surety": but they say that they are an insurance company; they were approached through insurance agents: this is a well known form of insurance business; and they have re-insured their risks with other persons carrying on business in the insurance world, notably at Lloyd's. On the other hand the contract demanded by the Dock Board was a guarantee; the defendants in the contract styled themselves sureties; the contract appears in substance to be a contract to answer for the debt, default or miscarriage of another; and the express provisions negativing release of the "surety" upon a variation of the contract or forbearance as to time indicate that the parties were thinking of the law as to guarantees. I entertain no doubt that this was a

---

1   [1985] 2 Lloyd's Rep 546 at 548.
2   [1937] AC 1.

guarantee, and the rights of the parties shall be regulated on that footing. I may be allowed to remark that it is difficult to understand why businessmen persist in entering upon considerable obligations in old fashioned forms of contract which do not adequately express the true transaction. The traditional form of marine policy is perhaps past praying for; but why insurance of credits or contracts, if insurance is intended, or guarantees of the same, if guarantees are intended, should not be expressed in appropriate language passes comprehension. It is certainly not the fault of lawyers.'[1]

5.10   In the mid-1990s, the Court of Appeal created confusion about the interpretation of conditional bonds in *Trafalgar House Constructions (Regions) Limited v General Surety and Guarantee Co Limited*.[2] In considering the standard form default bond, the Court of Appeal concluded that such bonds operated as on-demand ones. So long as Trafalgar House asserted in good faith that damages of a certain amount were due, and that amount exceeded the amount of the bond, the surety was obliged to pay the full amount of the bond. According to Saville LJ:

'Both those who seek and those who provide securities for forms of commercial obligations . . . would save much time and money if in future they heeded what Lord Atkin said so many years ago (in *Trade Indemnity v Workington Harbour and Dock Board*)[3] and set out their bargain in plain English without resorting to ancient forms which were doubtless designed for legal reasons which no longer exist.'

But the position remained:

'. . . what the Bond does is to impose upon the Surety an independent obligation to pay the damages sustained by the Main Contractor (up to the amount of the Bond) . . .'

5.11   The plaintiff was the main contractor for a leisure centre at Maidstone, costing approximately £9 million. The groundworks were sub-contracted to KD Chambers Limited, at a value of approximately £1 million. Chambers provided a standard 10 per cent performance bond, underwritten by General Surety. Chambers started work in October 1989 but went into receivership before completion. The bond was called in. The bondsman failed to pay, and, on 9 February 1993, Trafalgar House obtained summary judgment against them for the full amount of the bond. General Surety appealed, and to the surprise of many legal commentators, the Court of Appeal held the bond did not create a guarantee. That decision was the subject of an appeal to the House of Lords which reversed the Court of Appeal judgment.[4] The House of Lords held a performance bond to be what it had traditionally been thought to be, a guarantee. The provision which the House of Lords needed to consider was the standard one:

'Now the condition of the above-written bond is such that if the subcontractor shall duly perform and observe all the terms provisions conditions and stipulations of the said subcontract on the subcontractor's part to be performed observed according to the true purport intent and meaning thereof or if on default *by the subcontractors the surety shall satisfy and discharge the damages sustained by the main contractors thereby up to the amount of the above written bond* then this obligation shall be null and void . . .' [emphasis added][5]

---

1   [1937] AC 1 at 16–17.
2   (1994) CILL 912.
3   [1937] AC 1.
4   The decision of the House of Lords is to be found at [1995] 3 WLR 204.
5   [1995] 3 WLR 204 at 207–208.

5.12 There was a single judgment of the House of Lords; that of Lord Jauncey. He said:

> 'Bonds in similar form have existed for more than 150 years and have been treated by the parties thereto and by the courts as guarantees. Indeed the current standard ICE Conditions of Contract contain a specimen bond in terms identical to those in the Chambers bond. In the first place the bond itself contains indications that it was intended to be a guarantee. The appellants are described as "the surety". There is a provision to the effect that no alteration in the terms of the subcontract should release the surety from liability. In the absence of such provision a surety would normally be released from his obligation by any subsequent material alteration to the contractual provisions agreed between the contractor and subcontractor.'[1]

Further, he stated:

> '... it is interesting to note that in *Tins Industrial Co Limited v Kono Insurance Limited* (1987) 42 BLR 110 Hunter JA giving the judgment of the Court of Appeal of Hong Kong in a case concerning a bond in virtually identical terms to the Chambers bond stated, at p 121 that "a claimant under the bond has to prove first breach and secondly damages" ...
>
> My Lords I have no doubt that the Court of Appeal were in error in concluding that the bond was not a guarantee ...'[2]

Although the House of Lords decision in the *Trafalgar House* case was generally welcomed, the placing of default bonds firmly within the law of guarantees potentially causes problems. Guarantees are subject to the rule that any variation to the principal contract will operate to vitiate the guarantee entirely. Usually the operation of this rule is specifically excluded by wording to that effect in guarantees but, on occasions, particularly in bespoke contracts it can be omitted.

WHAT IS A DEFAULT?

5.13 Conditional bonds make it clear that the bondsman can only be called upon to pay if there has been a contractual default on the part of the contractor. Without proof of default, the bond is null and void.[3] There can be difficulties in establishing a default on the part of the contractor, particularly if the contractor has become insolvent. Strictly speaking, unless the contract deems insolvency to be a breach of contract for the purposes of activating a particular bond, in the absence of such wording, insolvency itself is not a circumstance of default, although the consequences of insolvency may be to place the contractor in breach of his obligations under the contract. What constitutes *default* was considered in *Northwood Development Co Limited v Aegon Insurance Company (UK) Limited*.[4] On 22 September 1988, Northwood entered into a JCT 87 with Declan Kelly Homes Limited ('Declan Kelly') for the construction of a block of flats. The contract provided, as did the JCT contracts at that time, that the management contractor's employment would determine automatically on insolvency. On 21 February 1991, Declan Kelly went into

---

1   [1995] 3 WLR 204 at 209.
2   Ibid at 211.
3   *Tins Industrial Co Limited v Kono Insurance Limited* (1987) 42 BLR 110 (Supreme Court of Hong Kong Court of Appeal).
4   (1994) 38 Con LR 1.

liquidation and the contractor's employment automatically determined. Five days later, Northwood itself went into administrative receivership. Aegon was bondsman under a bond for the building contract in the amount of £217,600. In the time-honoured tradition the bond contained the following provision:

> 'If the Contractors shall fully comply with all the terms, covenants and conditions of the Contract on their part to be kept and performed according to the Contract of if on default by the Contractors the surety shall satisfy and discharge the damages sustained by the Employer thereby up to the amount of this Bond then this obligation shall be null and void otherwise it shall remain in full force.'[1]

5.14   On Aegon's refusal to make payment under the bond, Northwood argued it was not necessary to establish a breach of contract on Declan Kelly's part. The bondsman responded that the bond required proven breaches of contract. Since insolvency brought an automatic determination of the contractor's employment under the contract, the contractor had been discharged from the requirement of further performance. In addition, the bondsman maintained the bond was a guarantee; Northwood's liabilities to Declan Kelly should be set off, thereby reducing Aegon's potential liability. Other arguments put forward by Aegon included the refusal to allow them to complete the works and the failure to commence proceedings 'within 6 months of the expiry of the maintenance period'. The Official Referee, Judge Richard Havery QC, did not equate *default* with breach of contract and, in distinguishing the *Trade Indemnity* case, held that the bond was not a contract of guarantee (p 11 of the judgment). The commercial purpose of the bond required it to cover any failure to fulfil the contractor's obligations, regardless of the existence of breach. The word *default* did not require a breach of contract. He stated:

> 'It is wide enough to cover something which does not give rise to a legal liability and . . . in the context of the whole bond the expression "damages" is wide enough to cover the case of the loss sustained by the employer resulting from the contractor's failure fully to comply with all the terms, covenants and conditions of the contract even if the contractor is not thereby in breach of contract.'[2]

5.15   In a second case, *Perar v General Surety & Guarantee Company Limited*,[3] the contractor, employed under a JCT 81 'design and build' contract, went into administrative receivership. The contractor's employment, in accordance with clause 27.2, automatically determined. The Court of Appeal had to decide whether the surety was liable under the bond where no breach of contract was alleged. Going into receivership was not a breach of contract, although counsel argued unsuccessfully that there was an anticipatory breach which had caused damage. In the view of the Court of Appeal, once the contractor's employment automatically determined, he had no further obligation in regard to the works. Clause 27.2 and 27.4 of JCT 81 were intended to provide a code for what should happen on the insolvency of the contractor. This code specified what were the employer's and the contractor's respective rights and duties consequent on the automatic determination. Clause 27.4 provided a framework whereby an employer could employ others to finish the works with a mechanism for ascertaining the account on completion. The cost of finishing the

1   (1994) 38 Con LR 1 at 3.
2   Ibid, at 7.
3   (1994) 66 BLR 52.

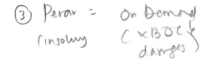

works would be calculated and an ascertainment made to show whether there was a net balance due from the employer to the contractor or vice versa. Any default would come, if at all, on that final account and the contractor's failure to pay any balance due, if owed. As a Court of Appeal decision, *Perar* was generally preferred to *Northwood*.

5.16   *Northwood* was not followed in *Oval (717) Limited v Aegon Insurance Company (UK) Limited,*[1] a decision of Mr Recorder Colin Reese QC. Here, Oval (717), a company owned by the University of Bristol, entered into a building contract with Woodward Construction Limited for the construction of halls of residence. The contract was based on JCT 81: With Contractor's Design. Aegon, the bondsman, issued a standard-form performance bond in the sum of £276,000. The bond included a typical clause drafted as follows:

> 'The Bond is executed by the Surety upon the following conditions which will be conditions precedent to the right of the Employer to recover hereunder. The Surety shall be notified by the Employer in writing of any non-performance or non-observance on the part of the Contractors of any of the stipulations or provisions contained in the said Contract and on their part to be performed and observed within one month after such non-performance or non-observance shall come to the knowledge of the Employer or his authorised representative(s) having supervision of the said Contract and the Employer shall insofar as it may be lawful, permit the Surety to perform the stipulations or provisions of the said Contract which the Contractor shall have failed to perform or observe.'

Woodward went into administrative receivership with the works incomplete and subsequently Oval demanded the sum of £276,000 under the bond. Aegon refused to pay, alleging breach of the condition precedent.

5.17   Certain facts were agreed. These were:

–   from 23 August 1994, Woodward were in breach of clause 23.1 of the contract by reason of their failure to complete by 23 August 1995;
–   23 August 1994 was the extended completion date under clause 25 of the contract;
–   Oval did not notify Aegon under the bond of non-performance or non-observance within one month after it had come to its knowledge or that of its authorised representatives;
–   the receiver's statement and/or failure to pay was a non-observance or non-performance of clause 27.4.5 of the contract;
–   Oval's solicitors notified Aegon's solicitors within one month of the non-performance or non-observance of 27.4.5.

5.18   The issues were as follows:

–   on the true construction of the bond and on the basis of the facts admitted in the pleadings and/or agreed, was the plaintiff entitled to make a call and recover under the bond? (the defendant relied in its defence on the condition precedent, being the time-limit of one month from breach);
–   was the bond a contract to which s 3 of the Unfair Contract Terms Act 1977 applied?; and

---

1   (1997) 15 CLD 08–16.

- (if the Unfair Contract Terms Act 1977 did apply) was the required condition precedent unreasonable and unenforceable?

5.19   The Recorder's findings were as follows:

- on the true construction of the bond, the plaintiff was not entitled to make a call and recover if, as it had done, the defendant elected to raise the issue of non-compliance with the first part of the first of the expressly stated conditions precedent;
- the bond was a contract where the plaintiff dealt on the defendant's written standard terms of business and was within s 3 of the 1977 Act;
- the condition precedent did not offend against s 3 of the Act.

5.20   Turning to the contents of the judgment itself, the Recorder concluded:

> 'To my mind, the meaning of "default" in this first part of the Bond is clear; it means a breach of the construction contract and I take note that in the *Perar* case … [this was] regarded … as the plain meaning of the word. By the use of such traditional words, what was created, so far as the parties were concerned was a conditional bonding obligation whereby the Defendant undertook to be answerable to the Plaintiff for any damage suffered if the Contractor breached the terms of the construction contract. In other words the Plaintiff was required to establish a breach or breaches of the construction contract and damage caused by that breach or those breaches before it could seek recovery from the Defendant under the Bond.'

The Recorder took a robust view on when the one month commenced:

> 'What is required by the first part of the first of the stipulated conditions is the giving of a written notice to the Defendant within one month of certain occurrences actually coming to the notice of the Plaintiff … the occurrences of which such written notice is to be given are any non-performance or non-observances on the Contractor's part of any terms of the construction contract.'

The Recorder considered that the word 'any' should be read without any qualification and did not mean, as counsel for the plaintiff argued 'any material'. Further, a non-performance or a stipulation or provision occurred whenever the contractor neglected or failed in the due carrying out or due fulfilment of any one of its contractual obligations. Counsel for the plaintiff argued that this would prejudice the beneficiary of a bond who failed to report an extremely trivial breach.

5.21   The further issue interestingly dealt with in the case was the impact of s 3 of the Unfair Contract Terms Act 1977 (the 1977 Act). Section 3 of the 1977 Act applies as between contracting parties where one of them deals as a consumer on the other's written standard terms of business so that, as against that party, the other could not, by reference to any contract term claim, be entitled to render a contractual performance substantially different from that which was reasonably expected of him or in respect of the whole part of his obligation to render no performance at all, except insofar as the contract term satisfied the requirement of reasonableness as defined in s 11(1) of the 1977 Act and subject to the guidelines in s 11(5). Oval submitted, for the purposes of s 3 of the 1977 Act, they were, for the purposes of this contract, a consumer dealing on Aegon's written standard terms of business. Aegon denied the applicability of the 1977 Act, further stating that the term was not unreasonable, was prominently stated on the face of the bond (which the Recorder concluded was written in the usual convoluted jargon), the contracting parties had similarly strong bargaining positions and compliance was entirely practicable. The Recorder concluded that Oval contracted in the ordinary course of business but that the bond did represent Aegon's written standard terms of business. On the face of it, s 3 of the 1977 Act applied. However, Oval could not rely on either s 3(2)(b)(i) or (ii). Aegon did not claim to be entitled to render a contract of performance substantially different from that which was reasonably expected of it not did it claim to render no performance at all. The argument simply related to non-compliance with a condition precedent. Further, the requirement of reasonableness was satisfied.

5.22   The question of how to interpret a default bond arose in *De Vere Hotels Limited v Aegon Insurance Company (UK) Limited,*[1] an Official Referee's decision. Here, the plaintiff, De Vere, employed Pentagon Holdings Limited and Pentagon Design and Construction Limited to construct a hotel at Southampton for a maximum price of £1.662 million, exclusive of VAT, in accordance with an amended version of JCT 81: With Contractor's Design. The contractor's obligations included one to enter into a bond in a sum equivalent to 10 per cent of the contract sum. A bond was issued by Aegon in the sum of £1.662 million and executed on 14 October 1993, prior to all the terms of the building contract being agreed, which occurred towards the end of September 1993. The building contract included the standard clauses. Clause 27, relating to contractor insolvency, included the right under clause 27.4.2 for the employer to 'employ and pay other persons to carry out and complete the design and construction of the Works . . .'. Following the contractor's insolvency on 2 December 1993, on 4 May 1994, De Vere entered into a new building contract with Amec to finish the uncompleted works. Amec achieved practical completion on 9 September 1994, with the certificate being issued on 13 September. The certificate identified the contract under which it was issued as being that dated 4 May 1994. By September 1996, the old contractor, Pentagon, had gone into liquidation and, by a letter dated 11 September 1996, the plaintiff's agent demanded payment from the liquidator of £2,738,869.05. This was said to be the amount of the expenses properly incurred by the plaintiff and the amount of direct loss and/or damage caused by the determination.

5.23   Under the terms of the bond, the bondsman was to:

> 'be released and discharged from its obligation under the above written Bond upon the issue of a Statement of Practical Completion of the Works by the Employer's Agent and if any suit at law or proceedings in equity are brought against the Surety to recover any claim hereunder the same must be instituted within 6 months after the date of Practical Completion named in the Statement and thereafter shall be absolutely barred.'

Aegon admitted that the plaintiff 'purported to make a demand under the bond by a letter dated 4 October 1996' but 'denied that the said demand was a valid and effective demand and the Bond provided for the Surety to be released and discharged from its obligations upon the issue of a Statement of Practical Completion of Works by the Employer's Agent. The said Statement of Practical Completion was issued on 13 September 1994'. Aegon further argued 'further or in the alternative' that 'the Bond provided that any proceedings to enforce the Surety's obligations under the Bond should be instituted within 6 months after the date of Practical Completion named in the Statement and thereafter shall be absolutely barred'. The proceedings were

---

1   (1998) 15 CLD 05–15.

commenced on 4 October 1996 outside the relevant period and in breach of the bond. The questions before the judge were:

–   was the document dated 13 September a certificate or statement of practical completion for the purposes of the proviso to the bond?;
–   if so, was the date appearing in that document the date of practical completion for the purposes of the proviso?;
–   was the defendant released from his obligations under the bond on the date named in the certificate under the completion contract?

The terms of the bond as a whole and the contract which was contemplated at the time of the bond's execution needed to be considered to determine the extent of the obligations undertaken by Aegon and thus the meaning to be given to the words of the proviso. In carrying out this simple exercise, it was clear that the bond referred to the works to be carried out by the old contractor and not to those of the completion contractor. Had the old contractor completed, the employer would have issued a statement of practical completion under clause 16.5 of the amended JCT 81. In those circumstances, it was difficult to see how a statement of practical completion of the works could be read as referring to any other such statement than the one which would have been issued to the old contractor had the works been completed. There was no ambiguity in the words 'a Statement of Practical Completion of the Works'. The bond related solely to the building contract contemplated at the time it was entered into.

5.24   The difficulty of establishing a default under a conditional bond also arose in *Laing & Morrison-Knudson v Aegon Insurance Company (UK) Limited*,[1] a decision of His Honour Judge Humphrey Lloyd QC. Aegon disputed liability under a sub-contract bond, following the appointment of administrative receivers. Two days after the appointment of the administrative receivers, the main contractor had sent a letter terminating the sub-contract and requiring delivery up of materials, equipment, etc, in accordance with the relevant contract provision. Under the termination clause, there was no automatic determination of the sub-contractor's employment on the appointment of administrative receivers; the contractor's entitlement was to terminate 'all or part of the sub-contract work at any time' with the clause being 'without prejudice to any other legal or equitable right or remedy . . . hereunder or as a matter of law'. The sub-contract between Laing & Morrison Knudson ('LMK') and Kentz related to the installation of mechanical works. The sub-contract permitted the contractor to complete or not complete the terminated sub-contract work (clause 25.5.2) but only provided for payment of sub-contractor work already done and made no reference to recovering the cost to complete outstanding sub-contract work. Further, the termination letter from main contractor to sub-contractor simply referred to the appointment of the administrative receivers under clause 20.2.2, and did not refer to the sub-contractor's repudiation, although expressly referred to in the sub-contract. The bondsman argued that the main contractor had both affirmed the sub-contract and had chosen not to accept or rely on the sub-contractor's repudiatory breach of contract. Therefore, the main contractor's only entitlements arose under clause 20 which did not include completion costs. The main contractor argued that, on its proper construction, the letter of termination did imply and accept the sub-contractor's repudiatory breach of contract. The judge rejected both the

---

1   (1997) 86 BLR 70.

bondsman's arguments. The bondsman had a further argument relating to the management nature of the main contract. Under clause 11 of the main contract, the main contractor was fully reponsible for all the acts and omissions of sub-contractors but subject to clause 6.22. They were 'deemed not to be liable' for sub-contractors unless they themselves were at fault or were unable to recover the client's damages or claims in respect of sub-contractors from the defaulting sub-contractors. Clause 11.3 of the main contract required a waiver by sub-contractors of any right to argue that, as a result of the terms of the main contract, the contractor had incurred no damage where breach of the sub-contract caused damage to the client. Aegon argued that under clause 6.22 of the main contract, the main contractor was entitled to recover completion costs from the client. The judge rejected these arguments, since first, there was no principle of law that a creditor under a bond would have to pursue other parties first before turning to the bondsman; secondly, the bondsman's liability was co-extensive with that of the sub-contractor; and thirdly, a failure to recover from a defaulting sub-contractor must include a defaulting sub-contractor's bondsman.

DISPUTING LIABILITY TO PAY UNDER BONDS

5.25   Under on-demand bonds, ordinarily the conditions to be complied with before the bond can be called are:

– that the employer makes a written demand on the bank or bondsman in question; and
– that the employer may be obliged to give written notice to the contractor of his intention to call the bond some days before actually calling it, detailing the breaches of contract relied upon and the likely losses.

5.26   To obtain payment under an on-demand bond, the employer must comply with any conditions precedent set out in the bond. However, the courts do not adopt too pedantic an approach. For instance, in *IE Contractors Limited v Lloyds Bank plc and Another*,[1] the Court of Appeal construed bonds relating to the construction of slaughterhouses in Iraq which were, according to Staughton LJ, '... prolix and vague' as requiring the demand to be in substance in accordance with the bond. According to Staughton LJ:

> 'I cannot attribute to the parties an intention that there had to be a strict degree of compliance.'[2]

5.27   Although, as a matter of fact, it may be difficult for a bondsman under a conditional bond to establish that a contractor was not in default, thereby causing loss to be occasioned to the employer, the grounds for impugning the operation of an on-demand bond are narrow and procedural. The grounds for attacking on-demand bonds are considered below.

Fraud

5.28   Fraud is not necessarily limited to strictly criminal behaviour. It can include, for civil law purposes, unconscionable conduct. What happens if the employer makes

---

1   (1990) 2 Lloyd's Rep 496.
2   Ibid, at 502.

a claim, knowing he has no legitimate claim or complaint against the contractor? In practical terms, on most construction projects it would be difficult, if not impossible, for the contractor to demonstrate that there were no defaults on his part which did not deserve reimbursement. Fraud is usually difficult to establish with a high standard of proof necessary. It may be difficult to treat an unfair call under a bond as fraudulent given the reluctance of the courts to enquire into the underlying dispute between the parties. In addition, the bondsman is not obliged to enquire into the performance of the underlying contract.

5.29   The courts have tended to treat on-demand bonds in the same manner as letters of credit. In *Edward Owen Engineering Limited v Barclays Bank International Limited*,[1] the principal contract was for the supply and installation of greenhouses in Libya. The contractor was subject to instalment payments under an irrevocable letter of credit. The contractor provided a 10 per cent performance bond which 'will be paid on your first demand.' The bond was called in *unfairly*. On learning of the demand, the contractor commenced High Court proceedings in England against Barclays Bank International and obtained an interim ex parte injunction to prevent Barclays reimbursing the Libyan bondsman under a guarantee. On discharge of the injunction and a first instance judgment that Barclays pay under the guarantee, the contractor appealed to the Court of Appeal. The Court of Appeal held that the courts could only intervene in cases of obvious fraud. In the words of Lord Denning MR:

> 'All this leads to the conclusion that the performance guarantee stands on a similar footing to a letter of credit. A bank which gives a performance guarantee must honour that guarantee according to its terms. It is not concerned in the least with the relations between the supplier and the customer; nor with the question whether the supplier has performed his contracted obligation or not; nor with the question whether the supplier is in default or not. The Bank must pay according to its guarantee, on demand if so stipulated, without proof or conditions. The only exception is when there is clear fraud of which the Bank has notice.'[2]

5.30   However, Lord Denning MR also said:

> 'It is obvious that course of action can be followed, not only where there are substantial breaches of contract, but also where the breaches are insubstantial or trivial in which case they bear the colour of a penalty or liquidated damages; or even when the breaches are merely allegations by the customer without any proof at all; or even where the breach is non-existent. The performance guarantee then bears the colour of a discount on the price of 10% or 5% or as the case may be ... The English supplier if he is wise will take it [the provision of an on-demand bond] into account when quoting his price for the contract.'[3]

5.31   The House of Lords took a similar stance in *United City Merchants (Investments) Limited and Others v Royal Bank of Canada ('the American Accord')*.[4]

5.32   On occasions, fraud on the part of the bondsman can be established. The bondsman must have actual knowledge that the call by the employer was fraudulent.

---

1   [1978] 1 All ER 976.
2   Ibid, at 983.
3   Ibid, at 982.
4   [1981] 3 All ER 142.

(*Edward Owen Engineering Limited v Barclays Bank plc,*[1] *Bolivinter Oil SA v Chase Manhattan Bank,*[2] *GKN Contractors Limited v Lloyds Bank plc*[3]).

PROCEDURAL REQUIREMENTS

5.33   What if the employer fails to comply with specific conditions in the bond? Non-compliance may mean that the bondsman refuses to pay up. Although a relaxed view was taken in *Esal (Commodities) Limited and Another v Oriental Credit Limited and Another,*[4] and *Attock Cement Co Limited v Romanian Bank for Foreign Trade,*[5] where the principal contract was for the construction of a cement works in Pakistan, the court stuck to the precise wording of the bond. The contractor was Romanian and the plaintiff a Cayman Islands-registered company. The contractor provided a performance bond for US$6.6 million which was called in following the determination of the contractor's employment in February 1987. The bond included conditions. There was a requirement which obliged the employer to accompany its demand with a declaration that Uzin Export Import (the Contractor) has failed to fulfil any of its obligations under Articles 3; 15; 16 and 17 of the above contract (referred to by Staughton LJ at p 1192). The employer's demand, dated 24 or 25 July 1987, referred to the specific articles. It was therefore valid.

5.34   In an unreported decision, *Fairclough Building Limited v Cigna Insurance and Zimmcor International Limited,*[6] Fairclough claimed against Zimmcor, its curtain walling sub-contractor, arising out of one of the London Docklands schemes. Zimmcor had provided a performance bond which stated that the bondsman, Cigna, was only liable on receipt of a written notice by the main contractor to the surety of default by the sub-contractor (such notice to provide full comprehensive and irrefutable evidence in substantiation of default). The requirement for *irrefutable evidence* required default to be established beyond all reasonable doubt rather than on the normal civil standard of the balance of probabilities.

5.35   A note of uncertainty was perhaps created by the decision of the Court of Appeal in *Potton Homes Limited v Coleman Contractors Limited.*[7] Even in the absence of specific wording, as is the case with on-demand bonds, the courts might decide that all bonds are provided as security for the due and proper performance of the contract in question. In *Potton Homes*, the principal contract was for the supply of prefabricated building units. The contractor provided three on-demand performance bonds; the second of which was subsequently called in. The plaintiff contractor sought an injunction to stop the defendant employer calling in the bond and, in addition, applied for summary judgment under RSC Ord 14. The plaintiff succeeded on the summary judgment application, although the judge held that he had no power to restrain a call on the bond. He tempered this approach by ordering that the proceeds of

1   [1978] QB 146.
2   [1984] 1 All ER 351.
3   [1985] 30 BLR 48.
4   [1985] 2 Lloyd's Rep 546.
5   [1989] 1 All ER 1189.
6   (1990) unreported.
7   (1984) 28 BLR 24.

the bond should be paid into a joint names account under RSC Ord 29, r 2(1). The employer appealed to the Court of Appeal. On-demand performance bonds should be treated in the same way as letters of credit. Although the Court of Appeal held in favour of the employer, Eveleigh LJ offered some possible support to contractors caught by unfair demands:

> 'As between buyer and seller, the underlying contract cannot be disregarded so readily. If the seller has lawfully avoided the contract *prima facie* it seems to me he should be entitled to restrain the buyer from making use of the performance bond. Moreover, in principle I do not think it possible to say that in no circumstances whatsoever, apart from fraud, will the court restrain the buyer. The facts of each case must be considered.'[1]

5.36   A further case on the interpretation of on demand bonds is *Erimis Sky Radio and Television v Banque Indosuez SA and Programma Europa.*[2] Here, Erimis agreed to buy television programmes from Programma, and Banque Indosuez provided an on-demand bond in favour of Programma. Erimis later alleged that Programma had repudiated their agreement and Programma made a demand under the bond. The bank refused to honour the bond, alleging a procedural irregularity. Erimis obtained an injunction restraining the bank from making payment and an order restraining Programma from seeking to receive payment under the bond. On the trial of various preliminary issues:

– there was no implied term that Programma would not make demands for sums which they did not honestly believe were due;
– where a bond contains a condition precedent that needs to be satisfied before a call is made, whether the condition has been complied with is wholly within the discretion of the bondsman;
– on the facts of the case, the demand was non-compliant, thereby entitling the bank to refuse to honour the claim.

5.37   If the bond is illegal or the demand made is illegal, then the call can be challenged.[3]

RESISTING THE CALL: CONDITIONAL BONDS

5.38   In the case of a conditional bond, the bondsman may be able to resist the call by using one of the defences already discussed in relation to on-demand bonds. However, depending on the circumstances, the bondsman can question:

– the existence or enforceability of the principal contract: has it been discharged, declared void, frustrated, rendered unenforceable by force majeure, etc;
– the discharge of the guarantor's obligations because of a non-permitted variation to the principal contract; or
– the existence of a breach of contract or, in the alternative, admit the breach but deny the level of damages claimed.

5.39   It is imperative to read the terms of a particular bond carefully. For instance, one well known bondsman included the following:

---

1   (1984) 28 BLR 24 at 28.
2   Unreported, 26 February 1997, Court of Appeal.
3   *Power Curber International v National Bank of Kuwait* [1981] 1 WLR 123.

'The Surety shall be notified by the Employer in writing of any non-performance or non-observance on the part of Contractors of any of the stipulations or provisions contained in the said Contract and on their part to be performed and observed within one month after such non-performance or non-observance shall have come to the knowledge of the Employer ...'

5.40   Such a clause replicates one that has been in existence for a great number of years and is referred to by Ian Duncan Wallace in his book, *Construction Contracts: Principles and Policies in Tort and Contract*:[1]

'one particular obnoxious provision, employed by the Fidelity Deposit Company of Maryland as long ago as 1909, and compounded by a highly controversial House of Lords' decision upon its wording in 1915 (which) has currently been resuscitated verbatim by ingenious bonding companies in the Far East.'

5.41   The particular decision of the House of Lords, alluded to by Wallace, was *Clydebank District Water Trustees v Fidelity Deposit of Maryland*.[2] The effect of that decision appears to be that any failure to notify the bondsman of delays giving a potential for a claim for liquidated and ascertained damages nullifies the whole bond. Therefore, a great onus is placed upon any employer's professional team to ensure that every conceivable feature of the contract which goes wrong is brought to the bondsman's attention.

5.42   The difficulty in obtaining summary judgment in regard to a conditional bond was seen in *Tower Housing Association Limited v Technical and General Guarantee Co Limited*,[3] a decision of His Honour Judge Humphrey Lloyd QC. Tower Housing Association employed Deltamar Construction ('Deltamar') under JCT 81. There was a performance bond in the value of £44,047. In May 1996, Deltamar went into administrative receivership and the employer's agent terminated Deltamar's employment under the contract. By April 1996, about £390,000 worth of work had been completed by Deltamar which meant, according to the original contract, approximately £80,000 worth of work remained to be completed. Tower Housing Association appointed a completion contractor and advised the bondsman of its intention to make a call on the bond, in July 1996. In September 1996, the employer's agent sent the bondsman a financial statement of known and anticipated costs, but showing a minimum additional cost of £88,956 to complete. Tower Housing Association claimed the amount of the bond. The relevant term of the bond was:

'In consideration of the Employer entering into the Contract with the Contractor, the Surety hereby guarantees to the Employer due and punctual performance by the Contractor of the obligations contained in the Contract (so that for the sole purposes of establishing breach and/or the net damages the terms and conditions of the Contract shall be deemed to be incorporated herein) and shall, in the event of a proven breach of the Contract by the Contractor and/or in the event of the determination of the Contractor's employment under the Contract for reasons of insolvency whether such determination is automatic or otherwise, and in each case subject to clause 2 of this Guarantee Bond, satisfy and discharge the net damages sustained by the Employer as established and ascertained pursuant to and in accordance with the provisions of the Contract, after taking into account all sums due or to become due to the Contractor thereunder and all retention

1   (Sweet & Maxwell, 1986) p 298.
2   [1916] SC 69.
3   (1997) 87 BLR 74.

monies held, provided that nothing therein contained shall oblige the Employer to await completion of the Works prior to making any proper demand hereunder.'

Following issue of a writ and service of a defence, Tower Housing Association issued a summons for summary judgment/interim payment. According to the Official Referee:

'As the claim is made on the bond, certain basic principles have to be borne in mind in approaching a bond of this kind. First of all, it is well established and it must, I assume, be taken to be common ground that a bondsman in the position of the defendant is entitled to avail itself of all the defences that might have been available to the contractor had the contractor either not been insolvent and obviously, where it is in either insolvent or in financial difficulties, then a defence is available to the administrative receivers. Secondly ... in general terms, one would approach the terms of the bond on the basis that they are to be "strictly construed and no liability is imposed which is not clearly and distinctly covered by the terms of the agreement.'[1]

The Official Referee summarised:

'Under this building contract, and it seems to be common ground, no liability to Tower would have arisen on the part of Deltamar because completion by its successor had not been achieved and in any event a statement has apparently not yet been served following completion by the employer ...

... [Tower] says, in essence, that the proviso at the end of clause 1 of the bond has the effect of nullifying any restrictions that there were in the contract, such as those set out in clause 27.6.6.2 and clause 26.6.7, and therefore it is free to recover sums which ... are indisputably due if one were to apply the "principles" ... as set out in clause 27.6.6 itself.'[2]

The Official Referee stated:

'The key, it seems to me, are the words at the end, "... prior to making a proper demand hereunder". A "proper demand hereunder" must mean a demand pursuant to and in accordance with the provisions of the contract. The only such demand for which Deltamar would be liable consequent upon determination is that created by the code set out in clause 27: see *Perar*, especially Peter Gibson LJ at page 83.

It seems to me plain that clauses 27.2 and 27.4 were intended to provide a code for what should happen on the insolvency of a contractor, and that this code specified what were the employer's and contractor's respective rights and duties consequent on the automatic determination.

So the proviso cannot apply to a liability under clause 27 for no proper demand could be made until after completion.'[3]

Dealing with the proviso to clause 1, the Official Referee concluded:

'Certainly, for the purposes of RSC Order 14, it seems to me that Tower's suggested reading of the proviso, namely that it imposes upon a surety an obligation to which the contractor was not subject, is clearly only an arguable proposition, as it conflicts with the general principles of interpretation ... I do not find clause 1 particularly easy to read. Its structure is not clear. The introduction of the brackets and the proviso at the end does nothing to assist its clarity. This is a clear case in which even for the purposes of RSC

---

1   (1997) 87 BLR 74 at 87.
2   Ibid, at 88.
3   Ibid, at 91.

Order 14, there is no point which can be dealt with shortly and summarily and the issue ought to go to trial.'[1]

IS IT ALWAYS A BLEAK OUTLOOK WITH ON-DEMAND BONDS?

5.43   On occasion, the courts will temper the full effect of an on-demand bond. In *Cargill International SA and Another v Bangladesh Sugar and Food Industries Corp*,[2] Morison J, sitting in the Commercial Court, considered the effect of an on-demand bond to a beneficiary who suffered no loss, or a loss which was less than the bond value. Cargill had agreed to sell sugar to the defendant, a government organisation. The sugar was to be delivered by a fixed date, 15 September 1994, and carried in a vessel which was less than 20 years old. The bond was 10 per cent of the contract sum. The terms of the bond were stipulated in the contract. They were:

> 'hereby undertake and guarantee due signing and acceptance and performance of the contract by the supplier [defined as Cargill] and we unconditionally and absolutely bind ourselves:
>
> (1) to make payment of US dollars 526,273.15 . . . to the corporation [the defendant] or as directed by the [defendant] in writing without any question whatsoever . . . The Guarantee is unconditional and it is expressly understood that the sole judge for deciding whether the suppliers have performed the contract and fulfilled the terms and conditions of the contract will be [defendant] . . .'

The preliminary issues before the court were as follows:

–   assuming the plaintiff was in breach of contract relating to the overage of the vessel and its late arrival, could the defendant make a call for the full value of the performance bond if the breach or breaches of contract either caused no loss to the defendant or caused a loss to the defendant less than the amount of the bond, or caused some loss to the defendant which was equal to or greater than the amount of the performance bond?;

–   if the defendant obtained payment under the performance bond as a result of any such call, was the defendant entitled to retain either all of the monies received, or only such amount as was equal to the loss suffered by it or some other, and if so, what amount?

5.44   The Commercial Court held that the defendant was entitled to make a call for the full amount of the bond even if the breach of contract had caused it no loss. The bond was not intended to represent an 'estimate' of the amount of damages to which it might be entitled under such a breach but was a 'guarantee' of due performance. However, it was implicit in the nature of the bond that, in the absence of clear words to the contrary, when a bond was called there would at some stage in the future be an 'accounting' between the parties to determine their rights and obligations. In the particular case, there was an implied contractual term that the defendant would account to the plaintiff for the proceeds received under the bond and would only retain the amount of any loss suffered as a result of the plaintiff's breach. Accordingly, if the

---

1   (1997) 87 BLR 74 at 92.

2   [1996] 4 All ER 563.

defendant had suffered no damage as a result of the plaintiff's breach, any money received by it under the bond was recoverable.

5.45   Morison J referred to the decision of Lord Denning MR in *State Trading Corp of India v ED & F Mann (Sugar) Limited:*[1]

> '... performance bonds fulfil a most useful role in international trade. If the seller defaults in making delivery, the buyer can operate the bond ... He can get the damages at once which are due to him for breach of contract. The bond is given so that, on notice of default being given, the buyer can have his money in hand to meet his claim for damages for the seller's non-performance ... If he receives too much, that can be rectified later at an arbitration ...'[2]

5.46   The judge found some assistance in Australian case-law, including *Australasian Conference Association Limited v Mainline Constructions Pty Limited (In Liq).*[3] There, the question was: when the builder went into liquidation, could the employer pay sub-contractors out of the performance bond monies? The bank argued that the employer was obliged to account for any surplus after the sub-contractors had been paid off. The employer conceded it was not entitled to retain the surplus and the court concluded that the surplus should be released to the contractor and not to the bank. In another Australian case, *Wood Hall Limited v Pipeline Authority*[4] the court held that the beneficiary was entitled to call the bond but that once paid the 'money must be held as security for the contractor's due and faithful performance of the work'.

5.47   The question of accountability was considered in Keating *Building Contracts,*[5] where the editors stated:

> 'Problems that they [on-demand bonds] raise include whether an employer who calls an on-demand bond has to account for the amount received, and if so, to whom and on what legal principles ... It is submitted that, where in relation to a building contract a contractor has at the request of the employer procured an unconditional bond, the court may depending on all the circumstances be able to imply into the building contract a term that the employer should account to the contractor for the proceeds of the bond. There may in some circumstances alternatively be a collateral contract to equivalent effect. If this were correct, where the employer's loss was either nil or less than the amount recovered under the bond, the contractor would be entitled to recover in part or in whole.'[6]

PREVENTING PAYMENT UNDER AN ON-DEMAND BOND

5.48   To prevent the bondsman from paying under an on-demand bond, an injunction will be necessary. However, an injunction will be granted only in the most limited of circumstances. The usual ground for such injunctions will be fraud. There are two methods of attack. First, the employer can be injuncted from making a call under the bond and second, the bondsman can be injuncted from paying out. Usually,

1   (1981) *The Times,* 22 July.
2   [1996] 4 All ER 563 at 569.
3   (1978) 141 CLR 335.
4   (1979) 141 CLR 443.
5   6th edn (Sweet & Maxwell, 1995) pp 275–276.
6   Morison J's judgment was upheld by the Court of Appeal and reported at [1998] 1 WLR 461.

the bondsman or employer will be able to show that there has been a default of some sort (however minor) on the part of the contractor.

GENERAL CONSIDERATIONS RELATING TO BONDS

5.49   The Insurance Companies Act 1982 states that only those insurance companies duly licensed by the Department of Trade and Industry under the relevant sections of the Act can provide performance bonds, the only exception being joint banks. Contractors have the principal choice of going to their bank or to an insurance company. Which is better? When an insurance company issues a bond, this does not affect the contractor's general credit. It is often quicker and simpler to get bonds from banks, although banks regard the issue of bonds as forming part of their customer's general credit facilities. If a contractor uses his bank, this digs into his general overdraft facilities with the bank and reduces the level of his working capital. The cost of obtaining a performance bond is, for a contractor, relatively low, although it will depend on circumstances. The stability and the experience of the contractor are, of course, important, but other features to be considered will include the level of retention, the contract period, onerous risk conditions in the contract and the bond percentage. When underwriting the bond, the following will be considered:

- the contractor's technical abilities;
- the nature of the contractor's usual business;
- the contractor's tender;
- the level of bonded contracts already entered into by the contractor;
- an appraisal of the contractor's general business.

Although there is at common law a right of indemnity from the bonded contractor in favour of the surety, ordinarily sureties will require a specific indemnity from the bonded contractor. As a matter of practice, this will usually be required from the ultimate parent company of the contractor. Where the contractor is a subsidiary, the surety will usually obtain a counter-guarantee from the holding company, particularly where the subsidiary is a limited liability company. Although many counter-indemnities require the reimbursement of monies actually paid out, others adopt an on-demand wording. Contractors need to look to how they support the counter indemnity. Obviously, a charge on the business is usually not possible because the bank has secured its position by a debenture to support the company's overdraft. Therefore, the contractor may need to offer collateral security to support the bond issue.

LOOKING TO THE FUTURE

5.50   In his report, *Constructing the Team*, Sir Michael Latham stated in para 5.10:

> 'Bonds have long been a controversial part of the construction process. The Secretary of State for the Environment announced in his speech last November that the DoE would prepare guidelines to apply throughout Government on the use of bonds. He was critical of on-demand bonds, as are the CIEC. Bonds were intended to be a protection against

failure or poor performance. As this DoE work is in progress, I do not need to duplicate it. But I believe that the DoE's guidance on bonds should be formulated within these principles:

1. They should be drafted in comprehensible and modern language.
2. They should not be on-demand and unconditional, but should have clearly defined circumstances set out in them for being called.
3. If the circumstances/conditions provided for in the bond are fulfilled, the beneficiary should be able to obtain prompt payment for that recourse to litigation.
4. They should have a clear end date.'

ABI MODEL FORM OF GUARANTEE BOND

5.51   According to the Association of British Insurers (ABI):

'The ABI Model Form of Guarantee Bond introduces an industry standard which provides clarity of purpose and equity to employer, contractor and surety. Its use should cut out many hundreds of different bond wordings currently in use and save all parties considerable time and legal expenses in the issue of bonds.

It should enable insurers to meet the increasing requirement for bonds arising from the difficult economic conditions facing the construction industry without blocking contractor's bank credit lines with on demand bonds at a time in the economic cycle when they will most probably need such bank loans to fund their business operations.

In consultation with the Department of the Environment and the construction industry, the ABI Surety Bond Panel is continuing its study of an equitable alternative to pay on-demand bonds.'

5.52   Further, according to the *ABI News Release* of 26 September 1995, taking on board the House of Lords' judgment in *Trafalgar House Construction (Regions) Limited v General Surety & Guarantee Co Limited*,[1] the ABI had issued a new model form of guarantee bond with the following purposes:

–   to satisfy the commercial requirements of the employer and contractor by providing a simple short-form document to meet their commercial purpose of affording the employer protection against financial loss as a consequence of default (usually upon insolvency) by the contractor;
–   to address the concerns of the construction industry regarding the use of 'on-demand' bonds and the statement of the Secretary of State for the Environment that 'on-demand bonds have no place in Government contracts . . .;[2]
–   to take into account the recommendations of the Latham report on bonds that they should be drafted in comprehensible and modern language; they should not be on-demand and unconditional but have clearly defined circumstances set out in them for being called; if the circumstances/conditions provided in the bond are

---

1   [1995] 3 WLR 204, in which Lord Jauncey commented:
      'In recent years there has come into existence a creature described as an "on-demand bond" in terms of which the creditor is entitled to be paid merely on making a demand for the amount of the bond . . . all that was required to activate it was a demand by the creditor stated to be on the basis of the events specified in the bond.'
2   (1994) CILL 912.

fulfilled, a beneficiary should be able to obtain prompt payment without recourse to litigation and they should have a clear end date;
- to ensure that the obligations and rights of the surety and the contractor are identical under the terms and conditions of the bond and the contract.

5.53 Usefully, the ABI has published *An Explanatory Guide* (September 1995) to which the new Guarantee Bond forms Appendix II. This document is well worth reading and can be obtained from the ABI.[1]

5.54 The ABI Bond is a guarantee, although described as a *guarantee bond*. The differences between it and existing performance bonds are ones of form rather than substance. Like any *default* bond, it requires the employer, when calling upon the bond, to prove his loss and to allow the surety to set off any sums due and owing from the employer to the contractor prior to payment of any residue due to the employer. The bond is generally written in clearer, more modern language and with reasonable brevity. The clauses are followed by a schedule which the parties will need to complete. That said, the bond still contains some time honoured phraseology including, for instance, 'no allowance of time by the Employer under or in respect of the Contract or the Works shall in any way release, reduce or affect the liability of the Guarantor under this Guarantee Bond'. As the editor of *Construction Industry Law Letter* indicated:[2]

> 'Is this supposed to mean that extensions of time are to be disregarded in calculating the Guarantor's liability for liquidated damages? An accomplished legal historian would recognise these words as a traditional antidote to the rule, dating back to *Rees v Berrington* in 1795, that extending the time for performance releases a surety. But the rule was mitigated in respect of express extension of time provisions as long ago as 1899 (in *Greenwood v Francis*).'

5.55 The ABI Bond has seven operative clauses. These are set out below.

Clause 1
The guarantee bites on a contractor's breach of contract. The older word, *default*, is omitted. Also, any rights of set-off counterclaim, etc vested in the guarantor are assessed expressly by reference to the principles under the principal contract.

Clause 2
This states the maximum aggregate liability of the guarantor. This is broadly similar to earlier provisions. However, what is expressly stated is that the liability of the guarantor is co-extensive with that of the contractor.

Clause 3
Alterations to the principal contract will not discharge the obligation of the guarantor. This replicates traditional provisions.

Clause 4
The guarantor's liability is discharged on the expiry. This is defined in the Schedule. There is an important proviso in that claims survive:

---

1   Telephone: 0171 600 3333.
2   At (1995) CILL 1103.

'... in respect of any breach of the Contract which has occurred and in respect of which a claim in writing containing particulars of such breach has been made upon the Guarantor before Expiry.'

The Explanatory Guide indicates that the date to be used for expiry is a matter for negotiation and discussion between employer and contractor in each instance. Often the date of issue of the Certificate of Practical or Substantial Completion will be inserted.

Clause 5

This could be seen as otiose. However, its insertion does emphasise the obligation of the contractor to perform and discharge its obligations under the contract properly and in such manner as to avoid potential calls on the bond.

Clause 6

There is an absolute prohibition on assignment without the prior written consent of the guarantor and the contractor. There are no qualifying words of the sort 'such consent not to be unreasonably or vexatiously delayed or withheld'. The Explanatory Guide notes that wherever there is an assignment of the principal contract, 'it is envisaged that the consent to the assignment of the benefit of the bond would be given by the Guarantor save in the most exceptional of circumstances'.

Clause 7

This is the dispute resolution clause. Unlike the position under other forms of bond, dispute resolution is exclusively via the medium of the courts. There is no option to arbitrate unless a specific amendment is included. The ABI missed the opportunity to include a fast-track adjudication procedure. This is contrary to the Latham culture that beneficiaries should be able to obtain prompt payment without litigation. The need to establish first a default or breach of contract and subsequently to agree quantification means that there will be no fast track available via the courts in many situations. Both RSC Ord 14 and RSC Ord 14A will be frequently inappropriate.

5.56   Deciding the expiry for inclusion in the Schedule may be difficult, particularly in the light of *Perar v General Surety & Guarantee Company Limited*.[1] Case-law has emphasised that insolvency of the contractor, unless specifically deemed to be a *default*, is not of itself a breach of contract. If the contractor's employment either determines automatically on insolvency or the employer has a right to determine the contractor's employment on insolvency, the contractor is discharged from the obligation to complete the works and cannot be in breach of contract if he fails to do so. Under the ABI Bond, liability of the surety only occurs when the contractor is in breach of the principal contract. This will continue to cause immense problems. In contracts of the JCT type, there is an accounting mechanism which suspends further payment to the insolvent contractor until such time as the finishing contractor has completed the works and a final audited account can be made to ascertain sums either due from employer to insolvent contractor or vice versa, examples being clause 27 of JCT 80 and JCT 81. If there is a net balance due from

---

1   (1994) 66 BLR 52.

insolvent contractor to employer, which is not paid, that would be the necessary breach for the purposes of activating the ABI Bond.

5.57 There may be difficulties if the expiry of the bond is expressed to be the date of practical completion under the principal contract. The final account of the new contractor and the necessary accounting mechanism will be completed post practical completion of the new contractor's contract. Rather confusingly, the ABI suggests in the Explanatory Guide that practical completion of the works by another contractor would not constitute practical completion under the principal contract, with the effect of extinguishing the liabilities of the guarantor. The ABI position is poorly reasoned, relying upon a decision of the Scottish courts (at best persuasive in England and Wales, which does not in fact appear to be in point). Any employer will seek to amend the bond to ensure that claims survive the insolvency of the principal contractor. A simple amendment required is to state in Clause 1 that 'Breach of Contract also means Contractor's insolvency or the determination of its employment because of insolvency'.

5.58 The second situation which might arise, and where the bondsman would escape liability, is if, before the employer's claim arises and becomes payable, the insolvent contractor ceases to exist as a legal entity. An example would be if the insolvent contractor were struck off the Companies Register. The bondsman is only liable as guarantor for a contractor in breach of contract. Can the bondsman be liable if the contractor no longer exists in a legal sense?

OTHER FORMS OF BOND

Tender/bid bonds

5.59 Tender/bid bonds compensate an employer in the event of the withdrawal of a tender before acceptance; or the tenderer's failure to enter into a contract with the employer. There are no standard form tender bonds, although ordinarily they are on demand. Some employers insist upon the deposit of a fixed sum in lieu of a tender bond. *Construction News*[1] reported a requirement on consortia tendering for the Midland Metro Line to provide a tender bond which could be called should any of them withdraw from the bidding. At the time, this was unprecedented in UK contracting and apparently caused great concern to the consortia members.

Advance payment bonds

5.60 Whenever an advance payment is made to a contractor, an advance payment bond or guarantee is essential. This ensures that any loss suffered by the employer as a result of making such payment, most probably because of the contractor's subsequent insolvency, can be recovered. The bond or guarantee is usually valued at the full amount of the advance payment made. However, as with any other legal document, the contents of any proposed advance payment bond or guarantee need to be reviewed carefully.

---

1   (1992) *Construction News*, 28 May.

5.61   The terms of one such advance payment bond were considered by the Court of Appeal in *Mercers Company of London v New Hampshire Insurance Company Limited.*[1] Mercers made an advance payment of £4.5 million to Rush & Tomkins in regard to a project carried out under a JCT contract. When Rush & Tomkins went into administrative receivership, approximately £3.5 million of the advance payment had not been expended for the purposes of the contract. In order to avoid liability, New Hampshire Insurance argued that Mercers had been in breach of contract by failing to give Rush & Tomkins possession of the site on the due date or within six weeks, as required by JCT 80. This breach meant that New Hampshire Insurance were not liable under the bond. It was a *performance* bond for a contract, the terms of which were varied without the consent of New Hampshire Insurance. A basic principle of the law relating to surety bonds and guarantees is that any variation to the terms of the underlying contract between the creditor and the debtor (whose obligations are guaranteed or underwritten) which might prejudice the surety will discharge the surety from liability.[2] Although this argument was accepted by the trial judge, the decision was reversed by the Court of Appeal on the following grounds:

–   late possession of the site was not a repudiatory breach of the contract giving rise to a variation and, as such, could not discharge the guarantor's liability to pay under the bond;

–   no special significance was expressed in the bond as attaching to the date of actual possession of the site. Mercers were, therefore, able to recover the £3.5 million, being the monies for which they had not received value in return for the advance payment;

–   the bond was one whereby New Hampshire Insurance had made themselves jointy and severally liable for any unearned balance.

Retention bonds

5.62   During the early 1990s, there was a spate of case-law decisions concerning the treatment of retention monies, particularly under the JCT contracts. These cases demonstrated that, in the absence of specific wording to the contrary, retention monies under such contracts were held by the employer on trust for the contractor and, if required by the contractor, the employer was obliged to place those retention monies in a separate designated bank account. The problem of dealing with retention monies encouraged certain employers to consider using retention bonds. On release of the retention by the employer to the contractor, a retention bond takes over. Retention bonds are common on complex mechanical and electrical contracts, including offshore oil and gas installations, to assist the contractor's cash flow, while at the same time providing protection to the employer. There is no standard form retention bond, although such bonds are generally payable *on demand*. The British Constructional Steelwork Association proposes its members offer a retention bond.

Payment guarantee bonds

5.63   These are common in some countries, for instance the USA, and require a contractor to obtain a bond to ensure payment to sub-contractors and suppliers.

---

1   (1992) 60 BLR 76.
2   *Holmer v Brunskill* (1877) 3 QBD 495. *Plant v Brown* (1862) 4 De GF & J 367.

The purpose is to avoid disruption resulting from non-payment of specialist contractors. Although not generally used in the UK, the Confederation of Construction Specialists has prepared a form of payment guarantee bond which has been recommended to its members. The level of 'take-up' is unclear but probably minimal.

Appendix

SHORT FORM PARENT COMPANY GUARANTEE

THIS AGREEMENT is made on [*date*] BETWEEN:

(1) [*name*] of [*address*] ('the Guarantor') of the first part; and

(2) [*name*] of [*address*] ('the Employer') of the second part.

WHEREAS:

(A) This agreement is supplemental to a Contract ('the Contract') of even date hereto and made between [*name*] ('the Contractor') and the Employer whereby the Contractor has agreed to carry out certain works more particularly described in the Contract and the Employer has agreed in consideration of the due performance of the said works to pay to the Contractor the contract price as defined in the Contract.

(B) In consideration of the Contractor and the Employer entering into that Agreement the Guarantor has agreed to guarantee for the benefit of the Employer the due performance by the Contractor of its obligations under the Contract.

NOW IT IS AGREED as follows:

1   If the Contractor shall in any respect fail to execute the works to be executed under the Contract or commits any breach of its obligations under the Contract the Guarantor shall indemnify the Employer against all losses, damages, costs and expenses which may be incurred by the Employer by reason of any default on the part of the Contractor in performing and observing the agreements and provisions on the Contractor's part contained in the Contract.

2   The Guarantor shall not be discharged or released from the Guarantee by any arrangements made between the Contractor and the Employer without the consent of the Guarantor or by any alteration in the obligations undertaken by the Contractor or by any forbearance as to payment, time, performance or otherwise.

3   This Guarantee shall be binding upon the Guarantor's successors in title and assigns and shall enure for the benefit of and be enforceable by the Employer, its successors in title and assigns.

IN WITNESS whereof this Agreement has been executed as a Deed the date and year first before written

THE COMMON SEAL of [*name*] was hereto affixed   }
in the presence of: }

....
Director

....
Secretary

LONGER FORM OF PARENT COMPANY GUARANTEE

THIS GUARANTEE is made on [*date*] BETWEEN:

(1) [*company name*] whose registered office is situated at [*address*] ('the Guarantor') of the one part; and

(2) [*company name*] whose registered office is situated at [*address*] ('the Beneficiary') of the other part.

WHEREAS:

(A) This Guarantee is supplemental to an agreement dated [*date*] ('the Agreement') and made between the Beneficiary and [*name*] ('the Contractor') for the procurement of the design, supply and installation of certain works as therein described ('the Works').

(B) the Contractor is a [wholly owned] subsidiary of the Guarantor.

(C) The Guarantor has agreed to guarantee the due performance by the Contractor of the Contractor's obligations under the Agreement in regard to the Works in the manner hereinafter appearing.

NOW THIS DEED WITNESSETH as follows:

1. In consideration of the Beneficiary entering into the Agreement with the Contractor the Guarantor hereby guarantees as follows:

   1.1 that the Contractor will duly and punctually perform and observe all those terms and obligations contained in the Agreement on the part of the Contractor to be performed and observed;

   1.2 that in the event of any breach of any such term or obligation by the Client the Guarantor shall make good or cause such breach to be made good in any event and otherwise perform and fulfil in place of the Contractor each and every obligation in respect of which the Beneficiary has defaulted or as may be unfulfilled by the Contractor;

   1.3 to indemnify and keep indemnified the Beneficiary against any loss damage expense or claim occasioned to the Contractor by any such failure or breach on the part of the Contractor.

2. The Guarantor's liability under this Guarantee shall not be discharged lessened or affected in any way by reason of any time forbearance or other indulgence on the part of the Beneficiary or by reason of the conduct or performance by the Beneficiary of its obligations under the Agreement or by any variation in the terms of the Agreement or by any other act omission or thing concerning the Agreement.

3. This Guarantee shall be an irrevocable continuing guarantee which shall be and continue in full force and effect notwithstanding the dissolution of the Contractor or any change in its status function control or ownership.

4. Any notice given by the Beneficiary under this Guarantee shall be deemed duly served on the Guarantor if sent to its registered office by recorded delivery post but not otherwise.

5.   This Guarantee shall be in addition to and not in substitution for any rights or remedies that the Beneficiary may have against the Contractor arising under the Agreement or otherwise. This Guarantee shall not be operated until such time as the Beneficiary has pursued and exhausted all remedies reasonably available against the Contractor.

6.   This Guarantee shall in all respects be construed and governed in accordance with English law and shall be subject to the jurisdiction of the English courts. The proceedings shall be conducted before the Technology and Construction Court in London.

IN WITNESS WHEREOF this Guarantee has been executed as a Deed the day and year first before written.

THE COMMON SEAL of [*name*] was hereto affixed   }
in the presence of: }

....
Director

....
Secretary

ADVANCE PAYMENT BOND: *THE MERCER'S COMPANY V NEW HAMPSHIRE INSURANCE COMPANY* (1991) CONST LJ 130

KNOW ALL MEN BY THESE PRESENTS:

That RUSH & TOMPKINS LIMITED as Principal, and NEW HAMPSHIRE INSURANCE COMPANY as Surety, are held and firmly bound unto THE MERCER'S COMPANY as Obligee, in the sum of Four Million Five Hundred and Twenty Nine Thousand Three Hundred and Forty Pounds (£4,529,340) for the payment of which sum, well and truly to be made, the Principal and Surety bind themselves, their heirs, executors, administrators, successors and assigns, jointly and severally, firmly by these presents.

WHEREAS the Principal has entered into a written contract dated 20th March 1989 with the Obligee for the reconstruction of Halton House; refurbishment of the Gatehouse and the Mercer's Dining Hall, Holborn, London, EC1 and

WHEREAS said contract provides for certain advance payments to be made by the Obligee to the Principal, as more fully set forth therein and

WHEREAS the Obligee has required the Principal to furnish a bond in the form and tenor of this instrument conditioned upon the faithful employment, for the purpose of the contract, of said monies so advanced and

WHEREAS this bond is given to save the Obligee harmless against any and all losses which may result from the failure of the Principal to faithfully employ for the purpose of the contract and liquidate in accordance with the terms and conditions of said contract all or any portion of the advance payments so made.

NOW, THEREFORE, THE CONDITION OF THIS OBLIGATION IS SUCH, that if the aforementioned advance so made is liquidated in accordance with the terms and conditions of said contract and is faithfully employed for the purpose of said contract, then this obligation shall be void; otherwise it shall remain in full force and effect.

PROVIDED HOWEVER THAT the Surety shall not be liable for any default of the Principal due in any way to causes beyond the control of the Principal including but not limited to force majeure, war, strikes, riots, civil commotion, or acts of God.

Signed Sealed and dated 30th March 1989

JCT 80: AMENDMENT 18 (1998) ADVANCE PAYMENT BOND

1   THE parties to this Bond are:

(1) _____

whose registered office is at _____

_____ ('the Surety'), and

(2) _____

of _____

_____ ('the Employer').

2   The Employer and _____ ('the Contractor')

have agreed to enter into a contract for building works ('the Works') at _____

_____ ('the Contract').

3   The Employer has agreed to pay the Contractor the sum of [_____] as an advance payment of sums due to the Contractor under the Contract ('the Advance Payment') for reimbursement by the Surety on the following terms:

(a)   When the Surety receives a demand from the Employer in accordance with Clause 3(b) the Surety shall repay the Employer the sum demanded up to the amount of the Advance Payment.

(b)   The Employer shall in making any demand provide to the Surety a completed notice of demand in the form of the Schedule attached hereto which shall be accepted as conclusive evidence for all purposes under this Bond. The signatures on any such demand must be authenticated by the Employer's bankers.

(c)   The Surety shall within 5 Business Days after receiving the demand pay to the Employer the sum so demanded. 'Business Day' means the day (other than a Saturday or a Sunday) on which commercial banks are open for business in London.

4   Payments due under this Bond shall be made notwithstanding any dispute between the Employer and the Contractor and whether or not the Employer and the Contractor are or might be under any liability one to the other. Payment by the Surety under this Bond shall be deemed a valid payment for all purposes of this Bond and shall discharge the Surety from liability to the extent of such payment.

5   The Surety consents and agrees that the following actions by the Employer may be made and done without notice to or consent of the Surety and without in any way affecting changing or releasing the Surety from its obligations under this Bond and the liability of the Surety hereunder shall not in any way be affected hereby. The actions are:

(a)   waiver by the Employer of any of the terms, provisions, conditions, obligations and agreements of the Contractor or any failure to make demand upon or take action against the Contractor;

(b)   any modification or changes to the Contract; and/or

(c)   the granting of any extentions of time to the Contractor without affecting the terms of clause 7(c) below.

6   The Surety's maximum aggregate liability under this Bond which shall commence on payment of the advance payment by the Employer to the Contractor shall be the amount of [_____] which sum shall be reduced by the amount of any reimbursement made by the Contractor to the Employer as advised by the Employer in writing to the Surety.

7   The obligations of the Surety and under this Bond shall cease upon whichever is the earliest of:

(a)   the date on which the Advance Payment is reduced to nil as certified in writing to the Surety by the Employer;

(b)   the date on which the Advance Payment or any balance thereof is repaid to the Employer by the Contractor (as certified in writing to the Surety by the Employer) or by the Surety; and

(c)   [longstop date to be given],

and any claims hereunder must be received by the Surety in writing on or before such earliest date.

8   This Bond is not transferable or assignable without the prior written consent of the Surety. Such written consent will not be unreasonably withheld.

9   This Bond shall be governed and construed in accordance with the laws of England and Wales.

IN WITNESS hereof this Bond has been executed as a Deed by the Surety and delivered on the date below:

EXECUTED as a Deed by: _____

    for an on behalf of the Surety: _____

EXECUTED as a Deed by: _____
    for and on behalf of the Employer: _____

Date: _____

SCHEDULE TO ADVANCE PAYMENT BOND

(clause 3(b) of the bond)

Notice of Demand

Date of Notice: _____

Date of Bond: _____

Employer: _____

Surety: _____

The bond has come into effect

We hereby demand payment of the sum of

£ _____ (amount in words)
which does not exceed the amount of reimbursement for which the Contractor is in default at the
date of this notice

Address for payment: _____

_____

This Notice is signed by the following persons who are authorised by the Employer to act for
and on his behalf:

Signed by _____

    Name _____

    Official Position: _____

Signed by _____

    Name _____

    Official Position: _____

The above signatures to be authenticated by the Employer's bankers

[Reproduced by kind permission of the Joint Contracts Tribunal.]

CONDITIONAL BOND: *TRADE INDEMNITY CO V WORKINGTON HARBOUR AND DOCK BOARD* [1937] AC 1

'Know all men by these presents that Messrs. Kirk & Randall, Ld., of 146/7 Grosvenor Road, London S.W.1 (hereinafter called the Contractors) and the Trade Indemnity Company Ld., of 13 Austin Friars, London, E.C.2 (hereinafter called the Surety) are held and firmly bound unto the Workington Harbour & Dock Board of Workington in the County of Cumberland (hereinafter called the Owners) in the full and just sum of Fifty thousand pounds sterling to the payment of which said sum of money well and truly to be made and done the said Contractors and the said Surety bind themselves and their successors jointly and severally firmly by these presents:

Signed Sealed and Dated this Eleventh day of October One thousand nine hundred and twenty-two.

Whereas the Contractors have entered into a certain written contract with the Owners bearing date the [twenty-third] day of October 1922 (hereinafter referred to as the contract) for the execution of certain works of demolition and the construction completion and maintenance of an extension of the Lonsdale Dock and a new entrance thereto and all other works in clause 1 of the contract mentioned (all of which works are more particularly shown described or referred to in the contract) subject to and in accordance with the provisions of the said clause 1 which contract with all its provisions covenants conditions and obligations is hereby made a part of the above written Bond to all intents and purposes as though the contract had been incorporated herein. Now therefore the condition of the above written Bond is such that if the Contractors shall execute construct and maintain the said recited works subject to and in accordance with the provisions of the said clause 1 of the contract and shall in all things whatsoever observe perform fulfil and keep all and singular the clauses and conditions agreements matters and things which on the part of the Contractors are and ought to be observed performed fulfilled and kept by them according to the contract then the above written Bond shall be null and void otherwise it shall remain in full force and virtue. Provided always and it is hereby agreed and declared that the Surety shall not be released or discharged from the above written Bond by any agreement which may either with or without the assent or notwithstanding the dissent of the Surety be made between the Contractors and the Owners or between the Contractors and the engineers in the contract mentioned for any alteration in or to the said works or the contract or any forbearance by the Owners or by the said engineers whether as to payment time performance or otherwise howsoever or by any dealing or transaction which may take place between the Contractors and the Owners or between the Contractors and the said engineers or by any act or default of the said engineers or by any act or omission to act by the Owners in consequence of the said engineers' acts or defaults and provided further that the Surety shall be bound by all decisions opinions orders directions requisitions and certificates of the engineers under the provisions of clauses 106 and 107 of the contract as the Contractors are so bound.'

SURETY OR PERFORMANCE BOND COMMONLY OFFERED BY BONDSMEN

Bond No.

The Contractors and the Surety are held and firmly bound to the Employer in the above Sum for the payment of which sum the Contractors bind themselves their heirs executors and administrators or their successors and assigns and the Surety binds itself its successor and assigns jointly and severally by this Bond.

> **Whereas** the Contractors have entered into a Contract for the work with the Employer which Contract with all its covenants and conditions shall be regarded as being incorporated herein.
> If the Contractors shall fully comply with all the terms covenants and conditions of the Contract on their part to be kept and performed according to the Contract or if on default by the Contractors the Surety shall satisfy and discharge the damages sustained by the Employer thereby up to the amount of this Bond then this obligation shall be null and void otherwise it shall remain in full force.

> **THIS BOND** is executed by the Surety upon the following conditions which shall be conditions precedent to the right of the Employer to recover hereunder:
>> The Surety shall be notified by the Employer in writing of any non-performance or non-observance on the part of the Contractors of any of the stipulations or provisions contained in the said Contract and on their part to be performed and observed within one month after such non-performance or non-observance shall have come to the knowledge of the Employer or his authorised representative(s) having supervision of the said Contract and the Employer shall in so far as it may be lawful permit the Surety to perform the stipulations or provisions of the said Contract which the Contractors shall have failed to perform or observe.

>> If any suits at law or proceedings in equity are to be brought against the Surety to recover any claim hereunder the same must be served within six months after the expiry of the maintenance period stated in the Contract.

PROVIDED ALWAYS that the liability of the Surety hereunder ceases upon issue of the certificate of practical completion.

Signed sealed and dated this   day of   19

> **WITNESS** the Seals of the said parties the day and year above written.

The Common Seal of the Contractors was   The Common Seal of [the *Bondsman*] was
hereunto affixed in the presence of: hereunto affixed in the presence of:

_____ DIRECTOR   _____

_____   _____

FORM OF PERFORMANCE BOND COMMONLY USED ON ENGINEERING CONTRACTS

BY THIS BOND [1]We [name] of [address]

[2]We [name] Ltd/plc whose registered office is at [address]

[3]We [name] and [name] carrying on business in partnership under the name or style of [name/style] at [address] ('the Contractor); and

[4][name] Ltd/plc whose registered office is at [address] ('the Surety')

are held and firmly bound unto [name] ('the Employer') in the sum of £[   ] for the payment of which sum the Contractor and the Surety bind themselves their successors and assigns jointly and severally by these presents.

SEALED with our respective seals and dated this [date].

WHEREAS the Contractor and the employer have entered into a Contract ('the said Contract') for the construction and completion of the Works as therein mentioned in conformity with the provisions of the said Contract.

NOW THE CONDITIONS of the above-written Bond are such that if:

(a)   the Contractor shall subject to condition (c) hereof duly perform and observe all the terms, provisions, conditions and stipulations of the said Contract on the Contactor's part to be performed and observed according to the true purport intent and meaning thereof; or if

(b)   on default by the Contractor the Surety shall satisfy and discharge the damages sustained by the Employer thereby up to the amount of the above-written Bond; or if

(c)   the Engineer defined in clause 1(1)(c) of the said Contract shall pursuant to the provisions of clause 61 thereof issue a Defects Correction Certificate then upon the date stated therein ('the Relevant Date')

this obligation shall be null and void but otherwise shall remain in full force and effect but no alteration in the terms of the said Contract made by agreement between the Employer and the Contractor or in the extent or nature of the Works to be constructed and completed thereunder and no allowance of time by the Employer or the Engineer under the said Contract nor any forbearance or forgiveness in or in respect of any matter or thing concerning the said Contract on the part of the Employer or the said Engineer shall in any way release the Surety from any liability under the above-written Bond.

PROVIDED ALWAYS that if any dispute or difference shall arise between the Employer and the Contractor concerning the Relevant Date or otherwise as to the withholding of the Defects Correction Certificate then for the purpose of this Bond only and without prejudice to the resolution or determination pursuant to the provisions of the said Contract of any dispute or difference whatsoever between the Employer and Contractor the Relevant Date shall be such as may be:

(a)   agreed in writing between the Employer and the Contractor; or

(b)   if either the Employer or the Contractor shall be aggrieved at the date stated in the said Defects Correction Certificate or otherwise as to the issue or withholding of the said Defects Correction Certificate the party so aggrieved shall forthwith by notice in writing to the other refer any such dispute or difference to the arbitration of a person to be agreed upon between the parties or (if the parties fail to appoint an arbitrator within one calendar month of the service of the notice as aforesaid) a person to be appointed on the application of either party by the President for the time being of the Institution of Civil Engineers and such arbitrator shall forthwith and with all due expedition enter upon the reference and make an award thereon which award shall be final and conclusive to determine the Relevant Date for the purposes of this Bond. If the arbitrator declines the appointment or after appointment is removed by order of a competent court or is incapable of acting or dies and the parties do not within one calendar month of the vacancy arising fill the vacancy then the President for the time being of the Institution of Civil Engineers may on the application of either party appoint an arbitrator to fill the vacancy. In any case where the President for the time being of the Institution of Civil Engineers is not able to exercise the aforesaid functions conferred upon him the said functions may be exercised on his behalf by a Vice-President for the time being of the said Institution.

Signed Sealed and Delivered as a Deed by [*name*] Ltd/plc

In the presence of [*name*]

Signed Sealed and Delivered as a Deed by [*Surety*]

In the presence of [*Name*]

NOTES:

1 Appropriate to an individual.
2 Appropriate to a limited company.
3 Appropriate to a firm.
4 Appropriate where the surety is a bank or insurance company.

SHORT FORM PERFORMANCE BOND WITH REDUCTION MECHANISM

THIS BOND was made the [*date*] BETWEEN:

(1) [*company name*] of [*address*] ('the Contractor') of the first part;

(2) [*company name*] of [*address*] ('the Surety') of the second part; and

(3) [*company name*] of [*address*] ('the Employer') of the third part.

1   By a contract dated [*date*] made between the Contractor and the Employer ('the Contract') the Contractor has agreed to carry out the Works specified in the Contract for the sum of £[   ] ('the Contract Sum').

2   The Contractor and the Surety are hereby jointly and severally bound to the Employer in the sum of £[   ] (not exceeding 10% of the original Contract Sum) which sum shall be reduced by an amount equal to 10% of the value of any part or parts of the Works taken into possession of the Employer under the provisions of the Contract [or of any Section of the Works upon the Architect/Contract Administrator certifying practical completion of that Section] provided that if the Contractor shall subject to clause 5 hereof duly perform and observe all the terms, conditions, stipulations and provisions contained or referred to in the Contract which are to be performed or observed by the Contractor or if on default by the Contractor the Surety shall subject to clause 3 hereof, satisfy and discharge the damage sustained by the Employer thereby up to the amount of this Bond then this agreement shall be of no effect.

3   If the Contractor has failed to carry out the obligations referred to in clause 2 hereof then written notice requiring the Contractor to remedy his failure, where possible, shall be given, and if the Contractor fails so to do or repeats his default the Employer shall be entitled to call upon the Surety in accordance with clause 2.

4   Any alteration to the terms of the Contract or any variations required under the Contract shall not in any way release the Surety from its obligations under this Bond.

5   The Contractor and the Surety shall be released from their respective liabilities under this Bond upon the date of Practical Completion of the Works as certified by the Architect/Contract Administrator appointed under the Contract.

IN WITNESS whereof the parties hereto have executed this Bond as a Deed the day and year first before written.

Contractor:
Signed by [*name of Director*]
and [*name of Company
Secretary or second Director*]
for and on behalf of

....
Director

....

....
Director/Company Secretary

Surety:
Signed by [*name of Director*]
and [*name of Company*
Secretary or second Director]
for and on behalf of

....
Director

....

....
Director/Company Secretary

Employer:
Signed by [*name of Director*]
and [*name of Company*
Secretary or second Director]
for and on behalf of

....
Director

....

....
Director/Company Secretary

TRADITIONAL FORM OF PERFORMANCE BOND: MECHANICAL AND ELECTRICAL WORKS

BY THIS BOND we:

[*name*] PLC/Limited, whose principal place of business (registered office) is at [*address*] ('the Contractor') and

[*name*] PLC/Limited whose principal place of business (registered office) is at [*address*] ('the Sureties')

are held and firmly bound unto [*name*] ('the Purchaser') in the sum of £[   ] for the payment of which sum the Contractor and the Sureties bind themselves and their assigns jointly and severally by these presents.

Sealed with our respective seals and dated this [*date*]

WHEREAS the Contractor by an Agreement made between the Purchaser of the one part and the Contractor of the other part has entered into a Contract ('the Contract') to design, manufacture, deliver, erect and test certain Works and correct defects therein as mentioned in and in conformity with the provisions of the Contract.

NOW THE CONDITION OF THE ABOVE WRITTEN Bond is such that if the Contractor shall duly perform and observe all the terms, provisions, conditions and stipulations of the Contract on the Contractor's part to be performed and observed according to the true purport, intent and meaning thereof or if on default by the Contractor the Sureties shall satisfy and discharge the damages sustained by the Purchaser thereby up to the amount of the above written Bond then this obligation shall be null and void but otherwise shall be and remain in full force and effect but no alteration in terms of the Contract or in the extent or nature of the Works to be designed, manufactured, delivered, erected and tested thereunder or in respect of the obligations to correct defects thereunder and no allowance of time by the Purchaser or the Engineer under the Contract nor any forebearance or forgiveness in or in respect of any matter or thing concerning the Contract on the part of the Purchaser or the said Engineer shall in any way release the Sureties from liability under the above written Bond.

PROVIDED ALWAYS that the above obligations of the Sureties to satisfy and discharge the damages sustained by the Purchaser shall arise only if a claim by the Purchaser is accompanied by either:

(a)   a written notice from the Purchaser and the Contractor that the Purchaser and the Contractor have mutually agreed that the amount of damages concerned is payable to the Purchaser; or
(b)   a legally certified copy of a Judgment of a Court having jurisdiction or of an award issued in arbitration proceedings carried out in conformity with the terms of the said Contract under which damages are payable by the Contractor to the Purchaser, together with a statement by the Purchaser showing the amount of the damages which remain unsatisfied at the date of the claim;

and the claim is made within one month after the issue of the final certificate of payment under the Contractor unless prior to the expiry of such period either party shall have commenced proceedings arising out of the Contract in which event any such claim shall be made not later than three months after such proceedings have been finally concluded.

THE COMMON SEAL of [*name*]
PLC/Limited was hereto affixed
in the presence of:

....
Director

THE COMMON SEAL of [*name*]
PLC/Limited was hereto affixed
in the presence of:

....
Director

THE AMERICAN INSTITUTE OF ARCHITECTS PERFORMANCE BOND

AIA Document A312

Performance Bond

Any singular reference to Contractor, Surety, Owner or other party shall be considered plural where applicable.

Contractor (Name and Address):

OWNER (Name and Address):

SURETY (Name and Principal Place of Business):

CONSTRUCTION CONTRACT
  Date:
  Amount:
  Description (Name and Location):

BOND
  Date (Not earlier than Construction
    Contract Date):
  Amount:
  Modification to this Bond: ☐ None   ☐ See Page 3

CONTRACTOR AS PRINCIPAL   SURETY
Company: (Corporate Seal)   Company: (Corporate Seal)

Signature: _____   Signature: _____
Name and Title: Name and Title:

(Any additional signatures appear on page 3)

(FOR INFORMATION ONLY – Name, Address and Telephone)
AGENT OR BROKER: OWNER'S REPRESENTATIVE
                                     (Architect, Engineer or other party):

1 The Contractor and the Surety, jointly and severally, bind themselves, their heirs, executors, administrators, successors and assigns to the Owner for the performance of the Construction Contract, which is incorporated herein by reference.

2 If the Contractor performs the Construction Contract, the Surety and the Contractor shall have no obligation under this Bond, except to participate in conferences as provided in Subparagraph 3.1.

3 If there is no Owner Default, the Surety's obligation under this Bond shall arise after:

3.1 The Owner has notified the Contractor and the Surety at its address described in Paragraph 10 below that the Owner is considering declaring a Contractor Default and has requested and attempted to arrange a conference with the Contractor and the Surety to be held not later than fifteen days after receipt of such notice to discuss methods of performing the Construction Contract. If the Owner, the Contractor and the Surety agree, the Contractor shall be allowed a reasonable time to perform the Construction Contract, but such an agreement shall not waive the Owner's right, if any, subsequently to declare a Contractor Default; and

3.2 The Owner has declared a Contractor Default and formally terminated the Contractor's right to complete the contract, such Contractor Default shall not be declared earlier than twenty days after the Contractor and the Surety have received notice as provided in Subparagraph 3.1; and

3.3 The Owner has agreed to pay the Balance of the Contract Price to the Surety in accordance with the terms of the Construction Contract or to a contractor selected to perform the Construction Contract in accordance with the terms of the contract with the Owner.

4 When the Owner has satisfied the conditions of Paragraph 3, the Surety shall promptly and at the Surety's expense take one of the following actions:

4.1 Arrange for the Contractor, with consent of the Owner, to perform and complete the Construction Contract; or

4.2 Undertake to perform and complete the Construction Contract itself, through its agents or through independent contractors; or

4.3 Obtain bids or negotiated proposals from qualified contractors acceptable to the Owner for a contract for performance and completion of the Construction Contract, arrange for a contract to be prepared for execution by the Owner and the contractor selected with the Owner's concurrence, to be secured with performance and payment bonds executed by a qualified surety equivalent to the bonds issued on the Construction Contract, and pay to the Owner the amount of damages as described in Paragraph 6 in excess of the Balance of the Contract Price incurred by the Owner resulting from the Contractor's default; or

4.4 Waive its right to perform and complete, arrange for completion, or obtain a new contractor and with reasonable promptness under the circumstances:

.1 After investigation, determine the amount for which it may be liable to the Owner and, as soon as practicable after the amount is determined, tender payment therefor to the Owner; or

.2 Deny liability in whole or in part and notify the Owner citing reasons therefor.

5 If the Surety does not proceed as provided in Paragraph 4 with reasonable promptness, the Surety shall be deemed to be in default on this Bond fifteen days after receipt of an additional written notice from the Owner to the Surety demanding that the Surety perform its obligations under this Bond, and the Owner shall be entitled to enforce any remedy available to the Owner. If the Surety proceeds as provided in Subparagraph 4.4, and the Owner refuses the payment tendered or the Surety has denied liability, in whole or in part, without further notice the Owner shall be entitled to enforce any remedy available to the Owner.

6 After the Owner has terminated the Contractor's right to complete the Construction Contract, and if the Surety elects to act under Subparagraph 4.1, 4.2, or 4.3 above, then the responsibilities of the Surety to the Owner shall not be greater than those of the Contractor under the Construction Contract, and the responsibilities of the Owner to the Surety shall not be greater than those of the Owner under the Construction Contract. To the limit of the amount of this Bond, but subject to commitment by the Owner of the Balance of the Contract Price to mitigation of costs and damages on the Construction Contract, the Surety is obligated without duplication for:

> **6.1** The responsibilities of the Contractor for correction of defective work and completion of the Construction Contract;

> **6.2** Additional legal, design professional and delay costs resulting from the Contractor's Default, and resulting from the actions or failure to act of the Surety under Paragraph 4; and

> **6.3** Liquidated damages, or if no liquidated damages are specified in the Construction Contract, actual damages caused by delayed performance or non-performance of the Contractor.

7 The Surety shall not be liable to the Owner or others for obligations of the Contractor that are unrelated to the Construction Contract, and the Balance of the Contract Price shall not be reduced or set off on account of any such unrelated obligations. No right of action shall accrue on this Bond to any person or entity other than the Owner or its heirs, executors, administrators, or successors.

8 The Surety hereby waives notice of any change, including changes of time, to the Construction Contract or to related subcontracts, purchase orders and other obligations.

9 Any proceedings, legal or equitable, under this Bond may be instituted in any court of competent jurisdiction in the location in which the work or part of the work is located and shall be instituted within two years after Contractor Default or within two years after the Contractor ceased working or within two years after the Surety refuses or fails to perform its obligations under this Bond, whichever occurs first. If the provisions of this Paragraph are void or prohibited by law, the minimum period of limitation available to sureties as a defense in the jurisdiction of the suit shall be applicable.

10 Notice to the Surety, the Owner or the Contractor shall be mailed or delivered to the address shown on the signature page.

11 When this Bond has been furnished to comply with a statutory or other legal requirement in the location where the construction was to be performed, any provision in this Bond conflicting with said statutory or legal requirement shall be deemed deleted herefrom and provisions conforming to such statutory or other legal requirement shall be deemed incorporated herein. The intent is that this Bond shall be construed as a statutory bond and not as a common law bond.

12 DEFINITIONS

> **12.1** Balance of Contract Price: The total amount payable by the Owner to the Contractor under the Construction Contract after all proper adjustments have been made, including allowance to the Contractor of any amounts received or to be received by the Owner in settlement of insurance or other claims for damages to which the Contractor is entitled,

reduced by all valid and proper payments made to or on behalf of the Contractor under the Construction Contract.

12.2 Construction Contract: The agreement between the Owner and the Contractor identified on the signature page, including all Contract Documents and changes thereto.

12.3 Contractor Default: Failure of the Contractor, which has neither been remedied nor waived, to perform or otherwise to comply with the terms of the Construction Contract.

12.4 Owner Default: Failure of the Owner, which has neither been remedied nor waived, to pay the Contractor as required by the Construction Contract or to perform and complete or comply with the other terms thereof.

MODIFICATIONS TO THIS BOND ARE AS FOLLOWS:

(Space is provided below for additional signature of added parties, other than those appearing on the cover page.)

CONTRACTOR AS PRINCIPAL   SURETY
Company: (Corporate Seal)   Company:
(Corporate Seal)

Signature _____   Signature

_____
Name and Title: Name and Title:
Address: Address:

[*Reproduced by kind permission of the American Institute of Architects.*]

ASSOCIATION OF BRITISH INSURERS MODEL FORM OF GUARANTEE BOND

THE GUARANTEE BOND is made as a deed BETWEEN the following parties whose names and [registered office] addresses are set out in the Schedule to this Bond ('the Schedule'):

(1) The 'Contractor' as principal

(2) The 'Guarantor' as guarantor, and

(3) The 'Employer'

WHEREAS:

(A) By a contract ('the Contract') entered into or to be entered into between the Employer and the Contractor particulars of which are set out in the Schedule the Contractor has agreed with the Employer to execute works ('the Works') upon and subject to the terms and conditions therein set out.

(B) The Guarantor has agreed with the Employer at the request of the Contractor to guarantee the performance of the obligations of the Contractor under the Contract upon the terms and conditions of this Guarantee Bond subject to the limitation set out in clause 2.

NOW THIS DEED WITNESSES as follows:

1   The Guarantor guarantees to the Employer that in the event of a breach of the Contract by the Contractor the Guarantor shall subject to the provisions of this Guarantee Bond satisfy and discharge the damages sustained by the Employer as established and ascertained pursuant to and in accordance with the provisions of or by reference to the Contract and taking into account all sums due or to become due to the Contractor.

2   The maximum aggregate liability of the Guarantor and the Contractor under this Guarantee Bond shall not exceed the sum set out in the Schedule ('the Bond Amount') but subject to such limitation and to clause 4 the liability of the Guarantor shall be co-extensive with the liability of the Contractor under the Contract.

3   The Guarantor shall not be discharged or released by any alteration of any of the terms and conditions and provisions of the Contract or in the extent or nature of the Works and no allowance of time by the Employer under or in respect of the Contract or the Works shall in any way release, reduce or affect the liability of the Guarantor under this Guarantee Bond.

4   Whether or not this Guarantee Bond shall be returned to the Guarantor the obligations of the Guarantor under this Guarantee Bond shall be released and discharged absolutely upon Expiry (as defined in the Schedule) save in respect of any breach of the Contract which has occurred and in respect of which a claim in writing containing particulars of such breach has been made upon the Guarantor before Expiry.

5   The Contractor having requested the execution of this Guarantee Bond by the Guarantor undertakes to the Guarantor (without limitation of any other rights and remedies of the Employer or the Guarantor against the Contractor) to perform and discharge the obligations on its part set out in the Contract.

6   This Guarantee Bond and the benefits thereof shall not be assigned without the prior written consent of the Guarantor and the Contractor.

7   This Guarantee Bond shall be governed by and construed in accordance with the laws of [England and Wales] [Scotland] and only the courts of [England and Wales] [Scotland] shall have jurisdiction hereunder.

THE SCHEDULE

The Contractor:	[*name*] whose registered office address is at [*address*]
The Guarantor:	[*name*] whose registered office address is at [*address*]
The Employer:	[*name*] whose registered office address is at [*address*]
The Contract:	A contract dated [*date*] [to be entered into] between the Employer and the Contractor in the form known as [ ] for the construction of works comprising [ ] for the original contract sum of [ ] pounds (£[ ])
The Bond Amount:	The sum of £[ ] pounds sterling (£[ ]) [*insert any provisions for reduction of the Bond Amount*]
Expiry:	[*insert details of the event agreed between the parties*] which shall be conclusive for the purposes of this Guarantee Bond

IN WITNESS whereof the Contractor and the Guarantor have executed and delivered this Guarantee Bond as a Deed on [*date*]

EXECUTED AND DELIVERED as a deed by [*name*] (Contractor)

EXECUTED AND DELIVERED as a deed by [*name*] (Guarantor)

[*Reproduced by kind permission of the Association of British Insurers.*]

INDEMNITY TO BANK WHERE BONDS/ INDEMNITIES/GUARANTEES GIVEN TO THIRD PARTY

To [   ] BANK PLC

1   The consideration for this indemnity shall be your giving and/or procuring the giving by your correspondents of a bond, indemnity, guarantee or other obligation in the terms of the copy endorsed hereon or attached hereto (which I/we have verified and signed) ('the Obligation').

2   I/We [jointly and severally] for myself/ourselves and my/our legal personal representatives hereby:

2.1   agree to keep you indemnified from and against all actions, proceedings, liabilities, claims, demands, damages, costs and expenses in relation to or arising out of or appearing to you to arise out of the Obligation and/or your indemnity in respect thereof and to pay to you on demand all payments, losses, costs, charges, damages and expenses suffered or incurred by you in consequence thereof or arising thereout whether directly or indirectly; and

2.2   irrevocably authorise you to debit to any of my/our account(s) with you all such payments, losses, costs, charges, damages and expenses, and further agree that you shall be at liberty without any notice to or further or other consent from me/us to apply or transfer any money now or at any time hereafter standing to my/our credit upon current deposit or any other account in payment or in part payment of any such sums of money as may be or hereafter may from time to time become due or owing to you from or by me/us hereunder or to a suspense account and that you may refuse payment of any cheque, bill, note or order drawn or accepted by me/us or upon which I/we may be otherwise liable and which if paid would reduce the amount of money standing to my/our credit as aforesaid to less than the amount for the time being so due or owing to you from or by me/us as aforesaid; and

2.3   irrevocably authorise and direct you to make any payments and comply with any demands which may be claimed or made or appear to you to be claimed or made under the Obligation and/or your indemnity in respect thereof without any reference to or further authority, confirmation or verification from me/us and agree that any payment which you shall make in accordance or appearing to you to be in accordance with the Obligation and/or your indemnity in respect thereof shall be binding upon me/us and shall be accepted by me/us as conclusive evidence that you were liable to make such payment or comply with such demand and further that you may at any time determine or procure the determination of the Obligation and/or your indemnity in respect thereof; and

2.4   agree (without prejudice to any other provision of this indemnity) that any demand made upon you and/or your correspondents for payment of sums specified in the Obligation shall for all purposes relating to this indemnity be deemed to be a valid and effective demand and you and your correspondents shall be entitled to treat it as such notwithstanding any actual lack of authority on the part of the person making the demand if the demand appears on its face to be in order and

2.4.1 the demand is made by or through a bank or any other person carrying on a banking business, or

      2.4.2 the demand appears to you or your correspondents to be made by or on behalf of the beneficiary; and

2.5   agree (without prejudice to any other provision of this indemnity) that in the event that the Obligation stipulates that a demand made upon you and/or your correspondents shall be accompanied by any document or documents then, provided that it or they appear on their face to be in accordance with the terms of the Obligation, such document or documents shall for all purposes relating to this indemnity be deemed to be genuine and in accordance with the terms of the Obligation; and

2.6   agree that my/our liability hereunder shall also apply to any extension or renewal of the Obligation (whether in the same terms or otherwise and whether arising with my/our agreement or by operation of law or otherwise) and/or your indemnity in respect thereof to the intent that all agreements, undertakings and authorities herein shall continue to be binding on me/us in relation to the Obligation and/or your indemnity in respect thereof as so extended or renewed; and

2.7   agree (without prejudice to any other provisions of this indemnity) that (at your discretion and/or the discretion of your correspondents and entirely at my/our risk) you and/or your correspondents may use the telex system or other telegraph service of any country or any other recognised telegraph or transmission system for the purpose of giving the Obligation or sending any message relating or appearing to relate to the Obligation and/or your indemnity in respect thereof and in this connection I/we specifically release and indemnify you and your correspondents (and each of you and them) from and against the consequences of your and/or their failure and/or the failure of any other person to receive any such message in the form in which it was despatched and from and against the consequences of any delay that might occur during the course of the transmission of any such message.

3   This indemnity shall be governed by English law and shall be additional to any other indemnity which you now or hereafter may hold.

Signed on [*date*] by me/us (or by and on behalf of [*name*] pursuant to a resolution of the Board of Directors dated [*date*] a copy of which is hereto annexed)

SIGNATURE(S)

WITNESS'S SIGNATURE

AND ADDRESS

FORM OF RESOLUTION TO ISSUE A BOND, INDEMNITY, GUARANTEE OR OTHER OBLIGATION

At a meeting of the Board of directors of [*name*] Limited /plc ('the Company') whose registered office is at [*address*] held on [*date*]

IT WAS RESOLVED:

1   [   ] Bank plc be requested to issue or procure the issue of a bond, indemnity, guarantee or other obligation ('Obligation') in the terms of the draft produced to and approved by the meeting; and

2   [*name*] and [*name*] be and are hereby authorised on behalf of the Company to sign [   ] Bank plc's standard form of counter indemnity, a copy of which has been produced to and approved by the meeting, a copy of the Obligation being attached to or endorsed on the original of the said counter indemnity.

Certified a true copy by:

CHAIRMAN   SECRETARY

FULL NAMES   SIGNATURES

will sign

will sign

GENERAL INDEMNITY TO BANK WHERE BONDS/INDEMNITIES/GUARANTEES GIVEN TO THIRD PARTIES

To [   ] BANK PLC

1   The consideration for this indemnity shall be your agreeing from time to time to give and/or to procure the giving by your correspondents of such bonds, indemnities, guarantees or other obligations ('the Obligations') as we may request in accordance with paragraph 3 below.

2   I/We [jointly and severally] for myself/ourselves and my/our legal personal representatives hereby

2.1   agree to keep you indemnified from and against all actions, proceedings, liabilities, claims, demands, damages, costs and expenses in relation to or arising out of or appearing to you to arise out of the Obligations and/or your indemnities in respect thereof and to pay to you on demand all payments, losses, costs, charges, damages and expenses suffered or incurred by you in consequence thereof or arising thereout whether directly or indirectly; and

2.2   irrevocably authorise you to debit to any of my/our account(s) with you all such payments, losses, costs, charges, damages and expenses, and further agree that you shall be at liberty without any notice to or further or other consent from me/us to apply or transfer any money now or at any time hereafter standing to my/our credit upon current deposit or any other account in payment or in part payment of any such sums of money as may be or hereafter may from time to time become due or owing to you from or by me/us hereunder or to a suspense account and that you may refuse payment of any cheque, bill, note or order drawn or accepted by me/us or upon which I/we may be otherwise liable and which if paid would reduce the amount of money standing to my/our credit as aforesaid to less than the amount for the time being so due or owing to you from or by me/us as aforesaid; and

2.3   irrevocably authorise and direct you to make any payments and comply with any demands which may be claimed or made or appear to you to be claimed or made under any of the Obligations and/or your indemnities in respect thereof without any reference to or further authority, confirmation or verification from me/us and agree that any payment which you shall make in accordance or appearing to you to be in accordance with any of the Obligations and/or your indemnities in respect thereof shall be binding upon me/us and shall be accepted by me/us as conclusive evidence that you were liable to make such payment or comply with such demand and further that you may at any time determine or procure the determination of the Obligations and/or your indemnities in respect thereof; and

2.4   agree (without prejudice to any other provision of this indemnity) that any demand made upon you and/or your correspondents for payment of sums specified in any of the Obligations shall for all purposes relating to this indemnity be deemed to be a valid and effective demand and you and your correspondents shall be entitled to treat it as such notwithstanding any actual lack of authority on the part of the person making the demand if the demand appears on its face to be in order and

2.4.1 the demand is made by or through a bank or any other person carrying on a banking business, or

2.4.2 the demand appears to you or your correspondents to be made by or on behalf of the beneficiary; and

2.5 agree (without prejudice to any other provision of this indemnity) that in the event that any of the Obligations stipulate that a demand made upon you and/or your correspondents shall be accompanied by any document or documents then, provided that it or they appear on their face to be in accordance with the terms of the relevant Obligation, such document or documents shall for all purposes relating to this indemnity be deemed to be genuine and in accordance with the terms of the relevant Obligation; and

2.6 agree that my/our liability hereunder shall also apply to any extension or renewal of the Obligations (whether in the same terms or otherwise and whether arising with my/our agreement or by operation of law or otherwise) and/or your indemnities in respect thereof to the intent that all agreements, undertakings and authorities herein shall continue to be binding on me/us in relation to the relevant Obligation and/or your indemnity in respect thereof as so extended or renewed; and

2.7 agree (without prejudice to any other provisions of this indemnity) that (at your discretion and/or the discretion of your correspondents and entirely at my/our risk) you and/or your correspondents may use the telex system or other telegraph service of any country or any other recognised telegraph or transmission system for the purpose of giving any of the Obligations or sending any message relating or appearing to relate to any of the Obligations and/or your indemnities in respect thereof and in this connection I/we specifically release and indemnify you and your correspondents (and each of you and them) from and against the consequences of your and/or their failure and/or the failure of any other person to receive any such message in the form in which it was despatched and from and against the consequences of any delay that might occur during the course of the transmission of any such message.

3   The Obligations to which this indemnity shall apply shall be those which may be requested by me/us [on our behalf by such person or persons as we may from time to time authorise by board resolution or in any other manner acceptable to you].

4   Notwithstanding the terms of paragraphs 1 and 3 above, it is agreed that nothing in this indemnity shall impose upon you a duty to give or procure the giving of every Obligation which is the subject of a request as aforesaid: you shall be free in each case to decide whether or not to accept the instructions contained in any such request, in what manner to act upon them (including an absolute discretion as to the form and substance of any communication to your correspondents and/or the Beneficiary), and upon what terms (in addition to those contained in this indemnity).

5   This indemnity shall be governed by English law and shall be additional to any other indemnity which you now or hereafter may hold.

Signed on [*date*] by me/us (or by [*name*] and [*name*] on behalf of [*name*] pursuant to a resolution of the Board of Directors dated [*date*] a copy of which is hereto annexed)

SIGNATURE(S)

WITNESS'S SIGNATURE

AND ADDRESS

FORM OF RESOLUTION TO SIGN A GENERAL INDEMNITY

At a meeting of the Board of Directors of [*name*] Limited/plc ('the Company') held on [*date*]

IT WAS RESOLVED:

1   [*name*] and [*name*] be authorised on behalf of the Company to sign the general indemnity
    to [   ] Bank plc produced to and approved by the meeting; and
2   [*name*] and [*name*] be authorised on behalf of the Company to issue to the said Bank any
    request under paragraph 3 of the indemnity.

Certified a true copy by:

CHAIRMAN   SECRETARY

NOTES:

1 Insert name(s) of officials authorised to sign the general indemnity.
2 Insert name(s) (or designations) of officials who are to be authorised to request the provision
   of indemnities and guarantees from time to time.

INSTITUTION OF CHEMICAL ENGINEERS MODEL FORM OF CONDITIONS OF CONTRACT FOR PROCESS PLANT: REIMBURSABLE CONTRACTS (Appendix II)

Form of bank guarantee for the release of retention money

This is a suitable text for a Guarantee to be given by a third party Guarantor to the **Purchaser**. It should be noted that the estimated final value of a reimbursable contract may well change as the work proceeds. In such a case, it may from time to time be desirable to cancel the existing Guarantee and replace it by one with a maximum liability more closely related to the latest estimate of the contract value. If this is to be mandatory, a Special Condition should be written to this effect. See also Guide Note FF.

'We .... (the Guarantor) .... understand that you intend to enter into a **Contract** with .... (the Contractor) for services relating to the design, engineering, procurement and construction of a .... (type of plant) .... at .... (place) ....

In consideration therefore of your paying the **Contractor** in full settlement of his invoices without any deduction by way of retention we hereby guarantee to pay to you on your first demand:

(i)   if before the issue of the **Acceptance Certificate**, the sum of 5%
      or
(ii) if after the issue of the **Acceptance Certificate**, the sum of 2% of the total of all agreed invoices for the **Contractor's Services**.

Our maximum liability under the Guarantee is limited under (i) above the sum of £.................... reducing under (ii) above to the sum of £....................

Your demand shall be in writing and shall state that the **Contractor** has failed without good reason to fulfil his contractual obligations and that you have given the **Contractor** fourteen days' notice in writing of your intention to make a claim under this Guarantee and you shall provide either:

(a)   a Statement that no **Acceptance Certificate** has been issued in accordance with the **Contract**; or
(b)   a copy of the **Acceptance Certificate**.

The giving of time by you or the neglect or forbearance by you in requiring or enforcing payment of the aforesaid sum or other indulgence shall not in any way prejudice our obligation under this Guarantee.

Any payment made by us to you hereunder shall be made by us as Principal and shall be used solely for the purpose of the due performance of the **Contract**. Any part of the said payment which is not required by you for such purpose shall be repaid to us as soon as practicable.

This Guarantee will expire three hundred and sixty five days from the date of the **Acceptance Certificate** and must be returned on expiry. This Guarantee has been made under seal.'

[*Reproduced by kind permission of the Institution of Chemical Engineers.*]

Chapter 6

COLLATERAL WARRANTIES

Why do we need collateral warranties? – Recovery of damages in contract – Recovery of damages in tort – Claims for pure economic loss – Negligent misstatement – Reliance – Collateral warranties – Reasonable skill and care/fitness for purpose – Indemnity provisions – Deleterious materials – Copyright – Insurance – Step-in rights – Contribution – Preservation of rights in tort – Limitation – BPF Warranty agreement – COWA/P&T – Latent defects insurance – Appendix

WHY DO WE NEED COLLATERAL WARRANTIES?

6.1   The collateral warranty became an intrinsic part of the paperwork for commercial developments in the 1980s, being a reflection of the numerous parties often involved in construction projects and the absence of contractual links between many of those parties. The relationship between the parties under traditional contracting and design and build are set out in the Appendix to this chapter. Collateral warranties are partly as a result of the boom in the commercial property market, but also because of certain changes that occurred to the law of tort. The law clearly recognises that party A is liable to be sued by party B for the consequences of the former's negligence which causes physical harm to party B. Here, a simple example would be a negligent driver who, in knocking down a pedestrian, causes the latter personal injury. Where the harm caused to party B by party A is pure financial loss, the courts have struggled over the years for consistency and a coherent response. This type of claim is often referred to as *pure economic loss*, and over recent years courts have tended to take a restrictive view of those financial losses that are recoverable. The major exception to pure economic loss being non-recoverable is the principle established in *Hedley Byrne & Co Limited v Heller & Partners Limited.*[1]

RECOVERY OF DAMAGES IN CONTRACT

6.2   Contract law compensates the plaintiff for his financial losses and puts him, as far as possible, in the position he would have been in if the contract had been carried out. The plaintiff is under a duty to mitigate his financial losses. He is only entitled to recoup from the defendant that part of his losses that he is unable to avert. The scope of damages for breach of contract was defined in *Hadley v Baxendale,*[2] which remains the principal test:

---

1   [1964] AC 465, HL.
2   (1854) 9 Exch 341.

'Where two parties have made a contract which one of them has broken, the damages which the other party ought to receive in respect of such breach of contract should be such as may fairly and reasonably be considered either as arising naturally, ie according to the usual course of things, from such breach of contract itself, or such as may reasonably be supposed to have been in the contemplation of both parties at the time they made the contract, as the probable result of the breach of it.'

The level of loss recoverable in contract is often limited by the terms of the contract itself. To cap the losses recoverable, any entitlement to consequential losses may be specifically excluded.

RECOVERY OF DAMAGES IN TORT

6.3.   The recovery of damages in tort is more complicated. Since 1932, when the famous 'snail in the ginger beer bottle' case, *Donoghue v Stevenson*,[1] was decided, where someone suffers physical injury, together with economic loss, the latter is recoverable. If A, a pedestrian, is knocked down and injured as a result of B's negligence in driving his car, A is entitled to damages for:

- his physical injury;
- lost earnings;
- future loss of earnings;
- damage to his property.

CLAIMS FOR PURE ECONOMIC LOSS

6.4   The courts have always been suspicious of claims for pure economic loss. These are instances where the injured party suffered no damage to either life or property, but has nevertheless incurred financial losses because of the defendant's behaviour. A well known example is *Spartan Steel & Alloys Limited v Martin & Co (Contractors) Limited*.[2] When digging up a road, a contractor severed an electricity mains cable which supplied power to the plaintiff's factory. The power was off for 14½ hours. At the time of the power failure a quantity of metal was in the plaintiff's furnace. As a result of the furnace losing temperature, the metal could not be used. The physical damage was £368. If the process had been completed, the plaintiff would have made a profit of £400 on the ingots produced. An additional four consignments of metal with a profit of £1,767 would also have been processed if there had been electricity available during the 14½-hour period.

There was no dispute over negligence. The court decided that the plaintiff could recover only the value of the wasted metal and the profit that would have been made on that metal if it had been processed. The subsequent loss of production was pure economic loss for which the defendant was not liable. The same principle was supplied in *SCM (United Kingdom) Limited v WJ Whittall & Sons Limited*.[3]

---

1   [1932] AC 562.
2   [1972] 3 WLR 502.
3   [1970] 3 WLR 694.

6.5   For many years, it was thought that pure economic loss could be recovered only in the special circumstances first developed in *Hedley Byrne & Co Limited v Heller & Partners Limited* (see **6.1**). Where one party relied on the professional expertise of another to give a professional opinion, if the opinion was given negligently, the injured party could recover its financial losses, notwithstanding the absence of any physical harm. The principle has been re-emphasised on a number of occasions, including the more recent House of Lords' decision, *Caparo Industries plc v Dickman and Others*.[1]

'Special rules'

6.6   At times, the courts have somewhat illogically treated the construction industry as subject to special rules outside the normal principles of English law. Prior to the late 1950s, it was thought that a builder could not be liable in the tort of negligence even if his negligence resulted in personal injury or damage to property. This principle was cut back in *Billings & Son Limited v Riden*.[2] The contractor was held liable to the occupier of a house adjoining a building site when the occupier was injured by the dangerous state in which the entrance path was left. Gradually, the application of *Donoghue v Stevenson* was extended until it was said, in *Dutton v Bognor Regis Urban District Council*[3] that if an architect or engineer 'designs a house or a bridge so negligently that it falls down, he is liable to every one of those injured in the fall'.

6.7   *Anns v Merton London Borough Council*[4] continued the process of relaxing the limitations on recovery in tort. A block of maisonettes had been constructed on inadequate foundations. The local authority was sued in negligence for allowing building to proceed when the foundations had not been taken to an adequate depth. The local authority had powers of inspection under the building byelaws. According to the House of Lords, a cause of action arose when the building was in such a condition as to pose a present or imminent danger to the health or safety of the persons occupying it.

6.8 .   *Anns* was applied in *Batty v Metropolitan Realisations Limited*.[5] No physical damage had occurred to a dwelling house when the claim was brought. The house and its foundations had been properly constructed on a hillside prone to landslips. Some three years after construction there was a landslip below the house. This did not cause actual damage either to the house or its foundations. The evidence was that within 10 years there would be further landslips which would undermine the foundations and the house. The house was, therefore, doomed and essentially worthless. Notwithstanding the present lack of any physical damage to the property, the Court of Appeal held that the owners or occupiers of the house were entitled to recover both from the builder and the developer their loss which was the value of the property.

---

1   [1990] 2 AC 605.
2   [1951] AC 240.
3   [1972] 2 WLR 299.
4   [1978] AC 728.
5   [1978] 2 WLR 500.

Scotland: pure economic loss

6.9　*Junior Books Limited v Veitchi Co Limited*[1] represented the high water mark for pure economic loss claims. In this Scottish case, the building owner recovered damages against a nominated sub-contractor in respect of a defectively laid factory floor which included a sum for loss of profit as if there had been a contract.

According to Lord Fraser, where a specialist sub-contractor had been nominated, 'the proximity between the parties is so close, falling only just short of a direct contractual relationship'.[2] Thus, according to Lord Keith:

> 'The appellants accordingly owed the respondents a duty to take reasonable care to see that their workmanship was not faulty, and are liable for the foreseeable consequences, sounding in economic loss, of their failure to do so.'[3]

The years since *Junior Books* have left the decision isolated and largely devoid of meaning. Disingenuously, the case has been explained as 'decided on its own particular facts'. The truth is that nomination is relatively common in the building industry and the situation was not exceptional. There followed a cluster of cases in 1989/90 which decided that *Dutton, Anns* and *Batty*, but oddly not *Junior Books*, were all wrongly decided.

Relaxing the limitations on recovery in tort

6.10　*D & F Estates v Church Commissioners*[4] commenced the retreat from *Anns*. The main contractor for the construction of a block of flats engaged a specialist contractor for interior plaster work. The plaster was wrongly applied and, during later decoration to one of the flats, began to drop off. The House of Lords held that:

- in negligence, the cost of repairing a defect which was discovered before the defect had caused personal injury or physical damage to property was irrecoverable. The costs of repairing/making good such damage was pure economic loss; and
- the main contractor's only obligation was to employ a competent specialist sub-contractor. This had been done and there was no further general duty to ensure that works were free from dangerous defects.

6.11　*Murphy v Brentwood District Council*[5] continued the process of undoing *Anns*. The local authority received plans for a proposed dwelling house and sent them out to consulting engineers, who approved them. The consulting engineers failed to spot errors in the calculations for the foundation design. The house was built with defective foundations. Appropriate remedials were assessed at £45,000. The plaintiff sold the house for £35,000, less than the market value of the property in good condition. Legal proceedings to recover the difference were commenced. According to the House of Lords, where a defect was discoverable before it caused damage or injury, the cost of putting the defect right was pure economic loss and non-

---

1　[1983] AC 520.
2　Ibid, at 533.
3　Ibid, at 536.
4　[1989] AC 177.
5　[1991] 1 AC 398.

recoverable. On the same day as its judgment in *Murphy*, the House of Lords also delivered its judgment in *Department of the Environment v Thomas Bates Limited.*[1] Soft concrete was used in constructing the pillars of an office block. The occupier, who had no contract with the contractor, sued the contractor claiming the cost of strengthening the pillars. The plaintiff was not using the building to its maximum load-bearing capacity and there was no danger of imminent collapse. The House of Lords held that, as the tower block was not unsafe, the plaintiff's claim was merely for pure economic loss and, therefore, failed. The decision in *Murphy* was subsequently applied in *Nitrigin Eireann Teoranta v Inco Alloys Limited.*[2] Inco was a specialist manufacturer and supplier of alloy tubing which was installed by other contractors at Nitrigin's factory. The manufacturer and supplier were under a contract made with Nitrigin in 1981. In July 1983, an allegedly defective pipe cracked and was repaired. On 27 June 1984, the pipe fractured and exploded, causing damage to the structure of the surrounding plant. A claim in contract was statute-barred and Nitrigin sued in tort. The dispute was whether or not the cause of action arose in 1983 or 1984. Applying *Murphy*, the cracking to the pipe in 1983 was damage to the thing itself, which resulted in pure economic loss which was irrecoverable in tort. Therefore, the cause of action arose in June 1984 when there was physical damage to property other than the defective item itself, ie the plant.

Sufficient proximity to give rise to duty of care

6.12   The right to recover pure economic loss, other than via a *Hedley Byrne* relationship, may survive by one of two methods. In *Murphy*, Lord Bridge said:

> 'There may, of course, be situations where, even in the absence of contract, there is a special relationship of proximity between builder and building owner which is sufficiently akin to contract to introduce the element of reliance so that the scope of the duty of care owed by the builder to the owner is wide enough to embrace purely economic loss. The decision in *Junior Books v Veitchi Co Limited*[3] can, I believe, only be understood on this basis.'[4]

Complex structures theory

6.13   The other method by which economic loss, not otherwise recoverable, may be recoverable is under the so-called *complex structures theory*. In *D & F Estates*[5] it was suggested that it might be possible to argue that a building was a complex structure. Where, for instance, a defect in the foundations causes the coping to crack and let in water, it might be possible to argue that the coping was so far removed from the defective area, in situation and in nature, that it could be treated as property other than the defective building itself. The artificiality of the complex structures theory needs no elaboration and, in *Murphy*, two Law Lords rejected it. However, although dismissed as 'quite unrealistic', *Murphy* opened the door to the equally confusing and unworkable notion of positive *malfunction* as a replacement for, or refinement of, the complex structures theory. In the words of Lord Bridge:

---

1   [1991] 1 AC 499.
2   [1992] 1 WLR 498.
3   [1983] 1 AC 520.
4   [1991] 1 AC 398 at 481.
5   [1989] AC 177; see also **6.10**.

'A critical distinction must be drawn here between some part of a complex structure which is said to be a "danger" only because it does not perform its proper function in sustaining the other parts and some distinct item incorporated in the structure which positively malfunctions so as to inflict positive damage on the structure in which it is incorporated. Thus, if a defective central heating boiler explodes and damages a house or a defective electrical installation malfunctions and sets the house on fire, I see no reason to doubt that the owner of the house, if he can prove that the damage was due to the negligence of the boiler manufacturer in the one case or the electrical contractor on the other, can recover damages in tort on *Donoghue v Stevenson* [1932] AC 562 principles. But the position in law is entirely different where, by reason of the inadequacy of the foundations of the building to support the weight of the superstructure, differential settlement and consequent cracking occurs. Here, once the first cracks appear, the structure as a whole is seen to be defective and the nature of the defect is known. Even if, contrary to my view, the initial damage could be regarded as damage to other property caused by a latent defect, once the defect is known the situation of the building owner is analogous to that of a car owner who discovers that the car has faulty brakes. He may have a house which, until repairs are effected, is unfit for habitation, but, subject to the reservation I have expressed with respect to ruinous buildings at or near the boundary of the owner's property, the building no longer represents a source of danger and as it deteriorates will only damage itself.'[1]

Assignment of rights

6.14   The deliberations of the House of Lords in *Linden Gardens Trust v Lenesta Sludge Disposals*; *St Martin's Property Corporation v Sir Robert McAlpine & Sons*[2] considered not only the proper interpretation to be placed upon the assignment provisions in JCT contracts, but also raised a further point of interest on the use of collateral warranties for commercial developments. The standard JCT assignment provision prevents any assignment of rights without the consent of the other party. Traditionally, third party users of a development have taken the benefit of the building contract and relating consultancy appointments by way of assignment at practical completion stage. In *St Martin's*, the House of Lords held that, provided certain conditions are met, the original employer under a building contract can claim substantial damages from the contractor for defects, even if he has sold the building at full value and is under no liability for repairs. It is not open to the contractor to argue that, because the employer has suffered no actual loss, the employer's entitlement is limited to nominal damages. The judgment was based on an old principle dating from *Dunlop v Lambert*[3] that a consignor of goods who had parted with the property in the goods before the date of breach could, even so, recover substantial damages for the failure to deliver the goods. In the words of Lord Browne-Wilkinson in *St Martin's*:

'In my judgment the present case falls within the rationale of the exceptions to the general rule that a plaintiff can only recover damages for his own loss. The contract was for a large development of property which, to the knowledge of both the Corporation and McAlpine, was going to be occupied, and possibly purchased, by third parties and not by Corporation itself. Therefore it could be foreseen that damage caused by a breach would cause loss to a later owner and not merely to the original contracting party, Corporation. As in contracts

---

1   [1991] 1 AC 398 at 478–479.
2   [1994] 1 AC 85.
3   (1839) 6 Cl & F 600.

for the carriage of goods by land, there would be no automatic vesting in the occupier or owners of the property for the time being who sustained the loss of any right of suit against McAlpine. On the contrary, McAlpine had specifically contracted that the rights of action under the building contract *could* not without McAlpine's consent be transferred to third parties who became owners or occupiers and might suffer loss. In such a case, it seems to me proper, as in the case of the carriage of goods by land to treat the parties as having entered into the contract on the footing that Corporation would be entitled to enforce contractual rights for the benefit of those who suffered from defective performance but who, under the terms of the contract, could not acquire any right to hold McAlpine liable for breach. It is truly a case in which the rule provides "a remedy where no other would be available to a person sustaining loss which under a rational legal system ought to be compensated by the person who has caused it.'[1]

6.15 The decision in *St Martin's* begs a number of questions. First, in what circumstances will parties be held to have contemplated a future sale or letting? The answer may be obvious in the case of a large, multi-unit shopping centre, but what about an industrial warehouse or office block, particularly of the speculative kind? Secondly, the Law Lords did not need to answer what happens if the sale occurs after the defective work is done and not before, as in *St Martin's*. Thirdly, the decision leaves open the amount of damages recoverable. The Law Lords assumed that the employer's claim would be for the cost of repairs. What of the traditional approach of adopting the difference in value between the development as it should have been and as it was built?

6.16 Similarly, the decision in *Darlington Borough Council v Wiltshier Northern Ltd*[2] is of interest. More recently, the question was considered again by the Court of Appeal, in *Alfred McAlpine Construction Ltd v Panatown Ltd*.[3] Panatown engaged McAlpine to design and build an office block and multi-storey car park. On completion, Panatown alleged defective performance of the building contract and served notice of termination on the contractor. The site owner and effective developer was an associated company of Panatown, Unex, who also had the benefit of a duty of care warranty. In arbitration, McAlpine argued that Panatown, not being the owner, could recover only nominal losses. The arbitrator, unlike the Official Referee on appeal, held Panatown could recover substantial losses. The Court of Appeal held Panatown was entitled to substantial losses notwithstanding the existence of a warranty. The argument was advanced by McAlpine that there was the risk of double recovery. The Court had little sympathy. If damages were recovered by the employer on behalf of the building owner, credit would have to be given for such recovery if there was a separate claim under the warranty. This has not entirely reassured contractors who may require a bar on double recovery to be expressly set out in warranties. The type of clause now beginning to appear is as follows:

> 'In any proceedings brought under this Deed the Beneficiary shall give credit for any monies received from the Developer pursuant to any proceedings brought by the Developer under the Building Contract and to the extent that any proceedings are brought under this Deed prior to any proceedings under the Building Contract there shall be no concurrent recovery of monies on behalf of the Beneficiary under any subsequent

---

1   [1994] 1 AC 85 at 114–115.
2   (1994) 69 BLR 1 (CA).
3   (1998) CILL 1353.

proceedings brought pursuant to the Building Contract to the extent that such recovery has already occurred under the Deed.'

6.17   The more relaxed views of the courts in permitting recovery of losses for the benefit of a third party can also be seen in *Phillips Petroleum Co (UK) Ltd and Norsea Pipeline Ltd v IT Corporation Ltd and Flaretec Alloys and Equipment Ltd.*[1] The first plaintiff, Phillips, operated a North Sea oil terminal. Phillips sued IT Corporation over the design, manufacture and delivery of a flare tip which was alleged defective in various regards. Much of the defence related to arguments that Phillips had suffered no loss because it had been fully reimbursed by Norsea under an internal funding arrangement. According to the Official Referee, His Honour Judge Cyril Newman QC, the case fell within the exception to the rule in *Dunlop v Lambert.*[2] The Official Referee quoted from counsel's submission on behalf of Phillips at p 1367:

> 'In a world of increasingly complex transactional structures, the courts are not willing to countenance genuine loss disappearing into a black hole as a side wind of an otherwise sensible commercial arrangement.'

6.18   On 30 March 1998, the Court of Appeal delivered its second judgment in *Alfred McAlpine Ltd v Panatown Ltd.*[3] This judgment concerned Panatown's rights to recover damages for delay. Here, counsel for McAlpine submitted that the judgment in *Darlington Borough Council v Wiltshier Northern Ltd*[4] precluded such recovery. The Court of Appeal rejected this argument although leave to appeal to the House of Lords was granted.

NEGLIGENT MISSTATEMENT

6.19   Another important recent development has been the re-emergence of the law of negligent misstatement and reliance generally. An earlier and well-known example of reliance, although not characterised as such by the House of Lords, was *Pirelli General Cable Works Limited v Oscar Faber & Partners.*[5] The defendant consulting engineers advised on the design of a chimney, built in 1969. Cracks developed near the top of the chimney not later than 1970. They remained undiscovered until 1977, with legal proceedings being commenced in 1978. The House of Lords held, in a case where the cause of action in contract was clearly statute-barred, that the cause of action in negligence accrued when the damage came into existence rather than when it was discovered. It was assumed that, although the parties were in contract, this was not a barrier to a claim being advanced in the tort of negligence. Although the existence of concurrent rights in contract and tort was doubted for a number of years, the wheel has now turned full circle. First, in *Wessex Regional Health Authority v HLM Design,*[6] the Official Referee awarded damages for economic losses suffered by a local authority as a result of late release of information and negligent certification by its consultant engineer and architect. Secondly, in *Conway v Crowe,*

---

1   (1998) CILL 1366.
2   (1839) 6 Cl & F 600.
3   (1998) CILL 1383.
4   [1995] 1 WLR 68.
5   [1983] 2 AC 1.
6   (1993) CILL 907.

Kelsey & Partners,[1] an engineer was held liable for losses caused by damage to the client's house as a result of negligent design and supervision of remedial works. These two rulings indicate that:

- where someone professing special skills, for which professional qualifications are necessary, enters into a contract for the exercise of those skills, he can be held liable in tort for economic loss, notwithstanding that for some years it was thought that concurrent liability could not exist; and
- more importantly, in the context of collateral warranties, liability in tort for economic loss is not limited to negligent misstatement, strictly of the *Hedley Byrne* type, but relates to all actions. To this extent, English law may have caught up with certain Commonwealth jurisdictions.

RELIANCE

6.20 The re-emergence of *reliance* arguments is seen in two House of Lords' decisions. The first, *Henderson v Merrett Syndicates Limited*,[2] related to an action by Lloyd's Names who were members of syndicates managed by the defendant underwriting agents. In some instances, the Name's underwriting was managed by an agent with whom he had a contract, while in others the Name's business was managed by a sub-agent with whom he had no contract. As far as the contracts were concerned, it was agreed that there was an implied duty on behalf of the agents to exercise reasonable skill and care. Two questions arose. First, did primary or sub-agents owe a duty of care in tort to a Name? Secondly, could an agent who was in contract with a Name owe concurrent duties in tort? The House of Lords held that the necessary duty of care arose on reliance principles. In the second case, *White and Another v Jones and Others*,[3] the House of Lords confirmed by a majority of 3:2 that a solicitor could be liable to the intended beneficiaries of a will for negligence in preparing that will. The House of Lords' majority held that the responsibility of a solicitor towards his client should be extended to an intended beneficiary who was reasonably foreseeably deprived of his intended legacy as a result of the solicitor's negligence in circumstances where there was no confidential or fiduciary relationship, and neither the testator nor his estate had a remedy against the solicitor. Otherwise, an injustice would occur. Lord Nolan thought that the principle was of wide application. He stated:

> 'A professional man or an artisan who undertakes to exercise his skill in a manner which, to his knowledge, may cause loss to others if carelessly performed, may thereby implicitly assume a legal responsibility towards them. The fact that he is doing so in pursuance of a contractual duty or a statutory function cannot of itself exclude that responsibility.'[4]

6.21 Lord Nolan went on to refer to an Australian case, *Voli v Inglewood Shire Council*,[5] in which the architect of the Shire Hall was held to have owed a duty to

---

1   (1993) CILL 927.
2   [1994] 3 WLR 761.
3   [1995] 1 All ER 691.
4   Ibid at 735.
5   (1963) 110 CLR 74.

visitors to the Hall to make the stage safe for the burden reasonably expected to be placed on it. In the words of Windeyer J:

> 'Whatever might have been thought to be the position before the broad principles of the law of negligence stated in modern form in *Donoghue v Stevenson*, it is now beyond doubt that, for the reasonably foreseeable consequences of careless or unskilled conduct, an architect is liable to anyone whom it could reasonably have been expected might be injured as a result of his negligence. Such a person owes a duty of care quite independently of his contract of employment.'[1]

COLLATERAL WARRANTIES

6.22   Of course, *Voli* dealt with the question of personal injury. The extension of *White v Jones* to other circumstances is less clear. It is unclear where *White v Jones* leaves the present state of the law and the need for collateral warranties. In *White v Jones*, the House of Lords' majority, to avoid leaving the proposed beneficiaries without a remedy because of the solicitor's negligence in failing to draw up a new will, invented a remedy. What the construction industry now needs is a further case where a party tries to build on the principles of *White v Jones* in the construction law context. Where a warranty is provided, this may place the consultant in a *special relationship* with the recipient, bringing liability in tort. Where there is no collateral warranty, the picture is less clear. However, the tenor of present case-law may indicate that the existence of a contract, whether in the form of a warranty or other, is not a necessary requirement for there to be a special relationship. It is not necessary for a claimant, on the *White v Jones* test, to have been known to the consultants at the time of the negligent acts in question. In addition, a recent Court of Appeal decision, *Holt and Another v Payne Skillington (A Firm) and Another*[2] held that, where party A had concurrent claims against party B, in contract and in tort the tortious duty could be greater.

6.23   However, to maintain an element of uncertainty, it was decided in the Scots case, *Strathford East Kilbride Limited v Film Design Limited*,[3] that an architect employed by an owner to design a building did not owe a duty of care to the tenant in the absence of a direct contractual relationship. The tenant vacated a garage temporarily for remedial works to be carried out. Lord MacLean, basing his judgment on the earlier Scots case, *Junior Books Limited v Veitchi Co Limited*,[4] held no duty of care in delict to exist; there was no sufficiently special relationship between architect and tenant to import a duty of care. Where this decision leaves the law in England, which in tort parallels the Scots law, is unclear.

What goes in a collateral warranty? The prime obligation

6.24   Here there is a clash of interests between the consultant or the contractor (usually design and build) giving the warranty and the funder, purchaser, or tenant requesting the warranty. In short, the contents of a warranty will be the subject of

---

1   (1963) 110 CLR 74 at 84.
2   (1995) *The Times*, 22 December.
3   (1997) *The Times*, 1 December.
4   [1983] AC 520; and see **6.9**.

negotiation between them. However, there can be irreconcilable conflicts between the two interest groups, particularly in regard to what the consultant or contractor is warranting. For instance, if dealing with contaminated land, the consultant (or design and construct contractor) may have devised a land remediation scheme to enable development to occur. The developer may request a fitness for purpose warranty in favour of his funder or end users. This will not be acceptable to the consultant or design and construct contractor (who may, like the developer, have an imprecise idea of what is to be built) who will wish to restrict their obligation to *due skill care and diligence* and, perhaps, to exclude or cap liability for the consequences of dealing with the after-effects of further pollution. It is unlikely that a consultant or contractor will accept a warranty under which his liability is greater than under the principal contract.

Designers and contractors: their liabilities

6.25   Before exploring the question of consultant or contractor warranties, it is useful to review the position of designers and contractors at law, and their liabilities. It is these liabilities they are warranting to third parties. Under traditional forms of contract, such as JCT 98 and its predecessors, JCT 80 and JCT 63 of the ICE Conditions of Contract 5th and 6th Editions, the employer and his professional team (usually the architect or the engineer) assume responsibility for the design of the works. The contractor's responsibility is to build in accordance with the design and any other obligations which are set out or to be implied in the contract. There are obligations:

(1)   to carry out the works in a workmanlike manner;
(2)   to use materials of good quality;
(3)   to ensure the materials and work will be reasonably fit for their respective purposes.

Some of these obligations dovetail into those arising under the Supply of Goods and Services Act 1982. Warranties (1) and (2) are not usually excluded, although the fitness for purpose warranty is inapplicable in traditional building contracts where the employer does not rely on the skill and care of the contractor in the selection of materials. However, under design and build contracts at common law (ie in the absence of express terms), a contractor who both designs and constructs is obliged to produce a finished product which is reasonably fit for its purpose. This is a higher obligation than an architect or an engineer owes to his employer at common law. Traditionally, an architect or engineer has been required to carry out his function with reasonable skill and care, although the interpretation of such a term is, of course, one of art. The leading authority is the House of Lords' decision *Independent Broadcasting Authority v EMI Electronics Limited and BICC Construction Limited.*[1] Lord Scarman said:

> 'In the absence of any term (express or to be implied) negativing the obligation, one who contracts to design an article for a purpose made known to him undertakes that the design is reasonably fit for the purpose.'[2]

---

1   (1980) 14 BLR 1.
2   Ibid, at 48.

6.26   The position had previously been stated by Lord Denning MR in *Greaves (Contractors) Limited v Baynham Meikle & Partners*:[1]

> 'Now, as between the building owners and the contractor, it is plain that the owners made known to the contractors the purpose for which the building was required so as to show that they relied on the contractors' skill and judgment. It was, therefore, the duty of the contractors to see that the finished work was reasonably fit for the purpose for which they knew it was required. It was not merely an obligation to use reasonable care. The contractors were obliged to ensure that the finished work was reasonably fit for the purpose ...'

This principle is now well established and its application can be seen in other cases, including *Viking Grain Storage Limited v TH White Installations Limited*[2] and *Consultants Group International v John Worman Limited*.[3] The principle in the design and build cases is derived from the famous 'false teeth' case, *Samuels v Davis*[4] where Du Parc LJ said:

> '... if someone goes to a professional man ... and says: "Will you make me something which will fit a particular part of my body?" ... and then a professional gentleman says: "Yes" without qualification, he is then warranting that when he has made the article, it will fit the part of the body in question ... If a dentist takes out a tooth or a surgeon removes an appendix, he is bound to take reasonable care and show such skill as may be expected from a qualified practitioner ...'

6.27   With the exception of 'small' builders, who, in the absence of a standard form contract, invariably take on fitness for purpose obligations, the most common situations in which a contractor will incur design liabilities arise where he is employed under the standard form design and build contracts (ie JCT 81 (With Contractor's Design), JCT 98 (With Contractor's Design) or ICE Design and Construct Conditions (1992)), or one of the contracts which allow for an element of design and construct, such as JCT 80, where the Contractor's Designed Portion Supplement is used, ICE 6th Edition or the ACE form of contract. The basic design provisions in those contracts are reviewed below. The JCT 98 suite of contracts show no material changes from earlier forms.

JCT 81

6.28   Under JCT 81, the contractor's basic obligations are set out as follows:

> '2.1 – The Contractor shall upon and subject to the Conditions carry out and complete the Works ... and for that purpose shall complete the design for the Works including the selection of any specifications for any kinds and standards of the materials and goods and workmanship to be used in the construction of the Works so far as not described or stated in the Employer's Requirements or Contractor's Proposals....
>
> 2.5.1 – Insofar as the design of the Works is comprised in the Contractor's Proposals and in what the Contractor is to complete under Clause 2 and in accordance with the Employer's Requirements and the Conditions (including any further design which the Contractor is to carry out as a result of a change in the Employer's Requirements), the

---

1   [1975] 1 WLR 1095 at 1098.
2   (1985) 33 BLR 103.
3   (1987) 9 Conv LR 46.
4   [1943] KB 526 at 529–530.

Contractor shall have in respect of any defect or insufficiency in such design the like liability to the Employer whether under statute or otherwise, as would an architect or, as the case may be other appropriate designer holding himself out as competent to take on work for such design who, acting independently under a separate contract with the Employer, had supplied such design for or in connection with Works to be carried out and completed by a building contractor not being the supplier of the design.'

6.29 The Government Works Contract, GC/Works/1 Edition 3, now superseded but materially not altered in this respect, allows for partial design by the contractor with the limitation on a contractor's design liability broadly mirroring that found in JCT 81. Clause 31 demands the following:

'The Contractor shall use the skill and care of an experienced and competent contractor to ensure that – ... (b) any Things for incorporation, whether or not the Contractor is required to choose or select any of them, are of good quality for their intended purpose and conform [with the specification, the Bills of Quantities and the drawings].'

ACA Conditions

6.30 Under the little-used ACA Conditions, the contractor's responsibilities are found in clause 1.2:

'Without prejudice to any expressed or implied warranties or conditions the Contractor shall exercise in the performance of his obligations under this Agreement all the skill care and diligence to be expected of a properly qualified and competent contractor experienced in carrying out works of a similar scope, nature and size to the Works.'

Clause 1.2 is importantly expressed to be 'without prejudice to any express or implied warranties or conditions'.

The contractor's duties are further clarified in clause 3.1:

'The Contractor shall be responsible for all mistakes, inaccuracies, discrepancies and omissions in all drawings, details, documents and information provided by him ... Without prejudice to any expressed or implied warranties or conditions, the Contractor warrants that:
(a)   the Works will comply with any performance specification or requirement contained in the Contract Documents;
(b)   those parts of the Works due to be designed by the Contractor will be fit for the purposes for which they are required.'

ICE 6th Edition

6.31 Under the main civil engineering contract, ICE 6th Edition, clause 8(2) requires the contractor to undertake the design of a part or parts of the permanent works in the following manner:

'The Contractor shall not be responsible for the design or specification of the Permanent Works or any part thereof (except as may be expressly provided in the Contract).'

6.32 Under the ICE Design and Construct Conditions, the contractor's obligations are found in clauses 8(1) and (2). The basic responsibility in clause 8(2)(a) is to 'exercise all reasonable skill care and diligence'. This has no fitness for purpose connotations. What is more problematic for civil engineering contractors is the responsibility under clause 8(2)(b) for the contractor to check and accept responsibility for design work carried out by the employer, subject to the contractor's right to modify the employer's design work with the consent of the employer's representative.

JCT 80 Supplement

6.33 Finally, JCT 80, although principally a traditional contract, with the contractor building in accordance with the architect's design, does have the Contractor's Designed Portion Supplement. Clauses 2.6.1 and 2.6.2 mirror precisely the contractor's design obligations under clauses 2.5.1 and 2.5.2 of JCT 81. The architect remains responsible for the integration of contractor's design within the design of the works as a whole (clause 2.1.3), subject to the contractor's right under clause 2.7 to challenge by written notice the opinion of the architect or contract administrator if any such instruction injuriously affects the efficacy of the design of the Contractor's Designed Portion.

Reasonable skill and care

6.34 Under most collateral warranties, the principal obligation mirrors that at common law for consultants – the consultant/contractor warrants that he has used reasonable skill, care and diligence in the design of the works. Leaving to one side developer lawyers who push for fitness for purpose, sometimes this obligation is embellished, perhaps without any real addition to the meaning, to read as follows:

> 'The Consultant/Contractor warrants to [   ] that he has in the design of the Works used and will continue to use all the reasonable skill care and diligence to be expected of an experienced and competent consultant/contractor experienced in carrying out the design of works of a similar size scope and complexity to the Works.'

The judges have tussled with what constitutes 'reasonable skill and care'. In *Bolam v Friern Hospital Management Committee*,[1] the test was stated to be 'the ordinary skill of an ordinary competent man exercising that particular art'. In practical terms, a designer will usually escape liability for design failure if he can show that he acted in accordance with the usual practice and building standards current at the time that the design was carried out. No designer is automatically to be pilloried for coming to the wrong conclusion. As was stated in *Saif Ali v Sidney Mitchell & Co*,[2] a case on barristers' negligence, by Lord Wilberforce:

> 'Those who hold themselves out as qualified to practise other [excluding that of barrister] professions, although they are not liable for damage caused by what in the event turns out to have been an error of judgment on some matter on which the opinions of reasonably informed and competent members of the profession might have differed, are nevertheless liable for damage caused by their advice, acts or omissions in the course of their professional work which no member of the profession who was reasonably well-informed and competent would have given or done or omitted to do.'

6.35 Sometimes, a fitness for purpose obligation emerges from the client brief in the form of compliance with particular performance criteria. In *Gloucestershire Health Authority and Others v MA Torpey & Partners*,[3] as part of a design and

---

1   [1957] 1 WLR 582.
2   [1978] 3 WLR 849 at 858.
3   (1997) 55 Con LR 124.

supervision contract for the provision of an incineration plant, the plaintiff required two boilers which would dispose of a specified amount of waste, working 8 hours per day. The boilers failed to meet this requirement in use. The judge held that the engineers were obliged to have the client requirements in mind. The judge also considered if the engineer, as one with extensive experience, should be assessed as a specialist. He decided against this proposition. The engineer was required to meet the standards of a general mechanical and building services engineer. However, a particular specialist may be judged by a higher standard of care and hence the introduction into collateral warranties of wording of the type described in **6.32** above. In a recent article[1] Rachel Barnes referred to *Matrix Securities v Theodore Goddard and Another*,[2] a case relating to tax advice provided in regard to capital allowances. Quoting from the judgment, it was stated that the barrister's duty of care had to be judged by that of 'a rather small and select group of silks specialising in tax matters' and similarly the solicitors were to be judged by reference to the existence within the firm of a specialist tax department. Although neither barrister nor solicitors were found liable on the facts, the article intimates much may turn on the use of the word 'specialist'. There may be only the higher duty of care if the word 'specialist' is very explicitly referred to in a particular contract clause.

Competence

6.36   The level of competence of a designer or contractor carrying out design work is judged, except where there is a fitness for purpose obligation, by the standards prevailing at the time of the alleged negligence and not with the benefit of hindsight. Although the courts do not wish to fetter developments in technology and increased knowledge of particulars fields, a designer or design and build contractor who over-enthusiastically embraces new techniques may not be able to rely on 'state of the art' defences. This particularly applies to the use of new techniques for their own sake which may still be little researched or tested. In *Victoria University, Manchester v Hugh Wilson and Lewis Womersley (a firm) & Pochin (Contractors) Ltd*,[3] the judge was asked to approve the use of untried or relatively untried materials or techniques. He qualified his remarks by stating:

> 'For architects to use untried, or relatively untried materials or techniques cannot in itself be wrong, as otherwise the construction industry can never make any progress. I think, however, that architects who are venturing into the untried or little tried would be wise to warn their clients specifically of what they are doing and to obtain their express approval.'

Fitness for purpose obligations

6.37   Problems arise when those who draft development agreements endeavour to impose obligations under building contracts, often in favour of a specified investor. In those instances, the investor, often advised by surveyors, requires the building contractor (if on a design and build contract) and the consultants to warrant that the building, as designed and constructed, will be fit for particular purposes. Consultants and design and construct contractors usually argue that fitness for purpose insurance is

---

1   Rachel Barnes (1998) *Building*, 1 May, p 35.
2   (Unreported) 13 November 1997.
3   (1984) 2 Con LR 43 at 74.

not available in the market place. However, the real problems are the vague terms in which the fitness for purpose obligations are drawn by investors. They adopt such formulae as 'the development, when completed, will be fit for the purpose of being let as prestigious office space'. Clearly, as far as insurers are concerned, that is not a definable risk and, with the end user of some developments being a matter of complete speculation, is not a risk which can be justifiably assumed on a fitness for purpose basis. It may be that the end-user will have very specific computer requirements for the building, eg the growth of services nowadays such as telebanking. The insurance market may look at providing cover for fitness for purpose obligations if those obligations are clearly defined as compliance with performance criteria. It may not be unreasonable for a designer (including a design and build contractor) to warrant that certain load-bearing objectives will be achieved, and mechanical and electrical plant within the building will achieve certain operating standards which can be properly measured.

End users

6.38   When collateral warranties began to take off in the late 1980s, their purpose was seen as being to cover the obligations of those with a major design responsibility for a development who did not have a contract with end users, including tenants and purchasers. Not unnaturally, the zeal with which collateral warranties have been sought has now extended to sub-contractors providing design services. Therefore, it is common for particular design and build sub-contractors, eg those supplying piling, structural steel or windows, to provide collateral warranty agreements in favour of the end-users of buildings and investors. The problem arises under development agreements when an investor's enthusiasm for sub-contractor warranties (which are often difficult to obtain and even more difficult to cover by adequate professional indemnity or product liability insurance) leads to warranties being requested of sub-contractors, carrying out *substantial* design. To define 'substantial' is an extremely subjective exercise. Therefore, in the package of documentation for commercial developments, it is preferable that the sub-contractors from whom warranties are required are clearly identified.

Parties covered by warranties

6.39   Ordinarily, consultants and the contractor will be expected to give warranties in favour of the following:

– any funder of the development;
– any proposed purchaser of the development;
– proposed tenants of the development.

In order to ensure that collateral warranties are binding obligations, they will either be executed as a deed or be subject to *fictitious* consideration in that they will contain words to the effect:

> 'IN CONSIDERATION of the payment of £1 by the Funder to the Consultant, receipt of which the Consultant hereby acknowledges ...'

Many consultants and contractors view the negotiation of collateral warranty agreements as a nuisance, and the words 'receipt of which the consultants/contractor hereby acknowleges' are often deleted. These consultants/contractors enjoy the nuisance value of writing to funders etc demanding the £1 payment to be made.

REASONABLE SKILL AND CARE/FITNESS FOR PURPOSE

6.40   The consultant's or contractor's duty should be defined in exactly the same terms as in the principal contract. The clause may be expressed to cover antecedent, present and future services of the consultant/contractor in connection with the project, subject to an express provision that the consultant or contractor shall have no greater liability under the terms of the warranty than under the principal contract. A typical clause may read:

> 'The Consultant hereby warrants that he has exercised and will continue to exercise reasonable skill, care and diligence in relation to all services performed and to be performed in relation to the Development ... provided that the Consultant shall have no greater liability to the [   ] hereunder than he has to the [   ] under the Principal Contract.'

On occasions, collateral warranties attempt to increase the level of exposure by embellishing the consultant's obligations:

> 'The Consultant represents and warrants to the Beneficiary that the Consultant has exercised and will continue to exercise in the performance of the Services under the Appointment all the reasonable skill, care and attention to be expected of a competent and fully qualified architect experienced in the provision of services for works of a similar nature, value, complexity and time scale to the Works to be carried out under the Building Contract.'

6.41   The consultant may be given a *fitness for purpose* obligation. He will be requested to 'ensure that when completed the development will be fit for its intended purpose' or requested to 'ensure that particular performance criteria are met'. Fitness for purpose causes problems, as follows:

−   the consultant may have a higher duty under the warranty than under the principal contract;
−   professional indemnity insurance does not usually cover consultants for fitness for purpose;
−   the limitation period under the warranty may be deferred. If the building was initially defective but nevertheless is fit for its purpose, the limitation period would not start until the property ceased to be fit for its purpose.

INDEMNITY PROVISIONS

6.42   Collateral warranties often state:

> 'The Consultant shall indemnify and keep indemnified the Beneficiary from and against any claims, actions, costs, losses and expenses made or suffered by the Beneficiary as a result of any breach by the Consultant of his warranties and undertakings under this Deed.'

Here the problems are:

–   possible delay to the start of the limitation period. Breach of contract does not occur until the third party incurs the loss against which the indemnity is sought;

–   indemnity provisions, set out in broad terms, which increase the scope of damages recoverable possibly beyond those recoverable under the *Hadley v Baxendale*[1] test.

DELETERIOUS MATERIALS

6.43   Such clauses, of prime interest to architects and design and build contractors, may also affect structural engineers. Clauses have tended to grow in length, to the extent of giving rise to numerous sterile arguments. Lawyers cannot, of course, assess what is and what is not a deleterious material, and rely on the technically qualified to advise which materials should be prohibited for incorporation and which are merely to be avoided if possible. It may be an apocryphal story, but one surveyor suggested that he included in a deleterious materials list a 'rogue' material which was taken up with gusto by City solicitors, and afterwards appeared in a large number of collateral warranty agreements. There may be a backlash against deleterious materials lists, led by the British Council for Offices. According to research carried out by Tony Carey of the University of Northumbia[2] and reported by Tony Bingham, the basis of the lists of deleterious materials usually put forward is questionable. Indeed, in one Scottish case the court ordered West Lothian District Council not to use lists of so-called banned materials. According to Carey, the decision not to use high alumina cement may have stemmed from a roof collapse in London in 1974 when two pre-cast concrete beams failed and collapsed into the school swimming pool. Although *Estates Gazette* apparently stated in 1989, 'The more common deleterious materials are asbestos, calcium chloride, galvanised wall ties, high alumina cement, wall slabs', Carey concluded that, with the exception of asbestos, none of the other items commonly cited as deleterious were necessarily so. Much depended on the use made of them. For instance, calcium silicate bricks have been in use for 103 years and can compare very well with clay. However, silicate brick requires provision for expansion and contraction, meaning that movement joints should be at shorter intervals than for clay. Again, wood-wool slabs can be effective, despite problems in 1972 with a Belfast office block. Faced with the random nomination of materials as deleterious, the British Council for Offices and the British Property Federation commissioned Ove Arup & Partners to produce outline guidance for clients and specifiers on the selection of materials.

6.44   According to Ann Minogue:[3]

'Why not delete the list of deleterious materials and insert something along the following lines:

"The consultant shall use the skill care and diligence required by this agreement to see that he selects materials for use on the project in accordance with the guidance contained in the publication *Good Practice in the Selection of Construction Materials*

---

1   (1854) 9 Ex 341.
2   *Building*, 23 May 1997, p 35.
3   *Building*, 20 June 1997, pp 28–29.

(1997): Ove Arup & Partners and he shall use such skill and care and diligence to see that materials as used in the construction of the project will be in accordance with such guidance." '

Minogue further stated:

'Is there still any role for lists? Almost certainly not. Product scares will still arise – some will be genuine, others not. Professional assessment of the risks with the project team will always win over the blanket blacklist approach. Where concern about materials will be likely still to arise is in situations where product bans are imposed – and sometimes (especially when EU-inspired) where there is a phasing-out period.'

An interesting technical resumé of this subject can be found in the British Research Establishment's *Lists of excluded materials, a change in practice,*[1] and the unpublished paper, *Origins and Effects of Lists of Excluded Materials* by Hobbs, Cliff and Ashall.[2]

6.45   A typical example of a deleterious materials clause as currently drafted is:

'The Consultant warrants to the Beneficiary that he has exercised and will continue to exercise all reasonable skill, care and attention to ensure that none of the following have been or will be specified by the Consultant for use in the Works:

1.   high alumina cement in structural elements;
2.   wood wool slabs in permanent formwork to concrete;
3.   calcium chloride in admixtures for use in re-inforced concrete;
4.   asbestos products;
5.   naturally occurring aggregates for use in re-inforced concrete which do not comply with British Standard 882: 1983 and/or naturally occurring aggregates for use in concrete which do not comply with British Standard 8110: 1985;
6.   urea formaldehyde foam or materials which may release formaldehyde in quantities which may be hazardous.'

The basic clause set out above may be modified to make it more onerous. First, it can be modified as follows:

'The Consultant [the Contractor] warrants to the Beneficiary that he has exercised and will continue to exercise all reasonable skill care and attention to ensure that none of the following have been or will be specified by the Consultant for use in the Works.'

6.46   Another technique to enlarge the responsibility of the consultant is to include a broad-brush, sweeping-up provision. Although the following may be acceptable to consultants:

'Any other substances which are not in accordance with British Standards and Codes of Practice current at the time of specification'

such a sub-clause would be made unacceptable if it were also to include 'or any other substance not in accordance with good building practice' – a phrase too meaningless to ascribe a meaning to.

6.47   In considering whether to accept a deleterious materials clause, a consultant or contractor needs to ascertain whether or not the principal contract, into which the

1   *Digest 425* (September 1997).
2   (Building Research Establishment, 15 May 1997).

consultant or contractor enters, expressly requires the use of particular substances or allows the client to substitute materials which may be deleterious. Warranties and principal contracts must be 'back to back', although collateral warranties are often negotiated as a separate and distinct contract.

6.48   Illustrative of the way in which deleterious materials lists have grown to ever-increasing and absurd length is the following example:

'1.4   that the Building Contractor has not used or specified and will not specify for use and has exercised and will continue to exercise reasonable skill care and diligence as aforesaid to see that the Development shall be carried out without the inclusion therein of any of the following:

1.4.1   high alumina cement in structural elements;

1.4.2   wood wool slabs in permanent formwork to concrete or in structural elements;

1.4.3   calcium chloride in admixtures for use in reinforced concrete;

1.4.4   aggregates in concrete mixes of such proportion as is likely to give adverse alkali silica reaction;

1.4.5   aggregates for use in reinforced concrete which do not comply with British Standard Specification 882:1992; and aggregates for use in concrete which do not comply with British Standard Specification 8110:1985;

1.4.6   concrete which does not comply with the provisions of British Standard Specification 8110:1985;

1.4.7   white asbestos (chrysotile), brown asbestos (amosite otherwise known as asbestiform cummingtonite-grunerite) or blue asbestos (crocidolite) or any asbestos or asbestos-containing products as defined in the Asbestos Regulations 1969 or 1987 or any statutory modification or re-enactment thereof;

1.4.8   urea formaldehyde foam or materials which may release formaldehyde in quantities which may be hazardous, with reference to the limits set from time to time by the Health and Safety Executive;

1.4.9   calcium silicate bricks or tiles;

1.4.10   pitch polymer damp proof courses in horizontal locations;

1.4.11   cavity wall insulation which entirely fills the cavity or which is installed after construction;

1.4.12   when manufactured from galvanised material, wall ties, cramps, straps restraint and support angles and lintols in cavity walls;

1.4.13   deeply recessed joints used in conjunction with perforated bricks;

1.4.14   any materials containing lead which may be ingested, inhaled or absorbed, except copper alloy fittings containing lead permitted in drinking water pipework by any relevant authorities;

1.4.15   materials which are generally comprised of mineral fibres either man-made or naturally occurring which have a diameter of 3 microns or less and a length of 200 microns or less or which contain any fibres not scaled or otherwise stabilised to ensure that fibre migration is prevented;

1.4.16   any other substance to which a British Standard or Code of Practice applies but which does not comply with such British Standard or Code of Practice or which is generally known to be deleterious at time of specification or use.

The Building Contractor shall within one month after practical completion of the Development if required issue written confirmation to the Company that:

(a)   it has not used or specified for use any such materials in relation to the Development or any part of it . . .'

6.49   Some lawyers and consultants have attempted to bring some common sense to the question of deleterious materials clauses. A more sensible version might read:

'Without prejudice to the generality of clause [   ] (warranting that it has exercised and will continue to exercise all reasonable skill, care and diligence in the performance of his duties under the appointment as may be reasonably expected of a properly qualified and competent [   ]) the Consultant covenants with [   ] that the Consultant has exercised and will continue to exercise the standard of skill, care and diligence not to specify any products or materials for use in the Works which at the time of specification:

–   do not conform with British Standards or Codes of Practice; or
–   are generally known within the Consultant's profession to be deleterious, in the particular circumstances in which they are specified for use, to health and safety and/or the durability of the building or structure.'

COPYRIGHT

6.50   Most collateral warranties state:

'The copyright in all drawings, designs and calculations produced by the Consultant shall remain vested in the Consultant but the Beneficiary and its nominees shall have an irrevocable royalty-free licence ...'

However, the following points need to be considered.

–   What is the scope of any licences granted? From a consultant's perspective, the beneficiary should not be permitted to use drawings and other documents other than for the completion of the development, its repair, extension or maintenance. The beneficiary will not usually be permitted to use design information for the construction of a totally new building.
–   To gain some protection, the consultant should ensure that the granting of any third-party licences can occur only when all fees owed to him have been paid.
–   Although many collateral warranties are silent on the point, the consultant should ensure that he is reimbursed for the production of what could be copious photocopying and that he is not asked to provide copies in an unrealistically short period of time.
–   Just as a seller can provide ordinarily only as good a title as he has got, similarly a consultant can grant a licence only to the extent that he can do this lawfully. If the consultant has used the design work of others he must be sure that he is able to grant licences in circumstances where there are third party interests.
–   Consultants should be wary of clauses which not merely provide the facility for the granting of licences, but also the granting of sub-licences which might lead to granting extended responsibilities. The following might be unacceptable:

'The Licence may be transferred to third parties and shall include the right to grant sub-licences.'

INSURANCE

6.51   All collateral warranties require the consultant to maintain professional indemnity insurance. A not untypical clause reads as follows:

'The Consultant has and shall maintain for the period expiring not less than 12 years after the date of practical completion of the Works as defined in the Building Contract professional indemnity insurance without any material excesses or unusual exclusions with a well-established insurance office or underwriter of good repute carrying on business in the United Kingdom of not less than £[   ],000,000 ([   ] million pounds) for each and every claim or series of claims arising out of any one event or series of events PROVIDED ALWAYS that such insurance is available in the market to the profession of the Consultant at commercially reasonable rates. The Consultant shall immediately inform the Beneficiary if such insurance ceases to be available at commercially reasonable rates and with the approval of the Employer which approval is not to be unreasonably withheld or delayed take out such lower level of insurance as is available in the market to the profession of the Consultant at commercially reasonable rates. As and when the Consultant is reasonably requested to do so by the Beneficiary the Consultant shall promptly produce for inspection documentary evidence that such professional indemnity insurance is being maintained in accordance with the terms of this clause but not in any way which may breach the terms of the policy in force at that time.'

6.52   The problems that arise include the following.

– Consultants should be reluctant to commit themselves to paying unquantified insurance premiums for a specified period of years. Insurance policies are annual contracts with cover given on the basis of claims made during the period of insurance.
– No one really knows what *weasel* words in collateral warranties, of the type, 'at commercially reasonable rates', really mean. The problem is most acute with contaminated land schemes. The insurance market is generally cutting back the level of cover which is available to consultants. Insurance cover is usually capped to cover claims in the aggregate.
– Consultants should always remember that it is essential for them to get the approval of their indemnity insurers to any warranty.
– Indemnity insurance is often requested of contractors. It is inappropriate for contractors, simply carrying out building work, to confirm that they have professional indemnity cover. However, if the contractor is a design and build contractor, it is legitimate to ask him for professional indemnity insurance. Many contractors have difficulty in obtaining and maintaining professional indemnity insurance. The problem is most acute with specialist sub-contractors who may combine the roles of fabricator and installer for particular bespoke systems and from whom product liability insurance may be required.

STEP-IN RIGHTS

6.53   Step-in clauses are crucial in collateral warranties for commercial developments. For instance, if a lender has provided development finance, the fund wishes to be protected if the developer becomes insolvent or is guilty of a material breach of contract and the fund would otherwise be left with an incomplete development on its hands. Step-in clauses permit the fund, as necessary, to replace the developer as the consultant's employer for the purposes of the consultant's appointment. Similarly, if the warranty is one given by a contractor, the fund can replace the employer, on insolvency or other material event occurring, under the building contract. The step-in clause operates as a novation. For that reason, the developer, or the employer, will be made a party to the collateral warranty simply to endorse its agreement to the fund, taking over its responsibilities in appropriate circumstances. For the consultant or contractor, it is essential that the fund or other beneficiary assumes responsibility for all fees due to the consultant or contractor.

6.54   Typical step-in rights are set out below:

'2.   The Building Contractor hereby agrees with the Company that:

2.1   in the event of the Company serving upon the Building Contractor a copy of any certificate issued by the Company's Surveyor stating that the Employer is in default under the Development Agreement; or

2.2   in the event that the Building Contractor notifies the Company that it intends to exercise any right it has to terminate the Building Contract (and the Building Contractor hereby undertakes to give the Company not less than 21 days' written notice of such intention).

In either case the Company shall be entitled (but without giving rise to any obligation to do so) to require the Building Contractor by notice in writing and subject to clause 3 to accept the instructions of the Company to the exclusion of the Employer upon the terms and conditions of the Building Contract. The Employer acknowledges that the Building Contractor shall be entitled to rely on a notice given to the Building Contractor by the Company under this clause and that acceptance by the Building Contractor of the instructions of the Company to the exclusion of the Employer shall not constitute any breach of the Building Contractor's obligations to the Employer under the Building Contract. Provided that, subject to clause 3, nothing in this clause shall relieve the Building Contractor of any liability it may have to the Employer for any breach by the Building Contractor of the Building Contract or where the Building Contractor has wrongfully served notice under the Building Contract that it is entitled to determine its employment or has wrongfully treated the Building Contact as having been repudiated by the Employer.

3.   It shall be a condition of any notice given by the Company under clause 2 that (subject to the provisions of the Development Agreement) the Company accepts liability for payment of the sums certified as properly due to the Building Contractor under the Building Contract and for performance of the Employer's obligations thereunder including payment of any sums outstanding at the date of such notice. Upon the issue of any notice by the Company under clause 2, the Building Contract shall continue in full force and effect as if no right of determination of its employment under the Building Contract, nor any right to the Building Contractor to treat the Building Contract as having been repudiated by the Employer had arisen and the Building Contractor shall be liable to the Company under the Building Contract in lieu of its liability to the Employer.'

CONTRIBUTION

6.55   There are enormous potential problems over the question of joint and several liability under collateral warranties. In reality, various members of the design team, as well as the contractor, will be responsible in part for the same defective work. The position on collective responsibility is governed by the Civil Liability (Contribution) Act 1978 which has proved to be legally complex in its operation. Section 1(1) provides:

'Subject to the following provisions in this section any person liable in respect of any damage suffered by another person may recover contributions from any other person liable in respect of the same damage (whether jointly with him or otherwise).'

Section 6(1) of the Act states:

'A person is liable in respect of any damage for the purposes of this Act if the person who suffered it ... is entitled to recover compensation from him in respect of that damage (whatever the legal basis of his liability whether tort, breach of contract, breach of trust or otherwise).'

6.56   Where a defendant seeks a contribution from another party in litigation, he has to establish that the other person would himself have been liable to the plaintiff for some or all of the plaintiff's losses had the other party, rather than he, been sued by the plaintiff. For that reason, it is important for each of the consultants that similar warranties are executed by their fellow consultants and the contractor so that no single consultant is more exposed than the others. Even then, a consultant may be at risk if another member of the consultancy team becomes insolvent in the meantime. To overcome this problem the following solutions are included in particular warranties:

'The Developer undertakes to the Consultant that it has obtained warranties in no less onerous terms in favour of the Beneficiary from: [*details of consultants*].'

or

'It is a condition precedent to the operation of this Agreement that effective warranty agreements shall be completed by any other consultant appointed by the Developer in connection with the Development and also the Building Contractor ...'

or, according to the British Property Federation's CoWa/P&T Form of Warranty:

'1.(b)   The Firm's liability for costs under this Agreement shall be limited to that proportion of such costs which it would be just and equitable to require the Firm to pay having regard to the extent of the Firm's responsibility for the same and on the basis that ... shall be deemed to have provided contractual undertakings on terms no less onerous than this Clause 1 ...'

It is questionable just how successful any of these permutations are. Such clauses cannot fully accommodate the Civil Liability (Contribution) Act 1978. The court is unable to apportion damages where one or more of the parties is not before the courts. It is questionable that the courts would give effect to such a provision: *Maxfield v Llewellyn* [1961] 3 All ER 95, CA.

PRESERVATION OF RIGHTS IN TORT

6.57   For some years, preservation of rights in tort was not a relevant consideration as a possible substitute for a collateral warranty, given the limitations on recovery in tort already referred to above in paras **6.17–6.21**. Traditionally, lawyers have prepared legal pleadings, arguing the plaintiff's case both under any relevant contract and in tort. Lord Scarman, in *Tai Hing Cotton Mill Limited v Liu Chong Hing Bank Limited*,[1] introduced an element of confusion into established

---

1   [1985] 3 WLR 317 at 329.

practice although, being part of a Privy Council decision, his words were not of binding effect in England:

'Their Lordships do not believe that there is anything to the advantage of the law's development in searching for a liability in tort where the parties are in a contractual relationship. This is particularly so in a commercial relationship.'

6.58 To some extent, Lord Scarman's comments were merely a reflection of what he felt the legal position should be. It was illogical for there to be any tortious liability in circumstances where the parties had the benefit of a contract. Such is consistent with the position in France where the doctrine of *non cumul* specifically prevents the concurrence of claims in contract and tort. Unfortunately, the English approach has been a switchback railway of uncertainties. The first significant modern decision was a first instance one of Oliver J in *Midland Bank Trust Co Limited v Hett Stubbs and Kemp*.[1] The case concerned a negligent solicitor who, in drawing up an option to purchase a parcel of land, failed to register the option as an estate contract. Although the contrary was argued by the defendant solicitor, the existence of a detailed written contract was no bar to tortious recovery. In the words of Oliver J:

'There is not and never has been any rule of law that a person having alternative claims must frame his action in one or the other. If I have a contract with my dentist to extract a tooth, I am not thereby precluded from suing him in tort if he negligently shatters my jaw ...'[2]

The case was very significant in that the judge rejected the proposition that a professional who had a contract with the client was thereby freed from any possible liability in negligence, a proposition apparently accepted in earlier cases.

6.59 At Court of Appeal stage, in *National Bank of Greece v Pinios Co (No 1)*[3] Lloyd LJ said:

'As far as I know it has never been the law that a plaintiff who has the choice of suing in contract or in tort can fail in contract yet nevertheless succeed in tort; ...'

He went on to state:

'The position would be different if the contract and the tort lay in different fields. Thus, if, to take a simple example, I give my employee a lift home, and injure him by my careless driving, then obviously he will not be prevented from recovering from me in tort, because of the existence between us of a contract of employment ...'[4]

Concurrent liability

6.60 In *Bell v Peter Browne & Co*,[5] a case concerning solicitors' negligence in the transfer of the former matrimonial home by the plaintiff to his wife subject to an interest in the proceeds of sale, Mustill LJ thought it a pity that English law recognised concurrent duties in contract and negligence which he considered to be an anomaly and unnecessary. He stated:

---

1   [1979] 3 All ER 571.
2   Ibid, at 596.
3   [1990] 1 AC 637 at 650.
4   Ibid, at 651.
5   [1990] 2 QB 495.

'I think it a pity that English law has elected to recognise concurrent rights of action in contract and tort. Other legal systems seem to manage quite well by limiting attention to the contractual obligations which are, after all, the foundation of the relationship between the professional man and his client; as for example, in the case of French law, via the doctrine of *non cumul*. That precisely the same breach of precisely the same organisation should be capable of generating causes of action which arise at different times is in my judgment an anomaly which our law could well do without. Nevertheless the law is clear and we must apply it.'[1]

6.61   Again, the reluctance to identify a tortious cause of action in circumstances where there was a written contract, was reflected in the decision of the Official Referee, Judge Newey QC in *Hiron v Legal and General Assurance Pynford South Limited and Others*:[2]

'In view of the cases, while it may be that the courts are moving towards a restrictive review of duties in tort where there is a contract between the parties, it seems clear that at present the mere existence of a contract does not preclude liability in tort.

... I think that the correct approach is where there was a contract between plaintiffs and defendants it should be treated as a very important consideration in deciding whether there was sufficient proximity between them and whether it is to be just and reasonable that the defendant should owe a duty in tort.'

6.62   1993 and 1994 brought a spate of decisions on the question of concurrent liability. First, Judge Michael Kershaw QC, sitting as an Official Referee, considered the issue in *Lancashire and Cheshire Associations of Baptist Churches Inc v Howard and Seddon Partnership*.[3] Here, the plaintiff's claim against a firm of architects resulted from alleged defects in the design of a new church sanctuary which caused ventilation and condensation problems. A writ was issued against the architects claiming damages for breach of contract and negligence. The judge concluded:

'... there can be a duty in tort despite the existence of a contract for professional services, albeit that the implied as well as the express terms of a contract will regulate the extent of that duty ... [I]t cannot be said that there is a duty in tort in all cases where the parties are in a contractual relationship.'[4]

The judge had in mind that a party's claim in tort might ultimately be defeated because it constituted a head of loss not recognised by the general law of tort, such as pure economic loss in circumstances where the facts did not fall within the *Hedley Byrne* principle as developed by the courts. In the case before the judge, the designs submitted by the defendants were to enable the plaintiff to consider the accommodation and appearance of the proposed building. The architects had made no express statement as to the building's technical adequacy via the design work; there was no reliance and therefore no right to recover the simple cost of correcting defects.

6.63   The Limitation Act 1980 operated separately from a party's general legal right as defined by the appropriate law. The judge stated:

'[I]n my judgment the flaw in [counsel's] reasoning is to treat the right given to a defendant by the Limitation Act 1980 as a right derived from a contract, whether from

---

1   [1990] 2 QB 495 at 511.
2   (1993) 60 BLR 78 at 89.
3   [1993] 3 All ER 467.
4   Ibid, at 477.

express or from implied terms of the contract. It is not. It is derived from the 1980 Act. That Act does not imply a term into a contract. On the contrary, it has rightly been said that the successive statutes of limitation merely bar a plaintiff's remedy, and not his cause of action. In my judgment the principle that where the parties choose to regulate their rights by contract tort cannot alter those rights applies only to rights created by the terms of the contract, and not to rights resulting from the application of the 1980 Act.'[1]

6.64   The question of concurrence then arose in other cases, including *Conway v Crowe Kelsey Partner and Another*[2] and the seminal decision of the House of Lords in *Henderson v Merrett Syndicates Limited*.[3] In *Conway*, the plaintiffs engaged the defendant consulting engineers in relation to structural damage caused to their property by heave. Subsequently, when any cause of action in contract was statute-barred, they sued the defendant in tort. The judge, His Honour Judge Cyril Newman QC, sitting on Official Referee's Business, analysed the legal position. He concluded that orthodoxy dictated that the two causes of action, in contract and tort, existed independent of each other, despite the paradox that a defendant might use a defence under the Limitation Act 1980 to defeat a claim in contract. Consistent with His Honour Judge Kershaw in *Lancashire and Cheshire Associations of Baptist Churches*,[4] the judge concluded:

'The Defence of limitation is a creature of statute; it is procedural in its effect; it gives a Defendant the right to plead the statute if he wishes; he will not always wish to do so ... If Parliament has therefore enacted different limitation periods for contract and tort it is not unfair or unreasonable to the Defendant that the defence of limitation has not arisen against the Plaintiffs' claim in tort.'[5]

His Honour Judge James Fox-Andrews QC had adopted a similar approach in the slightly earlier case of *Wessex Regional Health Authority v HLM Design Limited*.[6] In the words of the judge:

'I am satisfied that where there is a contractual relationship between a person and someone professing to special skills for which professional qualifications are necessary and the contract relates to the exercise of those skills and the case falls within the principles of *Hedley Byrne* as explained in *Caparo* and *Murphy* there may be a concurrent duty to take reasonable care to prevent or avoid economic loss so long as it is fair and reasonable.'[7]

6.65   These first instance decisions were complemented by the seminal decision of the House of Lords in *Henderson v Merrett Syndicates Limited*.[8] The case related to an action by Lloyd's Names who were members of syndicates managed by the defendant underwriting agents. In some instances, a Name's underwriting was managed by an agent with whom he had a contract, while in others a Name's business was managed by a sub-agent with whom he had no contract. As far as the contracts were concerned, it was agreed that there was an implied duty on behalf of the agents to

---

1   [1993] 3 All ER 467 at 574.
2   (1994) CILL 927.
3   [1994] 3 WLR 761.
4   [1993] 3 All ER 467; see also **6.62**.
5   (1994) CILL 927 at 928.
6   (1993) CILL 907.
7   Ibid, at 909.
8   [1994] 3 WLR 761.

exercise reasonable skill and care. Two questions arose. First, did primary or sub-agents owe a duty of care in tort to Names? Secondly, could an agent who was in contract with a Name owe concurrently a duty of care in tort? After a detailed consideration of the law, primarily found in the speech of Lord Goff, the issues were resolved in favour of the Names. Lord Goff thoroughly endorsed the first instance decision of *Midland Bank Trust Co Limited v Hett Stubbs and Kemp*[1] and found *Hedley Byrne* applicable to establish a duty of care in favour of the Names.

6.66   On whether or not professional men could have a concurrent liability in tort if they caused economic loss, clearly, since the decision in *Hedley Byrne*, professional men were potentially liable in tort for negligent misstatement. Lord Goff in *Henderson* commented as follows:

> 'At first, as is shown in particular by cases concerned with liability for solicitors' negligence, the courts adopted something very like the French solution, holding that a claim against a solicitor for negligence must be pursued in contract and not in tort ... Furthermore when, in *Bagot v Stevens Scanlan & Co Ltd*,[2] Diplock L.J. adopted a similar approach in the case of a claim against a firm of architects, he felt compelled to recognise (pp 204–205) that a different conclusion might be reached in cases "where the law in the old days recognised either something in the nature of the status like a public calling (such as common carrier, common inn keeper, or a bailor and bailee) or the status of master and servant." ... I must confess to finding it startling that, in the second half of the 20th Century, a problem of considerable practical imortance should be solved by reference to such an outmoded form of categorisation as this. ...
>
> If concurrent liability in tort is not recognised, a claimant may find his claim barred at a time when he is unaware of its existence. This must moreover be a real possibility in the case of claims against professional men, such as solicitors or architects, since the consequences of their negligence may well not come to light until long after the lapse of 6 years from the date when the relevant breach of contract occurred. Moreover the benefits of the Latent Damage Act 1986, under which the time of the accrual of the cause of action may be postponed until after the plaintiff has the relevant knowledge, are limited to actions in tortious negligence. This leads to the startling possibility that a client who has had the benefit of gratuitous advice from his solicitor may in this respect be better off than a client who has paid a fee. Other practical problems arise, for example, from the absence of a right to contribution as between negligent contract-breakers; and the rules as to remoteness of damage, which are less restricted in tort than they are in contract; and from the availability of the opportunity to obtain leave to serve proceedings out of the jurisdiction.'[3]

Further in his judgment he stated:

> 'Attempts have been made to explain how doctors and dentists may be concurrently liable in tort while other professional men may not be so liable, on the basis that the former cause physical damage whereas the latter cause pure economic loss ... But this explanation is not acceptable, if only because some professional men, such as architects, may also be responsible for physical damage. As a matter of principle, it is difficult to see why concurrent remedies in tort and contract, if available against the medical profession,

---

1   [1979] 3 All ER 571.
2   [1966] 1 QB 197.
3   [1994] 3 WLR 761 at 780–781.

should not also be available against members of other professions, whatever form the relevant damage may take.'[1]

6.67   Lord Goff quoted from a New Zealand decision, *Rowlands v Collow,*[2] concerning engineer's negligence:

'The issue is now virtually incontestable; a person who has performed professional services may be held liable concurrently in contract and in negligence, unless the terms of the contract preclude the tortious liability.'

This means that in the absence of the tortious duty of care being expressly excluded in a collateral warranty, the beneficiary will have a concurrent right to sue in contract and negligence.

Defences

6.68   On the basis that a professional may have concurrent liability in tort and contract, how does he best protect himself? The obvious response is for the professional to put an exclusion clause in his appointment with the client limiting the latter's right to seek any remedies for deficient performance by the professional to those arising in contract rather than tort. This was common at the end of the 1980s in collateral warranties. This was the approach of Judge Newman QC in *Conway v Crowe Kelsey*:

'If professional practitioners wish to avoid the longer limitation period afforded to their clients in tort resulting from their special relationship or proximity, they have, perhaps with the exception of National Health hospital doctors and dentists whose position is even more complicated today, only to include an express term in their contract excluding any liability in tort.'[3]

Despite Lord Goff's similar indication in *Henderson* that the concurrent obligation in tort might be avoided by a suitable contractual provision in that the law of tort was not 'supplementary to the law of contract' but 'the general law, out of which the parties can, if they wish, contract',[4] any exclusion clause must be read subject to the test of reasonableness under the Unfair Contract Terms Act 1977. Under s 2(2):

'In the case of other loss or damage, a person cannot so exclude or restrict his liability for negligence except insofar as the term or notice satisfies the requirements of reasonableness.'

6.69   Few, if any, lawyers will need reminding that the 'reasonableness' test is clarified in s 11, and in the 'Guidelines' set out in Sch 2 to the 1977 Act. There is potentially some interesting litigation ahead, particularly in the context of claims by private individuals, as professionals rush to disclaim any responsibility in negligence.

The recent cases have been extremely useful in that the long-standing question of the concurrent liability of a professional in contract and negligence has been fully clarified. The object lesson now for all professionals is to look carefully at the terms of their insurance and to take account of their potentially far longer liabilities in negligence just in case that exclusion clause does not work.

---

1   [1994] 3 WLR 761 at 785.
2   [1992] 1 NZLR 178.
3   (1994) CILL 927 at 928.
4   [1994] 3 WLR 761 at 785.

Assignment

6.70   Nowadays, warranties are not usually silent on the question of assignment, ie the transfer of the benefit of the warranty in favour of a third party. Most consultants wish to restrict assignment to two occasions only. They are reluctant to consider any further assignment, even with consent.

LIMITATION

6.71   Many warranties are silent on the question of the limitation period. Others simply state in the insurance provisions that the consultant 'has and shall maintain for a period expiring not less than 12 years after the date of Practical Completion of the Works as defined in the Building Contract professional indemnity insurance'. Other warranties, an example being the British Property Federation (BPF) CoWa/P&T Warranty, state in not dissimilar terms as follows:

> '9.   No action or proceedings for any breach of this Agreement shall be commenced against the Firm after the expiry of [   ] years from the date of Practical Completion of the Premises under the Building Contract.'

In the absence of agreement to the contrary, if the parties have not agreed any particular limitation period, the Limitation Act 1980 will apply:

–   12 years from the date of breach if the agreement was under seal;
–   six years from the breach if the agreement was under hand.

As far as a beneficiary to a collateral warranty is concerned, if the statutory limitation period is not modified, the limitation period will run from the date of execution of the collateral warranty. A consultant will be in breach of his obligations under a collateral warranty to the beneficiary on the date of execution of the relevant warranty even if the original breach of contract under the principal contract upon which the beneficiary can sue occurred some time before.

Consultants

6.72   The re-emergence of concurrent liabilities in negligence has important repercussions for consultants. If the message from *White v Jones* (above) is that consultants can be liable in negligence, consultants need to be advised of the possible implications of the Latent Damage Act 1986 which may modify ordinary limitation periods but provides an overall longstop of 15 years.

6.73   Often, collateral warranties are silent on the question of how disputes are to be resolved. On occasions, disputes have been subject to resolution as Official Referees' Business in London or in major provincial centres. References to the Official Referees have now been replaced by references to the Technology and Construction Court. Rarely, collateral warranties have arbitration as the means of dispute resolution. However, arbitration is unsatisfactory where there is the prospect of multi-party proceedings or the potential for findings of liability against the professional team in different legal fora. Nowadays, the possible impact of the Housing Grants, Construction and Regeneration Act 1996 cannot be disregarded. Even if collateral warranties are ordinarily construction contracts for the purposes of ss 104–105 of the Act, they are arguably caught if the warranty is a funder's agreement and the funder exercises step-in rights and becomes a principal party to the construction contract. Therefore, prudence may dictate that adjudication provisions are included in funder warranties and a choice of standard adjudication procedure made, whether it be the Construction Industry Council or another. If an election is not made and adjudication does apply to certain warranties, parties may wish to avoid the operation of the Scheme for Construction Contracts (England and Wales) Regulations 1998.

BPF WARRANTY AGREEMENT – COWA/P&T

6.74   In 1990, the British Property Federation (BPF) produced a standard form collateral warranty in favour of third party funders of developments. The 1990 version was criticised and this led, in 1992, to the publication of an amended standard form in favour of purchasers and tenants. The warranty was approved by the Association of Consulting Engineers, the Royal Incorporation of Architects in Scotland, the Royal Institute of British Architects and the Royal Institution of Chartered Surveyors. In addition, without amendment, it was approved by the Association of British Insurers. The form is inappropriate for use by building contractors and sub-contractors. Main contractors, on a JCT development, should be requested, in the absence of a *bespoke* form, to supply the standard JCT main contractor warranty, MCWa/P&T and MCWa/F, and, for specialist sub-contractors, particularly those with a design input, *bespoke* warranties will continue to be the order of the day. There is a revised BPF funders' warranty, CoWa/F. It is identical to the CoWa/P&T warranty in all material respects subject to the provision for step-in rights.

6.75   The main clauses of the warranty are as follows:

Clause 1: The consultant's obligation is one of reasonable skill. The words 'and care/care and diligence' are inserted in parentheses. Sub-clause (a) defines the extent of recoverable loss. Consequential loss is excluded. The apparent restriction on the recovery of consequential losses may now be somewhat illusory. There has been a long and sometimes contradictory case-law on the recovery of so-called indirect losses other than consequential. In recent times, the courts have re-examined the question. *British Sugar plc v NEI Power Projects and Another*[1] confirmed, in a Court of Appeal judgment, that consequential loss is a general reference to indirect loss which might fall within the first limb of *Hadley v Baxendale*.[2] However, the words 'to the extent that the Purchaser/the Tenant is liable either directly or by way of financial contribution for the same' are confusing. They seem to exclude all claims by persons not under an obligation to carry out remedial works. The net contribution provision (sub-clause 1(b)) is confusing and unwieldy. In addition, there is a cap on liability. Sub-clause (c), although strangely worded, appears to have as its intention no more than that the liability under the warranty should be no greater than under the principal agreement.

Clause 2: The deleterious materials obligations are weaker than in certain bespoke warranties.

---

1   (1997/1998) CILL 1328.
2   (1854) 9 Ex 341.

Clause 5: In the copyright provision the purchaser/tenant can obtain a licence of the usual sort but only if the consultant has received 'payment of any fees agreed as properly due under the Appointment'. If there is a dispute, the purchaser's/tenant's licence is delayed.

Clause 6: Professional indemnity insurance clauses always cause problems. The nature of cover is not defined and the obligation to insure is subject to whether such insurance 'is available at commercially reasonable rates'. Is the test subjective or objective? It appears that the consultant can avoid liability to insure if he decides that 'such insurance ceases to be available at commercially reasonable rates'.

Clause 7: Even if it is not a real problem, the question of assignment is always an *emotional* problem. The BPF warranty aims to limit the number of assignments. Importantly, any assignment needs to comply with the requirements of *legal* assignment. Equitable assignment is inadequate.

Clause 9: This provides for a negotiated specific limitation period.

A wide selection of contractor and consultant warranties in favour of third party interests is set out in the Appendix to this chapter.

LATENT DEFECTS INSURANCE

6.76   In the absence of guidance from the courts, no one really knows with confidence how collateral warranties may operate in practice. In addition, they are expensive and time-consuming to negotiate, sometimes not resolved and on occasions put in place alongside a defective or non-existent principal 'contract'. These difficulties have led some commerical users of buildings to look at latent defects insurance. Non-cancellable insurance cover is provided for a period of up to 12 years for claims arising from the cost of repairing, renewing and/or strengthening the particular development in the event or threat of a latent defect causing physical damage or imminent collapse of the building dating from practical completion. Resultant damage to other elements of the insured building, including the cost of getting at the defect and reinstating other elements of the building which need to be dismantled to enable repair to take place, also fall within the cover. Where the building requires strengthening because of the likelihood of further damage occurring due to the inherent defects, such costs are also met under the policy. The beneficiary of the policy has secondary costs cover, including the removal of debris, consultancy fees and changes in building methods necessitated by Building Regulations approvals etc. The cover extends to building owners, occupiers and others with an insurable interest in the development for a period up to 12 years and is assignable.

Calculating the insured sum

6.77   Calculation of the insured sum is based on the total re-build cost calculated at the date of commencement of the policy, including, if required, the removal of debris and associated costs. The level of premium charged is calculated by reference to some or all of the following:

–   the type of building and its intended use;

- the location of the building;
- design and type of construction;
- foundations and site conditions;
- amounts of excess and indexation;
- duration of the construction period;
- period of cover;
- contract value;
- identity of project team;
- level of cover, ie including or excluding ingress of water, subrogation rights waived or intact, and other qualifications.

The cost of the premium generally varies from 0.05 per cent to 1.5 per cent including the cost of the technical audit, with the insurers always appointing an independent technical auditor to carry out an audit on their behalf.

6.78 The purpose of the technical audit is:

- preparation of initial risk appraisal;
- a design audit to assess structural adequacy;
- periodic visits to the works to check progress, monitor design compliance and changes, monitor quality control, level of supervision etc;
- preparation of reports to the underwriters at key construction phases;
- issue of a certificate of approval to the underwriters at the time of practical completion.

6.79 The fee payment will be staggered over the course of the construction phase, with a deposit payable prior to the commencement of construction and the last instalment paid prior to or at practical completion of the development. The cost of the technical audit is either included within the deposit or is sometimes payable in instalments during the construction phase. Under the BILD Latents Defects Policy the cost of the audit is included within the deposit. BILD is underwritten by Commercial Union and General Accident. Under a standard latent defects policy, insurers have subrogation rights against the project team. Under BILD, if required, cover can be arranged on the basis that insurers waive their rights. In addition to the material damage latent defects policy, it is possible to arrange cover for loss of revenue and loss of rent as a result of a latent defect. The agreed insurance period usually commences on practical completion following a certificate of approval from the technical auditor.

A standard BILD policy as used in the construction industry is appended by kind permission of Griffiths & Armour.

6.80 Recourse to the collateral warranty may become less common following legislative change. The Law Commission published its proposals in a consultative document, *Consultative Paper on Third Party Rights*, Law Commission Paper No 242, 31 July 1996. At the date of writing, the Contracts (Rights of Third Parties) Bill is before Parliament. It is almost certain to become law. At its heart, the Bill provides a partial statutory abolition of the common law doctrine of privity of contract, which was vigorously opposed in sectors of the construction industry. Under cl 1 of the Bill, parties will be able to enforce contractual terms, if either a party to them, or those terms purport to confer a benefit on them. The editors of *Construction Industry Law*

Letter[1] argue that 'these principles do not translate very happily into the context of a construction contract' and then pose a number of hypothetical situations which might lead to a greater number of potential liabilities because of the subjective element in interpreting the Bill. One example they pose is of the sub-contractor providing craneage to the main contractor who effectively is providing craneage for the lifting of other sub-contractors' materials.

The arrival of the Act, if such it becomes, will probably not remove the reliance on collateral warranties, such being the natural caution of lawyers. For the construction industry, cl 2 of the Bill looks unsatisfactory. Where a third party has rights under a contract, the others may not ordinarily 'cancel the contract, or vary it in such a way as to extinguish, or alter his entitlement under that right'. There are complex provisions to make this work, including appeals to the High Court to dispense with third party consent. However, it is anticipated parties will be able to exclude the operation of the Act, thereby returning squarely to the collateral warranty.

---

1   (1999) CILL 1481–1482.

Appendix

RELATIONSHIP OF PARTICIPANTS IN A CONSTRUCTION PROJECT: TRADITIONAL CONTRACTING

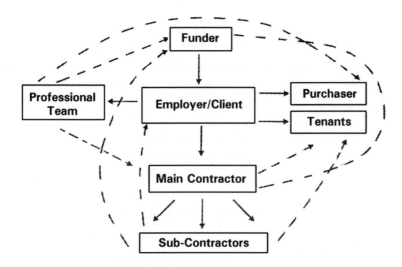

In traditional contracting, where the Professional Team continues to be employed by the Employer/Client the provision of collateral warranties will follow the broken lines.

RELATIONSHIP OF PARTICIPANTS IN A CONSTRUCTION PROJECT: DESIGN AND BUILD

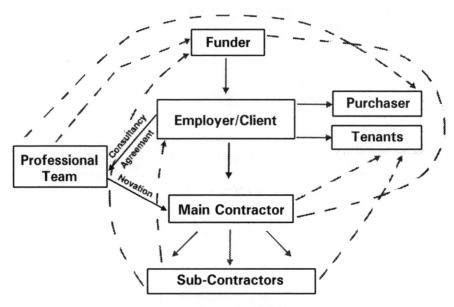

Under design and build schemes, the Professional Team will carry out preliminary design work for the Employer/Client but, on the appointment of the main contractor, will be novated to the Main Contractor for whom they will carry out the subsequent design work. The Employer/Client will, on novation, require a collateral warranty from the Professional Team, no longer being their Employer/Client. The other collateral warranties required remain as for traditional contracting.

JCT MAIN CONTRACTOR–FUNDER WARRANTY

Warranty Agreement

Note: This form is to be used where the Warranty is to be given to a company providing finance (Funder) for the proposed building Works to be carried out by a Contractor for an Employer. Where the Funder is acting as an agent for a syndicate of banks and/or other companies providing finance a recital should be added to refer to this as appropriate.

This Agreement

is made the   day of   19

Insert name of the Contractor.   (1) Between

of/whose registered office is situated at

('the Contractor') and

Insert name of the Employer.   (2)

of/whose registered office is situated at

('the Employer'), and

Insert name of the Funder.   (3)

of/whose registered office is situated at

('the Funder' which term

shall include all permitted assignees under this Agreement).

Whereas

A   The Funder has entered into an agreement ('the Finance Agreement') with the Employer for the provision of certain finance in connection with the carrying out of building works

Insert description of the building works.

at

('the Works' which term

shall include any changes made to the builidng works in accordance with the Building Contract referred to in recital B).

B   By a contract ('the Building Contract' which term shall include any enforceable agreements reached between the Employer and the Contractor and which arise out of and relate to the same)

Insert date.
Delete as
appropriate.

dated

the Employer has appointed the Contractor to carry out and
complete the Works/the Works by phased Sections.

Now it is hereby agreed

In consideration of the payment of one pound (£1) to the Contractor,
receipt of which the Contractor acknowledges:

1   The Contractor warrants that it has complied and will continue to
    comply with the Building Contract. In the event of any breach of this
    Warranty:

    (a) the Contractor's liability to the Funder under this Agreement
        shall be limited to that proportion of the Funder's loss by reason
        of the breach which it would be just and equitable to require the
        Contractor to pay having regard to the extent of the Contractor's
        responsibility for the same and on the basis that

Insert names of other
Warrantors.

*The Consultants'
warranty to a person
providing finance for
a proposed
development
prepared and
approved for use by
the British Property
Federation, the
Association of
Consulting
Engineers, the Royal
Incorporation of
Architects in
Scotland, the Royal
Institute of British
Architects and the
Royal Institution of
Chartered Surveyors.

    shall be deemed to have provided contractual undertakings in
    the terms of the *Warranty CoWa/F to the Funder in respect
    of the perforamance of their services in connection with the
    Works and shall be deemed to have paid to the Funder such
    proportion which it would be just and equitable for them to
    pay having regard to the extent of their responsibility;

    (b) the Contractor shall be entitled in any action or proceedings by
        the Funder to rely on any limitation in the Building Contract and
        to raise the equivalent rights in defence of liability as it would
        have against the Employer under the Building Contract.

2   Without prejudice to the generality of clause 1, the Contractor
    further warrants that, unless required by the Building Contractor or
    unless otherwise authorised in writing by the Employer or by the
    Architect/the Contract Administrator named in or appointed pursu-
    ant to the Building Contract (or, where such authorisation is given
    orally, confirmed in writing by the Contractor to the Employer
    and/or the Architect/the Contract Administrator), none of the
    following has been or will be used in the Works:

    (a) high alumina cement in structural elements;

    (b) wood wool slabs in permanent formwork to concrete;

    (c) calcium chloride in admixtures for use in reinforced concrete;

    (d) asbestos products;

    (e) naturally occurring aggregates for use in reinforced concrete
        which do not comply with British Standard 882: 1983 and/or
        naturally occurring aggregates for use in concrete which do not
        comply with British Standard 8110: 1985;

Further specific
materials may be
added by agreement.

    (f)

3   The Funder has no authority to issue any direction or instruction to the Contractor in relation to the Building Contract unless and until the Funder has given notice under clauses 4 or 5. The Funder has no liability to the Contractor in relation to amounts due under the Building Contract unless and until the Funder has given notice under clause 4 or clause 5.

4   In the event of the termination of the Finance Agreement by the Funder the Contractor will, if so required by notice in writing given by the Funder and subject to clause 6, accept the instructions of the Funder or its appointee to the exclusion of the Employer in respect of the Works upon the terms and conditions of the Building Contract. The Employer acknowledges that the Contractor shall be entitled to rely on a notice given to the Contractor by the Funder under this clause 4 as conclusive evidence for the purposes of this Agreement of the termination of the Finance Agreement by the Funder; and further acknowledges that such acceptance of the instructions of the Funder to the exclusion of the Employer shall not constitute any breach of the Contractor's obligations to the Employer under the Building Contract.

5(1)   The Contractor shall not exercise any right of determination of his employment under the Building Contract without having first

(a) copied to the Funder any written notices required by the Building Contract to be sent to the Architect/the Contract Administrator or to the Employer prior to the Contractor being entitled to give notice under the Building Contract that his employment under the Building Contract is determined, and

(b) given to the Funder written notice that he has the right under the Building Contract forthwith to notify the Employer that his employment under the Building Contract is determined.

5(2)   The Contractor shall not treat the Building Contract as having been repudiated by the Employer without having first given to the Funder written notice that he intends to so inform the Employer.

5(3)   The Contractor shall not

– issue any notification to the Employer to which clause 5(1)(b) refers

or

– inform the Employer that he is treating the Building Contract as having been repudiated by the Employer as referred to in clause 5(2)

Insert any different number that has been agreed and delete '7'.

before the lapse of 7   days from receipt by the Funder of the written notice by the Contractor which the Contractor is required to give under clause 5(1)(b) or clause 5(2).

Insert any different
number that has
been agreed and
delete '7'.

5(4)   The Funder may, not later than the expiry of the 7   days
referred to in clause 5(3) require the Contractor by notice in writing
and subject to clause 6 to accept the instructions of the Funder or its
appointee to the exclusion of the Employer in respect of the Works
upon the terms and conditions of the Building Contract. The
Employer acknowledges that the Contractor shall be entitled to rely
on a notice given to the Contractor by the Funder under clause 5(4)
and that acceptance by the Contractor of the instruction of the
Funder to the exclusion of the Employer shall not constitute any
breach of the Contractor's obligations to the Employer under the
Building Contract. Provided that, subject to clause 6, nothing in
clause 5(4) shall relieve the Contractor of any liability he may have
to the Employer for any breach by the Contractor of the Building
Contract or where the Contractor has wrongfully served notice
under the Building Contract that he is entitled to determine his
employment under the Building Contract or has wrongfully treated
the Building Contract as having been repudiated by the Employer.

6   It shall be a condition of any notice given by the Funder under clause
4 or clause 5(4) that the Funder or its appointee accepts liability for
payment of the sums certified as due/properly due to the Contractor
under the Building Contract and for performance of the Employer's
obligations thereunder including payment of any sums outstanding
at the date of such notice. Upon the issue of any notice by the Funder
under clause 4 or clause 5(4), the Building Contract shall continue in
full force and effect as if no right of determination of his
employment under the Building Contract, nor any right of the
Contractor to treat the Building Contract as having been repudiated
by the Employer, had arisen and the Contractor shall be liable to the
Funder and its appointee under the Building Contract in lieu of its
liability to the Employer. If any notice given by the Funder under
clause 4 or clause 5(4) requires the Contractor to accept the
instructions of the Funder's appointee, the Funder shall be liable to
the Contractor as guarantor for the payment of all sums from time to
time due to the Contractor from the Funder's appointee.

Delete if not
applicable.

7   The copyright in all drawings, reports, models, specifications, bills
of quantities, calculations and other documents and information
prepared by or on behalf of the Contractor in connection with the
Works (together referred to in this clause 7 as 'the Documents')
shall remain vested in the Contractor but, subject to the Employer
having discharged his obligation to pay all monies certified as
due/properly due under the Building Contract, the Funder or its
appointee shall have a licence to copy and use the Documents and to
reproduce the designs and content of them for any purpose related to
the Building Contract including, but without limitation, the construction, completion, maintenance, letting, promotion, advertisement, reinstatement, refurbishment and repair of the Works. Such
licence shall enable the Funder or its appointee to copy and use the
Documents for the extension of the Works but such use shall not
include a licence to reproduce the designs contained in them for any
extension of the Works. The Contractor shall not be liable for
any use by the Funder or its appointee of any of the Documents for

any purpose other than that for which the same were prepared by or on behalf of the Contractor.

Delete clause 8 except where the Building Contract is on the JCT Standard Form of Building Contract with Contractor's Design 1981 Edition (WCD81) **or** on the JCT Standard Form of Building Contract 1980 Edition (JCT80) which is modified by the Contractor's Designed Portion Supplement and/or includes Performance Specified Work to which clause 42 of JCT80 applies.

*Insert Amount.
**Insert period.

8   The Contractor shall take out and maintain professional indemnity insurance in an amount of* pounds (£   ) for any one claim and in all in any one period of insurance for a period of** years from the date of Practical Completion of the Works (or of practical completion of a Section of the Works where the Building Contract is modified for completion by phased sections) under the Building Contract, provided such insurance is available at commercially reasonable rates. The Contractor shall immediately inform the Funder if such insurance is not or ceases to be available at commercially reasonable rates in order that the Contractor and the Funder can discuss the means of best protecting the Contractor in the absence of such insurance. As and when it is reasonably requested to do so by the Funder or its appointee, the Contractor shall produce for inspection documentary evidence that its professional indemnity insurance is being maintained.

9   This Agreement may be assigned by the Funder by way of absolute legal assignment to another person providing finance or re-finance in connection with the carrying out of the Works without the consent of the Employer or the Contractor being required and such assignment shall be effective upon written notice thereof being given to the Employer and to the Contractor. No further or other assignment of this Agreement shall be permitted save as is expressly provided for herein.

10   Any notice to be given by the Contractor or the Employer hereunder shall be deemed to be duly given if it is delivered by hand at or sent by registered post or recorded delivery to the Funder at its registered office; and any notice given by the Funder hereunder shall be deemed to be duly given if it is delivered by hand, or sent by registered post or recorded delivery to the Employer or the Contractor at its registered office; and, in the case of any such notices, the same shall if sent by registered post or recorded delivery be deemed (subject to proof to the contrary) to have been received forty-eight hours after being posted.

Insert number of years.

11   No action or proceedings for any breach of this Agreement shall be commenced against the Contractor after the expiry of   years from the date of Practical Completion of the Works under the Building Contract or, where the Building Contract is modified for completion by phased sections, no action or proceedings for any breach of this Agreement shall be commenced against the Contractor in respect of any Section after the expiry of   years from the date of practical completion of such Section.

12   The construction validity and performance of this Agreement shall be governed by English law and the parties agree to submit to the non-exclusive jurisdiction of the English Courts.

Notes

[A1] **AS WITNESS THE HANDS OF THE PARTIES HERETO**

[A1] For Agreement
executed under hand and
NOT as a deed.

[A1] Signed by or on behalf of the Funder

    in the presence of:

[A1] Signed by or on behalf of the Employer

    in the presence of:

[A1] Signed by or on behalf of the Contractor

    in the presence of:

- -

[A2] For Agreement
executed as a deed under the
law of England and Wales by
a company or other body
corporate: insert the name of
the party mentioned and
identified on page 1 and then
use *either* [A3] and [A4] *or*
[A5].
If the party is an *individual*
see note [A6].

[A2] **EXECUTED AS A DEED BY THE FUNDER**
    hereinbefore mentioned namely

[A3]   by affixing its common seal

[A4]   in the presence of:

[A3] For use if the party is
using its common seal, which
should be affixed under the
party's name.

[A4] For use of the party's
officers authorised to affix its
common seal.

    *OR -

[A5] For use if the party is a
company registered under the
Companies Acts which is not
using a common seal: insert
the names of the two officers
by whom the company is
acting *who MUST be either a
director and the company
secretary or two directors*,
and insert their signatures
with 'Director' or 'Secretary'
as appropriate. *This method
of execution is NOT valid for
local authorities or certain
other bodies incorporated by
Act of Parliament or by
charter if exempted under
s 718(2) of the Companies
Act 1985.*

[A5]   acting by a director and its secretary*/two directors*
    whose signatures are here subscribed:
      namely

    [Signature]   *DIRECTOR*

    and

    [Signature]   *SECRETARY*/DIRECTOR**

[A2] For Agreement executed as a deed under the law of England and Wales by a company or other body corporate: insert the name of the party mentioned and identified on page 1 and then use *either* [A3] and [A4] *or* [A5].
If the party is an *individual* see note [A6].

[A3] For use if the party is using its common seal, which should be affixed under the party's name.

[A4] For use of the party's officers authorised to affix its common seal.

[A5] For use if the party is a company registered under the Companies Acts which is not using a common seal: insert the names of the two officers by whom the company is acting *who MUST be either a director and the company secretary or two directors*, and insert their signatures with 'Director' or 'Secretary' as appropriate. *This method of execution is NOT valid for local authorities or certain other bodies incorporated by Act of Parliament or by charter if exempted under s 718(2) of the Companies Act 1985.*

[A2] **EXECUTED AS A DEED BY THE EMPLOYER**
hereinbefore mentioned namely

[A3]   by affixing its common seal

[A4]   in the presence of:
*OR ---

[A5]   acting by a director and its secretary*/two directors* whose signatures are here subscribed:
      namely

    [Signature]   *DIRECTOR*

    and

    [Signature]   *SECRETARY*/DIRECTOR**

[A2] **AND AS A DEED BY THE CONTRACTOR**
hereinbefore mentioned namely

[A3]   by affixing hereto its common seal

[A4]   in the presence of:

*OR ---

[A5]   acting by a director and its secretary*/two directors* whose signatures are here subscribed:
      namely

    [Signature]   *DIRECTOR*

    and

    [Signature]   *SECRETARY*/DIRECTOR**

[A6] If executed as a deed by
an *individual* ... insert the
the name at [A2], delete the
words at [A3], substitute
'whose signature is here
subscribed' and insert the
individual's signature. The
individual MUST sign in the
presence of a witness who
attests the signature. Insert at
[A4] the signature and name
of the witness. Sealing by an
individual is not required.   **Delete as appropriate*

[Reproduced by kind permission of the Joint Contracts Tribunal.]

JCT MAIN CONTRACTOR–PURCHASER/TENANT WARRANTY

Warranty Agreement

This Agreement

is made the   day of   19

Insert name of the Contractor.

(1) Between

of/whose registered office is situated at

('the Contractor') and

Insert name of the Purchaser/the Tenant.

(2)

of/whose registered office is situated at

Delete as appropriate.

('the Purchaser'/'the Tenant' which term shall include all permitted assignees under this Agreement).

Whereas

Delete as appropriate.

A   The Purchaser/the Tenant has entered into an agreement to purchase/and agreement to lease/a lease with

('the Employer')

Insert description of the premises agreed to be purchased/leased.

relating to

Delete as appropriate.

forming the whole/a part of

Insert description and address of the Works.

at

('the Works')

B   By a contract ('the Building Contract' which term shall include any enforceable agreements reached between the Employer and the Contractor and which arise out of and relate to the same)

Insert date of Building Contract.

dated

The Employer has appointed the Contractor to carry out and complete

*   the Works which reached Practical Completion

Insert date.

on   (date)

**   the Works by phased Sections, where the Building Contract is modified for completion by such Sections, and the relevant Section reached practical completion

Insert date.

on   (date)

Delete as
appropriate.

as certified by the Architect/the Contract Administrator/as stated by the Employer under the relevant provisions of the Building Contract.

* Delete if the
Works are to be
completed by phased
Sections in
accordance with the
Building Contract.
** Delete if the
Works are not to be
completed by phased
Sections.

Now it is hereby agreed

In consideration of the payment of one pound (£1) by the Purchaser/the Tenant to the Contractor, receipt of which the Contractor acknowledges:

1   The Contractor warrants that it has carried out the Works in accordance with the Building Contract. In the event of any breach of this warranty:

2   (a) subject to paragraphs (b) and (c) of this clause, the Contractor shall be liable for the reasonable costs of repair renewal and/or reinstatement of any part or parts of the Works to the extent that
– the Purchaser/the Tenant incurs such costs and/or
– the Purchaser/the Tenant is liable either directly or by way of financial contribution for such costs.

The Contractor shall not be liable for other losses incurred by the Purchaser/the Tenant;

(b) the Contractor's liability for costs under this Agreement shall be limited to that proportion of such costs which it would be just and equitable to require the Contractor to pay having regard to the extent of the Contractor's responsibility for the same and on the basis that

Insert names of other
intended Warrantors.

*The Consultants' Warranty to a Purchaser or Tenant issued by the British Property Federation and approved for use by the British Property Federation, the Association of Consulting Engineers, the Royal Incorporation of Architects in Scotland, the Royal Institute of British Architects and the Royal Institution of Chartered Surveyors.

shall be deemed to have provided contractual undertakings in the terms of the *Warranty CoWa/P&T to the Purchaser/the Tenant in respect of the performance of their services in connection with the Works and shall be deemed to have paid to the Purchaser/the Tenant such proportion which it would be just and equitable for them to pay having regard to the extent of their responsibility;

(c) the Contractor shall be entitled in any action or proceedings by the Purchaser/the Tenant to rely on any limitation in the Building Contract and raise the equivalent rights in defence of liability as it would have against the Employer under the Building Contract;

(d) the obligations of the Contractor under or pursuant to this clause 1 shall not be increased or diminished by the appointment of any person by the Purchaser/the Tenant to carry out any independent enquiry into any relevant matter.

Without prejudice to the generality of clause 1, the Contractor further warrants that, unless required by the Building Contract or unless otherwise authorised in writing by the Employer or by the Architect/the Contract Administrator named in the Building Contract (or, where such authorisation is given orally, confirmed in writing by the Contractor to the Employer and/or the Architect/the Contract Administrator), none of the following has been used in the Works:

(a) high alumina cement in structural elements;

(b) wood wool slabs in permanent formwork to concrete;

(c) calcium chloride in admixtures for use in reinforced concrete;

(d) asbestos products;

(e) naturally occurring aggregates for use in reinforced concrete which do not comply with British Standard 882: 1983 and/or naturally occurring aggregates for use in concrete which do not comply with British Standard 8110: 1985;

Further specific materials may be added by agreement.

(f)

In the event of any breach of the warranty in this clause the provisions of clauses 1(a), 1(b), 1(c) and 1(d) shall apply.

3 The Contractor acknowledges that the Employer has duly discharged his obligation to pay all sums properly due/certified as due to the Contractor under the Building Contract up to the date of this Agreement or up to the date of Practical Completion of the Works (or of practical completion of a Section of the Works where the Building Contract is modified for completion by phased sections) whichever date is the later.

4 The Purchaser/the Tenant has no authority to issue any direction or instruction to the Contractor in relation to the Building Contract.

Delete clause 5 where not applicable.

5   The copyright in all drawings, reports, models, specifications, bills of quantities, calculations and other documents and information prepared by or on behalf of the Contractor in connection with the Works (together referred to in this clause 5 as 'the Documents') shall remain vested in the Contractor but, subject to the Employer having duly discharged his obligation to pay all monies properly due/certified as due under the Building Contract, the Purchaser/the Tenant and its appointee shall have a licence to copy and use the Documents and to reproduce the designs and content of them for any purpose related to the Building Contract including, but without limitation, the construction, completion, maintenance, letting, promotion, advertisement, resinstatement, refurbishment and repair of the Works. Such licence shall enable the Purchaser/the Tenant and its appointee to copy and use the Documents for the extension of the Works but such use shall not include a licence to reproduce the designs contained in them for any extension of the Works. The Contractor shall not be liable for any use by the Purchaser/the Tenant or its appointee of any of the Documents for any purpose other than that for which the same were prepared by or on behalf of the Contractor.

Delete clause 6 except where the Building Contract is on the JCT Standard Form of Building Contract with Contractor's Design 1981 Edition (WCD 81) or on the JCT Standard Form of Building Contract 1980 Edition (JCT 80) which is modified by the Contractor's Designed Portion Supplement and/or includes Performance Specified Work to which clause 42 of JCT 80 applies.

6   The Contractor shall take out and maintain professional indemnity insurance in an amount of* pounds (£) for any one claim and in all in any one period of insurance

for a period of** years from the date of Practical Completion of the Works (or of practical completion of a Section of the Works where the Building Contract is modified for completion by phased sections) under the Building Contract, provided always that at the date of this Agreement and thereafter such insurance is available at commercially reasonable rates. The Contractor shall immediately inform the Purchaser/the Tenant if such insurance is not or ceases to be available at commercially reasonable rates in order that Contractor and the Purchaser/the Tenant can discuss the means of best protecting the Contractor in the absence of such insurance. As and when it is reasonably requested to do so by the Purchaser/the Tenant or its appointee, the Contractor shall produce for inspection documentary evidence that its professional indemnity insurance is being maintained.

*Insert amount.   **Insert period.

Insert number of times.

7   This agreement may be assigned by the Purchaser/the Tenant by way of absolute legal assignment to another person taking an assignment of the Purchaser's/the Tenant's interest in the Works without the consent of the Contractor being required and such assignment shall be effective upon written notice thereof being given to the Contractor. No further or other assignment of this Agreement shall be permitted save as is expressly provided for herein.

8   Any notice to be given by the Contractor hereunder shall be deemed to be duly given if it is delivered by hand at or sent by registered post or recorded delivery to the Purchaser/the Tenant at its registered office and any notice given by the Purchaser/the Tenant hereunder shall be deemed to be duly given if it is delivered by hand at or sent by registered post or recorded delivery to the Contractor at its registered office, and, in the case of any such notices, the same shall if sent by registered post or recorded delivery be deemed (subject to proof to the contrary) to have been received forty-eight hours after being posted.

Insert number of years.

9   No action or proceedings for any breach of this Agreement shall be commenced against the Contractor after the expiry of   years from the date of Practical Completion of the Works under the Building Contract or, where the Building Contract is modified for completion by phased sections, no action or proceedings for any breach of this Agreement shall be commenced against the Contractor in respect of any Section after the expiry of   years from the date of practical completion of such Section.

10   The construction validity and performance of this Agreement shall be governed by English law and the parties agree to submit to the non-exclusive jurisdiction of the English Courts.

Notes

[A1] AS WITNESS THE HANDS OF THE PARTIES HERETO

[A1] Signed by or on behalf of the Purchaser/the Tenant

      in the presence of:

[A1] Signed by or on behalf of the Contrator

      in the presence of:

- -

[A2] For Agreement
executed as a deed under the
law of England and Wales by
a company or other body
corporate: insert the name of
the party mentioned and
identified on page 1 and then
use *either* [A3] and [A4] *or*
[A5].
If the party is an *individual*
see note [A6].

[A3] For use if the party is
using its common seal, which
should be affixed under the
party's name.

[A4] For use of the party's
officers authorised to affix its
common seal.

[A2] EXECUTED AS A DEED BY THE PURCHASER/THE TENANT
      hereinbefore mentioned namely

[A3]   by affixing its common seal

[A4]   in the presence of:

*OR -

[A5] For use if the party is a
company registered under the
Companies Acts which is not
using a common seal: insert
the names of the two officers
by whom the company is
acting *who MUST be either a
director and the company
secretary or two directors,*
and insert their signatures
with 'Director' or 'Secretary'
as appropriate. *This method
of execution is NOT valid for
local authorities or certain
other bodies incorporated by
Act of Parliament or by
charter if exempted under
s 718(2) of the Companies
Act 1985.*

[A5]   acting by a director and its secretary*/two directors*
    whose signatures are here subscribed:
       namely

    [Signature]   *DIRECTOR*

    and

    [Signature]   *SECRETARY*/DIRECTOR**

[A2] AND AS A DEED BY THE CONTRACTOR
      hereinbefore mentioned namely

[A3]   by affixing its common seal

[A4]   in the presence of:

*OR -

[A6] If executed as a deed by an *individual* … insert the the name at [A2], delete the words at [A3], substitute 'whose signature is here subscribed' and insert the individual's signature. The individual MUST sign in the presence of a witness who attests the signature. Insert at [A4] the signature and name of the witness. Sealing by an individual is not required.

[A5]   acting by a director and its secretary*/two directors* whose signatures are here subscribed:

  namely

[Signature]   DIRECTOR

and

[Signature]   SECRETARY*/DIRECTOR*

*Delete as appropriate.

[Reproduced by kind permission of the Joint Contracts Tribunal.]

BESPOKE SHORT FORM OF MAIN CONTRACTOR WARRANTY

THIS DEED is made on [*date*] BETWEEN:

(1)   [*name*] ('the Purchaser/Tenant') (which expression shall where the context so admits include its successors in title and assigns) whose registered office is situated at [*address*];

(2)   [*name*] ('the Contractor') whose registered office is situated at [*address*]; and

(3)   [*name*] ('the Employer') (which expression shall, where the context so admits, include its successors in title and assigns) whose registered office is situated at

WHEREAS:

(A)   The Contractor has entered into an agreement with the Employer dated [*date*] ('the Building Contract') to carry out the construction of certain works as described therein in connection with a development at [*address*] ('the Development').

(B)   The Purchaser/Tenant intends to enter or has entered into an agreement to purchase/lease from the Employer the whole or part of the Development when completed.

(C)   Pursuant to the Building Contract the Contractor has agreed with the Employer to execute a deed of warranty in the form of this Deed in favour of the Purchaser/Tenant.

NOW IT IS HEREBY AGREED as follows:

1   The Contractor hereby warrants to and undertakes with the Purchaser/Tenant that he has carried out and will carry out each and all of his obligations, duties and undertakings under the Building Contract strictly in accordance with its terms. Provided that the Contractor shall have no greater liability to the Purchaser/Tenant under this Deed than he would have had if the Purchaser/Tenant had been named as 'the Employer' under the Building Contract.

2   Notwithstanding the date of the Deed, no action may be commenced by the Purchaser/Tenant under this Deed after the expiry of 12 years from the date of practical completion of the Development under the Building Contract.

   In any action brought by the Purchaser/Tenant, for alleged breach of this Deed the Contractor shall have available to him the rights to all the defences that may have been available to him under the Building Contract.

IN WITNESS whereof the parties hereto have executed this Document as a Deed the day and the year before written

Purchaser/Tenant:

Director [*and insert name of* ....
Company Secretary or second   Director
Director] for and on behalf of

....
                                             Director/Company Secretary

Contractor: . . . .
Signed by [*insert name of*   Director
Director] and [*insert name of*
Company Secretary or second
Director] for and on behalf of

. . . .
                                                  Director/Company Secretary

Employer: . . . .
Signed by [*insert name of*   Director
Director] and [*insert name of*
Company Secretary or second
Director] for and on behalf of

. . . .
                                                  Director/Company Secretary

BESPOKE FORM OF CONTRACTOR–BANK/FUND WARRANTY

THIS DEED is made on [*date*] BETWEEN:

(1)   [*name*] ('the Bank/Fund') (which expression shall, where the context so admits, include its successors in title and assigns) and whose registered office is situated at [*address*];

(2)   [*name*] ('the Contractor') whose registered office is situated at [*address*];

(3)   [*name*] ('the Employer') (which expression shall, where the contract so admits, include its successors in title and assigns) whose registered office is situated at

WHEREAS:

(A)   The Employer has entered into an agreement with the Contractor dated [*date*] ('the Building Contract') to carry out the construction of certain works as described therein in connection with a development at [*address*] ('the Development').

(B)   The Bank/Fund intends to enter into or has entered into an agreement ('the Finance Agreement') with the Employer for the provision of finance in connection with the Development.

(C)   Pursuant to the Building Contract the Contractor has agreed with the Employer to execute a deed of warranty in the form of this Deed in favour of the Bank/Fund.

NOW IT IS HEREBY AGREED as follows:

1   The Contractor hereby warrants to and undertakes with the Bank/Fund that he has carried out and will carry out each and all of his obligations, duties and undertakings under the Building Contract strictly in accordance with its terms. Provided that the Contractor shall have no greater liability to the Bank/Fund under this Deed than he would have had if the Bank/Fund had been named as 'the Employer' under the Building Contract.

[2   The Contractor undertakes to ensure that the Bank/Fund is named as a joint insured under any policy of insurance taken out by the Contractor in accordance with Clause [   ] of the Building Contract. Upon execution of this Agreement and from time to time thereafter when reasonably requested by the Bank/Fund the Contractor shall provide to the Bank/Fund written evidence that such policy of insurance has been taken out and is being maintained by the Contractor.]

3   This Deed may, without the consent of the Contractor, be assigned by the Bank/Fund by way of absolute legal assignment to another person who from time to time intends to enter into or who has from time to time entered into an agreement with the Employer to the Employer's assigns for the provision of finance in connection with the Development and the assignment of this Deed shall be effective upon written notice thereof being given to the Contractor.

4   Any notice to be given by any party under this Deed shall be deemed to be duly given if it is delivered by hand or sent by registered post or recorded delivery to the registered office or place of business from time to time of the recipient and if so sent by registered post or recorded delivery shall be deemed to have been received 48 hours after being posted.

5   The Contractor agrees that, in the event of the termination of the Finance Agreement by the Bank/Fund, the Contractor will, if so required by notice in writing given by the Bank/Fund, accept the instructions of the Bank/Fund or its appointee in respect of the carrying out and completion of the Development upon the terms and conditions of the Building Contract. Provided always that the Bank/Fund or its appointee shall, by such notice, accept liability for payment of the amounts payable to the Contractor and for performance of the Employer's obligations under the Building Contract, including payment of any such amounts outstanding at the date of such notice.

6   The Contractor further agrees that he will not without first giving the Bank/Fund not less than 14 days' previous notice in writing, exercise any right he may have to terminate the Building Contract or to treat the same as having been repudiated by the Employer or discontinue the performance of any duties to be performed by the Contractor pursuant thereto. The Contractor's right to terminate the Building Contract or treat the same as having been repudiated, or to discontinue performance shall cease if, within such period of notice, the Bank/Fund shall give notice in writing to the Contractor requiring the Contractor to accept the instructions of the Bank/Fund or its appointee in respect of the carrying out and completion of the Development upon the terms and conditions of the Building Contract. Provided always that the Bank/Fund or its appointee shall, by such notice, accept liability for payment of the amounts payable to the Contractors under the Building Contract and for performance of the Employer's obligations under the Building Contract, including payment of any such amounts outstanding at the date of such notice.

7   Notwithstanding the date of the Deed, no action may be commenced by the Bank/Fund under this Deed after the expiry of 12 years form the date of practical completion of the development under the Building Contract.

8   In any action brought by the Bank/Fund, for alleged Breach of this Deed the Contractor shall have available to him the rights to all the defences that may have been available to him under the Building Contract.

IN WITNESS whereof the parties hereto have executed this Document as a Deed the day and year first before written.

Bank/Fund:
Signed by [*insert name of*   . . . .
Director] and [*insert name of*   Director
Company Secretary or second
Director] for and on behalf of

. . . .
                                               Director/Company Secretary

Contractor: . . . .
Signed by [*insert name of*   Director
Director] and [*insert name of*
Company Secretary or second
Director] for and on behalf of

. . . .
                                               Director/Company Secretary

Employer:

Signed by [*insert name of Director*] and [*insert name of Company Secretary or second Director*] for and on behalf of

. . . .

. . . .

Director

. . . .

Director/Company Secretary

BESPOKE CONTRACTOR'S WARRANTY DEED WITH PROVISION FOR FULL DELETERIOUS MATERIALS AND GUARANTOR OF OBLIGATIONS

DATE

BETWEEN:

(1) [*name*] (Company No. [*company number*]) whose registered office is at [*address*] ('the Building Contractor')

(2) [*name*] (Company No. [*company number*]) whose registered office is at [*address*] ('the Employer')

(3) [*name*] whose registered office is at [*address*] which expression where the context admits shall include its successors in title and assigns ('the Company')

(4) [*name*] (Company No. [*company number*]) whose registered office is at [*address*] and [*name*] (Company No. [*company number*]) whose registered office is at [*address*] and whose address for service in the United Kingdom is [*address*] (together 'the Guarantor')

WHEREAS:

(A) This Deed is supplemental to a building contract ('the Building Contract') dated [*date*] made between the Employer of the one part and the Building Contractor of the other part whereby the Building Contractor undertook to carry out the total design and construction of the development briefly described in the Schedule to this Deed and more particularly described in the Building Contract ('the Development').

(B) The Company has agreed under the provisions of an agreement ('the Development Agreement') dated [*date*] to engage the Employer in connection with the Development conditionally upon (inter alia) the Building Contractor entering into direct obligations towards the Company in the manner hereinafter appearing.

(C) The Company has an interest in the performance of the Building Contract by the Building Contractor and the Building Contractor and the Guarantor have agreed to enter into this Deed for the Company's benefit.

(D) The Company has appointed [*name*] ('the Company's Surveyor') to act on its behalf in connection with the Development.

NOW in consideration of £1 (one pound) paid by the Company to the Building Contractor (receipt of which the Building Contractor hereby acknowledges)

THIS DEED WITNESSETH as follows:

1   The Building Contractor hereby warrants to and undertakes with the Company:

1.1   that it has been engaged by the Employer under the Building Contract as building contractor to carry out the total design and construction of the Development;

1.2   that the Building Contractor has or will fully carry out its duties in respect of the Development in accordance with the terms of the Building Contract in a good substantial and workmanlike manner and that it has exercised and will continue to exercise all the reasonable skill care and diligence to be expected of a properly qualified and competent contractor experienced in designing and carrying out projects of a similar scope size and complexity as the Development;

1.3   without prejudice to the generality of Clause 1.2 the Building Contractor hereby warrants to the Company as follows:

  1.3.1   that the Building Contractor has exercised and will exercise all reasonable skill, care and diligence as aforesaid in the selection of goods and materials for the Development or any part of the Development;

  1.3.2   that the Development is/when completed will be fit for use and occupation;

  1.3.3.   that all the materials and components to be incorporated in the Development comply/shall comply with the provisions of any contract documents referred to in the Building Contract;

1.4   that the Building Contractor has not used or specified and will not specify for use and has exercised and will continue to exercise reasonable skill care and diligence as aforesaid to see that the Development shall be carried out without the inclusion therein of any of the following:

  1.4.1   high alumina cement;

  1.4.2   wood wool slabs in permanent formwork;

  1.4.3   calcium chloride in admixtures for use in concrete or mortar;

  1.4.4   asbestos or asbestos based products;

  1.4.5   concrete which does not comply with British Standard 882: 1983 and/or naturally occurring aggregates for use in concrete which do not comply with British Standard 8110: 1985;

  1.4.6   aggregates susceptible to alkali reaction;

  1.4.7.   urea formaldehyde foam;

  1.4.8   silicate bricks or tiles or board;

  1.4.9   PCB transformers;

  1.4.10   equatorial hardwoods from renewable sources;

  1.4.11   re-wirable fuses;

  1.4.12   ionizing lightning conductors;

  1.4.13   halons or chlorofluorocarbons;

  1.4.14   materials involving the release of chlorofluorocarbons in their manufacture or use or disposal;

  1.4.15   chipboard for flooring (other than as an infill material to steel raised access floor panels) and cill boards;

  1.4.16   lead or materials containing lead in circumstances where they may be ingested inhaled or absorbed;

  1.4.17   mineral wool or similar in a form which could readily result in the release of fibres in the course of normal occupancy or maintenance or materials containing fibres of less than three microns in diameter and a length of 22 microns or less or which contain any fibres not sealed or otherwise stabilised to ensure that fibre migration is prevented;

  1.4.18   polyisocynurate or polyurethane foam;

  1.4.19   any other materials or combination of materials which do not comply with any relevant British Standard Specification or Code of Practice at the time of specification or which an appropriately qualified and competent building contractor experienced in projects of a similar size scope and complexity to the Development would know to be deleterious;

  AND the Building Contractor shall within one month after practical completion of the Development if required issue written confirmation to the Company that:

| 1.4.19.1 | it has not used or specified for use any such materials in relation to the Development or any part of it; |
| 1.4.19.2 | the Development has been designed and constructed in accordance in all respects with all planning permissions and building regulation consents for the Development and all other statutory requirements; |

1.5   that the Building Contractor agrees that the Company shall be deemed to have relied exclusively upon the reasonable skill, care and diligence of the Building Contractor in relation to the performance by the Building Contractor of its obligations under the Building Contract

Provided always that the Building Contractor shall have no greater liability to the Company than it would have had if the Company had been named as employer under the Building Contract.

2   The Building Contractor hereby agrees with the Company:

2.1   in the event of the Company serving upon the Building Contractor a copy of any certificate issued by the Company's Surveyor stating that the Employer is in default under the Development Agreement; or

2.2   in the event that the Building Contractor notifies the Company that it intends to exercise any right it has to terminate the Building Contract (and the Building Contractor hereby undertakes to give the Company not less than 21 days' written notice of such intention);

the Company shall be entitled (but without giving rise to any obligation to do so) to serve on the Building Contractor notice of novation of the Building Contract such notice to be in writing.

3   In the event that the Company shall serve notice of novation pursuant to Clause 2 then with effect from the date of service of such notice the Building Contract shall be read and construed and continue in full force and effect as though the Company had originally executed the same as employer to the intent that all obligations and liabilities due by or to the Employer to or from the Building Contractor (whether arising before or after the date of such notice) shall be undertaken, performed and accepted by or to the Company.

4   The Company shall have no liability to the Building Contractor under the terms of this Deed save and to the extent that the Building Contract is novated pursuant to Clause 2 hereof.

5   The Employer by its execution of these presents acknowledges and agrees to the terms of this agreement and in particular agrees that the Building Contractor may accept the instructions of the Company in the circumstances envisaged by Clause 2 hereof accepting any certificate of the Company's Surveyor that the Employer is in default under the Development Agreement but nothing herein shall as between the Company and the Employer affect the rights and obligations of the parties thereunder.

6   The Building Contractor hereby agrees that the Company may assign the benefit of the covenants warranties and undertakings contained in this Deed to its successors in title on terms that only one such further assignment of this Deed shall be permitted.

7

7.1   The copyright in all drawings, reports, specifications, bills of quantities, calculations and other similar documents ('the Documents') provided by the Building Contractor in connection with the Development shall remain vested in the Building Contractor but the Company and its successors in title shall have an irrevocable licence without payment of any further fee to the Building Contractor to copy and use the Documents for all purposes connected with the Company's interests in the Development and those of its successors in title including but without limitation any rebuilding, repair, construction, completion, maintenance, letting, promotion, advertisement and reinstatement of the Development or any part thereof. The Building Contractor shall upon demand and subject to the payment of the Building Contractor's reasonable copying charges promptly supply the Company with copies of the Documents.

7.2   The Building Contractor undertakes to procure that there shall be granted to the Company and its successors in title an irrevocable licence as referred to in Clause 7.1 in relation to the documents of the same nature as the Documents provided by any party other than the Building Contractor for the purposes of or in connection with the Building Contract.

8

8.1   The Building Contractor hereby confirms that it currently maintains and agrees that it will use its best endeavours to continue to maintain suitable professional indemnity insurance with a reputable insurer carrying on business in the United Kingdom for such amounts and upon such terms as cover the Building Contractor's responsibilities in relation to the Development and hereunder for a sum insured of not less than £[   ] in respect of each and every claim in connection with the Development for a period of at least 12 years from the date of the issue of the Certificate of Completion of Making Good Defects provided always that such insurance is generally available in the market on such terms and at commercially reasonable rates and will on reasonable demand from time to time supply the Company with full particulars of such insurance and documentary evidence confirming that the premium is paid and up to date.

8.2   Full and current details of all the Building Contractor's relevant insurances are appended hereto and the premiums for the current period of insurance have been duly paid to the insurer.

8.3   The Building Contractor will use its best endeavours to ensure that such insurances are not to be invalidated or prejudiced in any way by any act, default or omission by it or its employees servants or agents.

8.4   The Building Contractor is not aware of any subsisting claim or any circumstances likely to give rise to any claim under such insurance or which might reduce the current level of cover.

8.5   The Building Contractor shall immediately inform the Company if such insurance ceases to be available on such terms and at commercially reasonable rates in order that the Building Contractor and the Company can discuss means of best protecting the respective positions of the Company and the Building Contractor in the absence of such insurance.

9

9.1   The Guarantor hereby guarantees as primary obligator the due and punctual performance by the Building Contractor of each and all its obligations warranties duties and undertakings whatsoever hereunder and hereby agrees and undertakes with the Company that it will make good any default hereunder on the Building Contractor's part or for which the Building Contractor is responsible and will indemnify the Company against and will pay on demand and make good all losses damages costs and expenses which the Company would be entitled to recover from the Building Contractor hereunder by reason or in consequence of any default omission or non-performance hereunder on the part of the Building Contractor or for which the Building Contractor is responsible or by reason or in consequence of any determination of the Building Contract (and for the avoidance of doubt the Guarantor shall have available to it the same counterclaims and defences hereunder as if the Guarantor had been named as the Building Contractor under the Building Contract).

9.2   Without prejudice to the generality of the provisions of Clause 9.1 the Guarantor agrees to pay to the Company on demand any sums which the Company is entitled to receive from the Building Contractor which the Building Contractor has failed to pay seven days after demand therefor having been made by the Company or on the Company's behalf.

9.3   None of the following shall in any way prejudice or diminish the Guarantor's liability under this Guarantee:

9.3.1   the giving of time by or to the Building Contractor;

9.3.2   any forbearance, forgiveness, indulgence or concession granted to the Building Contractor;

9.3.3   any failure by the Company to pursue any other remedy which might be available to it before calling on this Guarantee;

9.3.4   any variation of or addendum to the provisions of the Building Contract or other dealings or arrangement between the Building Contractor and the Employer (and for the avoidance of doubt the Guarantor's obligations under this Guarantee shall also apply to any such variation or addendum);

9.3.5   the determination or reputation of the Building Contract or its disclaimer by a liquidator;

9.3.6   any change in the structure or legal form of the Building Contractor or any change in the relationship between the Building Contractor and the Guarantor;

9.3.7   any other act or thing which but for this Clause 9.3 would cause the guarantee contained in Clause 9.1 to be released.

9.4   The Guarantor undertakes that it shall not by paying any sum due under this Guarantee or by any means or on any ground claim or recover such sum from the Building Contractor by the institution of proceedings or the threat of proceedings or otherwise or claim any set-off or counterclaim against the Building Contractor or prove in competition with the Company in respect of any payment by the Guarantor hereunder or be entitled in competition with the Company to claim or have the benefit of any security which the Company holds or may hold for any money or liabilities due or incurred by the Building Contractor to the Company and in case the Guarantor receives any sums from the Building Contractor in respect of any payment by the Guarantor hereunder the Guarantor shall hold such monies in trust for the Company so long as any sums are payable (contingency or otherwise) under this Guarantee.

9.5   The obligations on the part of the Guarantor contained in this clause shall be deemed to be joint and several obligations on the part of the parties comprising the Guarantor and references to the Guarantor shall include references to either of those parties.

10   Any notice provided for in accordance with this Deed shall be deemed to be duly given if delivered by hand or sent by prepaid registered or recorded delivery post to the party named therein at the address of such party shown in this Deed or such other address as such party may by notice in writing nominate as its address for service.

11   No action or proceedings for any breach of this Deed shall be commenced againt the Building Contractor after the expiry of 12 years from the date of the issue of the Certificate of Completion of Making Good Defects.

The parties or their duly authorised representatives have signed and delivered this Deed on the date shown on page one.

THE SCHEDULE

The Development

[   ]

THE COMMON SEAL of [*name*] was hereunto affixed
in the presence of:

....
                                                        Director

....
                                                        Secretary

THE COMMON SEAL of [*name*] was hereunto affixed
in the presence of:

....
                                                        Director

....
                                                        Secretary

THE COMMON SEAL of [*name*] was hereunto affixed
in the presence of:

....
                                                        Director

....
                                                        Secretary

THE COMMON SEAL of [*name*] was hereunto affixed
in the presence of:

....
                                                        Director

....
                                                        Secretary

THE COMMON SEAL of [*name*] was hereunto affixed
in the presence of:

....
                                                        Director

....
                                                        Secretary

COLLATERAL WARRANTY PURCHASERS/ TENANTS (CoWa/P&T)

Form of Agreement for

The forms in this pad are for use where a warranty is to be given to a purchaser or tenant of a whole building in a commercial and/or industrial development, or a part of such a building. It is essential that the number of warranties to be given to tenants in one building should sensibly be limited.

Collateral Warranty for purchasers & tenants CoWa/P&T

General advice

1. The term "collateral agreement", "duty of care letter" or "collateral warranty" is often used without due regard to the strict legal meaning of the phrase. It is used here for agreements with tenants or purchasers of the whole or part of a commercial and/or industrial development.

2. The purpose of the Agreement is to bind the party giving the warranty in contract where no contract would otherwise exist. This can have implications in terms of professional liability and could cause exposure to claims which might otherwise not have existed under Common Law.

3. The information and guidance contained in this note is designed to assist consultants faced with a request that collateral agreements be entered into.

4. The use of the word 'collateral' is not accidental. It is intended to refer to an agreement that is an adjunct to another or principal agreement, namely the conditions of appointment of the consultant. It is imperative therefore that before collateral warranties are executed the consultant's terms and conditions of appointment have been agreed between the client and the consultant and set down in writing.

5. Under English Law the terms and conditions of the consultant's appointment may be 'under hand' or executed as a Deed. In the latter case the length of time that claims may be brought under the Agreement is extended from six years to twelve years.

6. Under English Law this Form of Agreement for Collateral Warranty is designed for use under hand or to be executed as a Deed. It should not be signed as a Deed when it is collateral to an appointment which is under hand.

7. The acceptance of a claim under the consultant's professional indemnity policy, brought under the terms of a collateral warranty, will depend upon the terms and conditions of the policy in force at the time when a claim is made.

8. Consultants with a current indemnity insurance policy taken out under the RIBA, RICSIS, ACE or RIASIS schemes will not have a claim refused simply on the basis that it is brought under the terms of a collateral warranty provided that warranty is in this form. In other respects the claim will be treated in accordance with policy terms and conditions in the normal way. **Consultants insured under different policies** must seek the advice of their brokers or insurers.

9. **Amendment to the clauses should be resisted.** Insurers' approval as mentioned above is in respect of the unamended clauses only.

Commentary on Clauses

Recital A.

This needs completion.

When this warranty is to be given in favour of a purchaser or tenant of part of the Development, the following words in square brackets must be deleted.

["The Premises" are also referred to as "the Development" in this Agreement.]

Care must be taken in describing "the Premises" accurately.

When this warranty is to be given in favour of a purchaser or tenant of the entire development, the terms "the Premises" and "the Development" are synonymous.

The following words in square brackets must be deleted

[forming part of. .... at. .... ("the Development").]

Recitals B & C

These are self explanatory but need completion.

Clause 1

This confirms the duty of care that will be owed to the Purchaser/the Tenant. The words in square brackets enable the clause to reflect exactly the provisions contained within the terms and conditions of the Appointment.

Paragraphs (a), (b) and (c) qualify and limit in three ways the Firm's liability in the event of a breach of the duty of care.

1(a) By this provision, the Firm is liable for the reasonable costs of repair renewal and or reinstatement of the Development insofar as the Purchaser/the Tenant has a financial obligation to pay or contribute to the cost of that repair. Other losses are expressly excluded.

1(b) By this provision the Firm's potential liability is limited. The intention is that the effect of "several" liability at Common Law is negated. When the Firm agrees – probably at the time of appointment – to sign a warranty at a future date, the list should include the names, if known, or otherwise the description or profession, of those responsible for the design of the relevant part of the Development and the general contractor. When the warranty is signed, the list should be completed with the names of those previously referred to by description or profession.

1(c) By this clause, the Purchaser/the Tenant is bound by any limitations on liability that may exist in the conditions of the Appointment. Furthermore, the consultant has the same rights of defence that would have been available had the relevant claim been made by the Client under the Appointment.

1(d) This states the relationship between the Firm and any consultant employed by the Purchaser/the Tenant to survey the premises.

Clause 2

As a consultant it is not possible to give assurances beyond those to the effect that materials as listed have not been nor will be specified. Concealed use of such materials by a contractor could possibly occur, hence the very careful restriction in terms of this particular warranty. Further materials may be added.

Clause 3

This obliges the consultant to ensure that all fees due and owing including VAT at the time the warranty is entered into have been paid.

Clause 4

This is included to make it clear that the Purchaser/the Tenant has no power or authority to direct or instruct the Firm in its duties to the Client.

Clause 5

Reasonable use by the Purchaser/the Tenant of drawings and associated documents is necessary in most cases. By this clause, the Purchaser/the Tenant is given the rights that might be reasonably expected but it does not allow the reproduction of the designs for any purpose outside the scope of the Development.

Clause 6

This confirms that professional indemnity insurance will be maintained in so far as it is reasonably possible to do so. Professional indemnity insurance is on the basis of annual contracts and the terms and conditions of a policy may change from renewal to renewal.

Clause 7

This allows the Purchaser/the Tenant to assign the benefit of this Warranty provided it is done by formal legal assignment and relates to the entire interest of the original Purchaser/Tenant. By this clause any

right of assignment may be limited or extinguished. If it is to be extinguished the word "not" shall be inserted after "may" and all words after "the Purchaser/the Tenant" deleted. If it is agreed that there should be a limited number of assignments, the precise number should be inserted in the space between "assigned" and "by the Purchaser/the Tenant".

Clause 7S

This is applicable in Scotland in relation to assignations. Completion is as for Clause 7.

Clause 8

This identifies the method of giving Notice under Clause 7 & 7S.

Clause 9

This needs completion. The clause makes clear that any liability that the Firm has by virtue of this Warranty ceases on the expiry of the stated period of years after practical completion of the Premises. (Note: the practical completion of the Development may be later).

Under English law the period should not exceed 6 years for agreements under hand, nor 12 years for those executed as a Deed.

In Scotland, the Prescription and Limitations (Scotland) Act 1973 prescribes a 5 year period.

Clause 10 and Attestation below

The appropriate method of execution by the Firm and the Purchaser/the Tenant should be checked carefully.

Clause 10S and Testing Clause below

This assumes the Firm is a partnership and the Purchaser/the Tenant is a Limited Company. Otherwise legal advice should be taken.

N.B.   The above advice and commentary is not intended to affect the interpretation of this Collateral Warranty. It is based on the terms of insurance current at the date of publication. All parties to the Agreement should ensure the terms of insurance have not changed.

Published by
The British Property Federation Limited
35 Catherine Place, London SW1E 6DY
Telephone: 0171–828 0111

© The British Property Federation, The Association of Consulting Engineers, The Royal Incorporation of Architects in Scotland, The Royal Institute of British Architects and The Royal Institution of Chartered Surveyors. 1992.

ISBN 0 900101 08 7

[Reproduced by kind permission of the British Property Federation.]

Warranty Agreement   CoWa/P&T

(In Scotland, leave blank. For applicable date see Testing Clause on page 4)

THIS AGREEMENT

is made the .... day of 199

BETWEEN:-

(insert name of the Consultant)

(1) ....

of/whose registered office is situated at ....

....("the Firm"), and

(insert name of the Purchaser/the Tenant)

(2) ....

whose registered office is situated at ....

....

(delete as appropriate)

("the Purchaser"/"the Tenant" which term shall include all permitted assignees under this Agreement).

WHEREAS:-

(delete as appropriate)

A. The Purchaser/the Tenant has entered into an agreement to purchase/an agreement to lease/a lease with

....

.... ("the Client") relating to

(insert description of the premises)

....

....

.... ("the Premises")

(delete as appropriate)

[forming part of ....

(insert description of the development)

....

....

(insert address of the development)

at ....

.... ("the Development").**]**

(delete as appropriate)

["The Premises" are also referred to as "the Development" in the Agreement.**]**

(insert date of appointment)
(delete/complete as appropriate)

B. By a contract ("the Appointment") dated ....
the Client has appointed the Firm as [architects/consulting structural engineers/ consulting building services engineers/   surveyors] in connection with the Development.

C. The Client has entered or may enter into a contract ("the Building Contract") with

(insert name of building contractor or "a building contractor to be selected by the Client")

....

....

for the construction of the Development.

NOW IN CONSIDERATION OF THE PAYMENT OF ONE POUND (£1) BY THE PURCHASER/THE TENANT TO THE FIRM (RECEIPT OF WHICH THE FIRM ACKNOWLEDGES) IT IS HEREBY AGREED as follows:-

(delete as appropriate to reflect terms of the Appointment)

1. The Firm warrants that it has exercised and will continue to exercise reasonable skill [and care] [care and diligence] in the performance of its services to the Client under the Appointment. In the event of any breach of this warranty:

   (a) subject to paragraphs (b) and (c) of this clause, the Firm shall be liable for the reasonable costs of repair renewal and/or reinstatement of any part or parts of the Development to the extent that

   – the Purchaser/the Tenant incurs such costs and/or
   – the Purchaser/the Tenant is or becomes liable either directly or by way of financial contribution for such costs.

   The Firm shall not be liable for other losses incurred by the Purchaser/the Tenant.

   (b) The Firm's liability for costs under this Agreement shall be limited to that proportion of such costs which it would be just and equitable to require the Firm to pay having regard to the extent of the Firm's responsibility for the same and on the basis that ....

(insert the names of other intended warrantors)

   ....

   ....

   ....

   ....

   .... shall be deemed to have provided contractual undertakings on terms no less onerous than this Clause 1 to the Purchaser/the Tenant in respect of the performance of their services in connection with the Development and shall be deemed to have paid to the Purchaser/the Tenant such proportion which it would be just and equitable for them to pay having regard to the extent of their responsibility;

   (c) the Firm shall be entitled in any action or proceedings by the Purchaser/the Tenant to rely on any limitation in the Appointment and to raise the equivalent rights in defence of liability as it would have against the Client under the Appointment;

   (d) the obligations of the Firm under or pursuant to this Clause 1 shall not be released or diminished by the appointment of any person by the Purchaser/the Tenant to carry out any independent enquiry into any relevant matter.

(delete where the Firm is the quantity surveyor)

2. [Without prejudice to the generality of Clause 1, the Firm further warrants that it has exercised and will continue to exercise reasonable skill and care to see that, unless authorised by the Client in writing or, where such authorisation is given orally, confirmed by the Firm to the Client in writing, none of the following has been or will be specified by the Firm for use in the construction of those parts of the Development to which the Appointment relates:-

   (a) high alumina cement in structural elements;

   (b) wood wool slabs in permanent formwork to concrete;

   (c) calcium chloride in admixtures for use in reinforced concrete;

   (d) asbestos products;

   (e) naturally occurring aggregates for use in reinforced concrete which do not comply with British Standard 882:1983 and/or naturally occurring aggregates for use in concrete which do not comply with British Standard 8110:1985.

(further specific materials may be added by agreement)

   (f)

   In the event of any breach of this warranty the provisions of Clauses 1a, b, c and d shall apply.   ]

3. The Firm acknowledges that the Client has paid all fees and expenses properly due and owing to the Firm under the Appointment up to the date of this Agreement.

4. The Purchaser/the Tenant has no authority to issue any direction or instruction to the Firm in relation to the Appointment.

5. The copyright in all drawings, reports, models, specifications, bills of quantities, calculations and other documents and information prepared by or on behalf of the Firm in connection with the Development (together referred to in this Clause 5 as "the Documents") shall remain vested in the Firm but, subject to the Firm having received payment of any fees agreed as properly due under the Appointment, the Purchaser/ the Tenant and its appointee shall have a licence to copy and use the Documents and to reproduce the designs and content of them for any purpose related to the Premises including, but without limitation, the construction, completion, maintenance, letting, promotion, advertisement, reinstatement, refurbishment and repair of the Premises. Such licence shall enable the Purchaser/the Tenant and its appointee to copy and use the Documents for the extension of the Premises but such use shall not include a licence to reproduce the designs contained in them for any extension of the Premises. The Firm shall not be liable for any use by the Purchaser/the Tenant or its appointee of any of the Documents for any purpose other than that for which the same were prepared by or on behalf of the Firm.

6. The Firm shall maintain professional indemnity insurance in an amount of not less (insert amount) than _____ pounds (£ _____) for any one occurrence or series of occurrences arising out of any one event for a (insert period) period of _____ years from the date of practical completion of the Premises under the Building Contract, provided always that such insurance is available at commercially reasonable rates. The Firm shall immediately inform the Purchaser/ the Tenant if such insurance ceases to be available at commercially reasonable rates in order that the Firm and the Purchaser/the Tenant can discuss means of best protecting the respective positions of the Purchaser/the Tenant and the Firm in the absence of such insurance. As and when it is reasonably requested to do so by the Purchaser/the Tenant or its appointee the Firm shall produce for inspection documentary evidence that its professional indemnity insurance is being maintained.

(insert number of times)

(*delete if under Scots law*)

[7. This Agreement may _____ be assigned _____ by the Purchaser/the Tenant by way of absolute legal assignment to another person taking an assignment of the Purchaser/the Tenant's interest in the Premises without the consent of the Client or the Firm being required and such assignment shall be effective upon written notice thereof being given to the Firm. No further assignment shall be permitted.]

(insert number of times)

(*delete if under English law*)

[7S. *The Purchaser/the Tenant shall _____ be entitled to assign or transfer his/their rights under this Agreement _____ to any other person acquiring the Purchaser's/the Tenant's interest in the whole of the Premises without the consent of the Firm subject to written notice of such assignation being given to the Firm in accordance with Clause 8 hereof. Nothing in this clause shall permit any party acquiring such right as assignee or transferee to enter into any further assignation or transfer to anyone acquiring subsequently an interest in the Premises from him.*]

8. Any notice to be given by the Firm hereunder shall be deemed to be duly given if it is delivered by hand at or sent by registered post or recorded delivery to the Purchaser/the Tenant at its registered office and any notice given by the Purchaser/ the Tenant hereunder shall be deemed to be duly given if it is addressed to "The Senior Partner"/"The Managing Director" and delivered by hand at or sent by registered post or recorded delivery to the above-mentioned address of the Firm or to the principal business address of the Firm for the time being and, in the case of any such notices, the same shall if sent by registered post or recorded delivery be deemed to have been received forty eight hours after being posted.

(complete as appropriate)

9. No action or proceedings for any breach of this Agreement shall be commenced against the Firm after the expiry of _____ years from the date of practical completion of the Premises under the Building Contract.

(delete if under Scots law) [10.   The construction validity and performance of this Agreement shall be governed by English law and the parties agree to submit to the non-exclusive jurisdiction of the English Courts.

(alternatives: delete as appropriate)   **[AS WITNESS** the hands of the parties the day and year first before written.

Signed by or on behalf of the Firm ....

(for Agreement executed under hand and NOT as a Deed)   in the presence of: ....

Signed by or on behalf of the Purchaser/the Tenant ....

in the presence of: ....]

(this must only apply if the Appointment is executed as a Deed)   **[IN WITNESS WHEREOF** this Agreement was executed as a Deed and delivered the day and year first before written.

by the Firm

....

....

....

....

by the Purchaser/the Tenant

....

....

....

....]]

(delete if under English law)   10S.   *This Agreement shall be construed and the rights of the parties and all matters arising hereunder shall be determined in all respects according to the Law of Scotland.*

IN WITNESS WHEREOF these presents are executed as follows:-

SIGNED by the above Firm at ....

on the .... *day of* .... *Nineteen hundred and* ....

as follows:-

.... *(Firm's signature)*

Signature .... *Full Name* ....

Address ....

.... *Occupation* ....

Signature .... *Full Name* ....

Address ....

.... *Occupation* ....

SIGNED by the above named Purchaser/Tenant at ....

on the .... *day of* .... *Nineteen hundred and* ....

as follows:-

For and on behalf of the Purchaser/the Tenant

.... *Director/Authorised Signatory*

.... *Director/Authorised Signatory*]

CoWa/P&T   2nd Edition   Page 4
© BPF, ACE, RIAS, RICS, RIBA 1993

[Reproduced by kind permission of the British Property Federation.]

STANDARD CONSULTANT–FUNDER WARRANTY (Co/Wa/F)

THIS AGREEMENT is made on [*date*] BETWEEN:

(1) [*name*] whose registered office is situated at [*address*] ('the Firm'); and

(2) [*name*] whose registered office is situated at [*address*] ('the Client'); and

(3) [*name*] whose registered office is situated at [*address*] ('the Company' which term shall include all permitted assignees under this Agreement).

WHEREAS:

(A) The Company has entered into an agreement ('the Finance Agreement') with the Client for the provision of certain finance in connection with the carrying out of [*details of development at address*] ('the Development').

(B) By a contract ('the Appointment') dated [*date*] the Client has appointed the Firm as [   ] in connection with the Development.

(C) The Client has entered or may enter into a building contract ('the Building Contract') with [*name*] for the construction of the Development.

NOW in consideration of the payment of one pound (£1) by the Company to the Firm (receipt of which the Firm acknowledges) it is hereby agreed as follows:

1   The Firm warrants that it has exercised and will continue to exercise reasonable skill, care and diligence in the performance of its duties to the Client under the Appointment, provided that the Firm shall have no greater liability to the Company by virtue of this Agreement than it would have had if the Company had been named as a joint client under the Appointment.

2   Without prejudice to the generality of Clause 1, the Firm further warrants that it has exercised and will continue to exercise reasonable skill and care to see that, unless authorised by the Client in writing or, where such authorisation is given orally, confirmed by the Firm to the Client in writing, none of the following has been or will be specified by the Firm for use in the construction of those parts of the Development to which the Appointment relates:

(a)   high alumina cement in structural elements;
(b)   wood wool slabs in permanent formwork to concrete;
(c)   calcium chloride in admixtures for use in reinforced concrete;
(d)   asbestos products;
(e)   naturally occurring aggregates for use in refinforced concrete which do not comply with British Standard 882: 1983 and/or naturally occurring aggregates for use in concrete which do not comply with British Standard 8110: 1985.

3   The Company has no authority to issue any direction or instruction to the Firm in relation to performance of the Firm's duties under the Appointment unless and until the Company has given notice under Clause 5.

4   The Firm acknowledges that the Client has paid all fees and expenses due and owing to the Firm under the Appointment up to the date of this Agreement. The Company has no liability to the Firm in respect of fees and expenses under the Appointment unless and until the Company has given notice under Clause 5.

5   The Firm further agrees that it will not without first giving the Company not less than 21 days' notice in writing exercise any right it may have to terminate the Appointment or to treat the same as having been repudiated by the Client or to discontinue the performance of any duties to be performed by the Firm pursuant thereto. The Firm's right to terminate the Appointment with the Client or treat the same as having been repudiated or discontinue performance shall cease if, within such period of notice and subject to Clause 6, the Company shall give notice in writing to the Firm requiring the Firm to accept the instructions of the Company or its appointee to the exclusion of the Client in respect of the Development upon the terms and conditions of the Appointment.

6   It shall be a condition of any notice given by the Company under Clause 5 that the Company or its appointee accepts liability for payment of the fees payable to the Firm under the Appointment and for performance of the Client's obligations including payment of any fees outstanding at the date of such notice. Upon the issue of any notice by the Company under Clause 5, the Appointment shall continue in full force and effect as if no right of termination on the part of the Firm had arisen and the Firm shall be liable to the Company or its appointee under the Appointment in lieu of its liability to the Client. If any notice given by the Company under Clause 5 requires the Firm to accept the instructions of the Company's appointee, the Company shall be liable to the Firm as guarantor for the payment of all sums from time to time due to the Firm from the Company's appointee.

7   The copyright in all drawings, reports, specifications, bills of quantities, calculations and other documents provided by the Firm in connection with the Development shall remain vested in the Firm but the Company and its appointee shall have a licence to copy and use such drawings and other documents and to reproduce the designs contained in them for any purpose related to the Development including, but without limitation, the construc-tion, completion, maintenance, letting, promotion, advertisement, reinstatement, and repair of the Development. The Company and its appointee shall have a licence to copy and use such drawings and other documents for the extension of the Development but such use shall not include a licence to reproduce the designs contained in them for any extension of the Development. The Firm shall not be liable for any use by the Company or its appointee of any of the drawings and other documents for any purpose other than that for which the same were prepared and provided by the Firm.

8   The Firm shall maintain professional indemnity insurance in an amount of £[   ] for any occurrence or series of occurrences arising out of any one event for a period of 12 years from the date of Practical Completion of the Development for the purposes of the Building Contract, provided always that such insurance is available at commercially reasonable rates. The Firm shall immediately inform the Company if such insurance ceases to be available at commercially reasonable rates in order that the Firm and the Company can discuss the means of best protecting the respective positions of the Company and the Firm in respect of the Development in the absence of such insurance. As and when it is reasonably requested to do so by the Company or its appointee under Clause 5, the Firm shall produce for inspection documentary evidence that its professional indemnity insurance is being maintained.

9   The Client has agreed to be a party to this Agreement for the purposes of Clause 11 and for acknowledging that the Firm shall not be in breach of the Appointment by complying with the obligations imposed on it by Clause 5.

10   This Agreement may be assigned twice by the Company by way of absolute legal assignment to another company providing finance or re-finance in connection with the Development without the consent of the Client or the Firm being required and such assignment shall be effective upon written notice thereof being given to the Client and to the Firm. Two further assignments of this Agreement shall be permitted with the prior written consent of the Firm which consent shall not be unreasonably withheld or delayed.

11   The Client undertakes to the Firm that warranty agreements in this form or in substantially similar form have been or will be entered into between

[*name*]

[*name*]

on the one hand and the Company on the other hand.

12   Any notice to be given by the Firm hereunder shall be deemed to be duly given if it is delivered by hand at or sent by registered post or recorded delivery to the Company at its registered office and any notice given by the Company hereunder shall be deemed to be duly given if it is addressed to 'the Managing Director' and delivered by hand at or sent by registered post or recorded delivery to the above-mentioned address of the Firm or to the principal business address of the Firm for the time being and, in the case of any such notices, the same shall if sent by registered post or recorded delivery be deemed to have been received 48 hours after being posted.

IN WITNESS whereof this Agreement has been executed as a Deed and delivered the day and year first before written.

EXECUTED as a DEED by [*the Firm*]
in the presence of:

EXECUTED as a DEED by [*the Client*]
in the presence of:

SUB-CONTRACTOR–PURCHASER/TENANT WARRANTY

THIS AGREEMENT is made on [*date*] BETWEEN:

(1)   [*name*] of/whose registered office is situated at [*address*] ('the Sub-Contractor'); and

(2)   [*name*] of/whose registered office is situated at [*address*] ('the Purchaser/Tenant' which term shall include all permitted assignees under this Agreement).

WHEREAS:

(A)   The Purchaser/Tenant has entered into an agreement to purchase/an agreement to take a lease from [*name*] relating to [*specify premises*] ('the Premises').

(B)   By a sub-contract ('the Building Sub-Contract') between the sub-contractor and [*name*] ('the Contractor') and the Contractor has appointed the Sub-Contractor to carry out and complete the works specified in the Building Sub-Contract ('the Sub-Contract Works').

NOW IT IS HEREBY AGREED:

In consideration of the payment of one pound (£1) to the Sub-Contractor, receipt of which the Sub-Contractor acknowledges:

1   The Sub-Contractor warrants that it has exercised and will continue to exercise all proper skill and care in relation to the performance of its duties under the Building Sub-Contract and that it will carry out the construction and complete the design of the Sub-Contract Works (insofar as the Sub-Contractor is responsible under the Building Sub-Contract for such design) in accordance with the terms of the Building Sub-Contract:

(a)   the Sub-Contractor's liability under this Agreement shall be limited to that proportion of any losses incurred by the Purchaser/Tenant arising from any breach of this Agreement which it would be just and equitable to require it to pay having regard to the extent of its responsibility for the same;

(b)   the Sub-Contractor shall be entitled in any action or proceedings by the Purchaser/Tenant to rely on any limitation in the Building Sub-Contract and to raise the equivalent rights in defence of liability as it would have against the Contractor under the Building Sub-Contract;

(c)   the obligations of the Sub-Contractor under or pursuant to this Clause 1 shall not be increased or diminished by the appointment of any person by the Purchaser/Tenant to carry out any independent enquiry into any relevant matter.

2   Without prejudice to the generality of Clause 1, the Sub-Contractor further warrants that, unless required by the Building Sub-Contract or unless otherwise authorised in writing by the Contractor (or, where such authorisation is given orally, confirmed in writing by the Sub-Contractor to the Contractor) none of the following has been or will be used in the Sub-Contract Works:

(a)   high alumina cement in structural elements;

(b)   wood wool slabs in permanent formwork to concrete;

(c)   calcium chloride in admixtures for use in reinforced concrete;

(d)   asbestos products;

(e)   naturally occurring aggregates for use in reinforced concrete which do not comply with British Standard 882: 1983 and/or naturally occurring aggregates for use in concrete which do not comply with British Standard 8110: 1985;

(f)   **[Further specific materials may be added by agreement]**

In the event of any breach of the warranty in this clause the provisions of Clauses 1(a), 1(b) and 1(c) shall apply.

3   The Sub-Contractor acknowledges that the Contractor has duly discharged his obligation to pay all sums properly due/certified as due to the Sub-Contractor under the Building Sub-Contract up to the date of this Agreement or up to the date of Practical Completion of the Sub-Contract Works whichever date is the later.

4   The Purchaser/Tenant has no authority to issue any direction or instruction to the Sub-Contractor in relation to the Building Sub-Contract.

5   The copyright in all drawings, reports, models, specifications, bills of quantities, calculations and other documents and information prepared by or on behalf of the Sub-Contractor in connection with the Sub-Contract Works (together referred to in this Clause 5 as 'the Documents') shall remain vested in the Sub-Contractor but, subject to the Contractor having discharged his obligation to pay all monies certified as due/properly due under the Building Sub-Contract, the Purchaser/Tenant or its appointee shall have a licence to copy and use the Documents and to reproduce the designs and content of them for any purpose related to the Building Sub-Contract including, but without limitation, the construction, completion, maintenance, letting, promotion, advertisement, reinstatement, refurbishment and repair of the Premises. Such licence shall enable the Purchaser/Tenant or its appointee to copy and use the Documents for the extension of the Premises but such use shall not include a licence to reproduce the designs contained in them for any extension of the Premises. The Sub-Contractor shall not be liable for any use by the Purchaser/Tenant or its appointee of any of the Documents for any purpose other than that for which the same were prepared by or on behalf of the Sub-Contractor.

6   The Sub-Contractor shall take out and maintain professional indemnity insurance in an amount of [*specify amount*] pounds (£[   ]) for any one claim and in all in any one period of insurance for a period of 12 years from the date of Practical Completion of the Sub-Contract Works under the Building Sub-Contract, provided such insurance is available at commercially reasonable rates. The Sub-Contractor shall immediately inform the Purchaser/Tenant if such insurance is not or ceases to be available at commercially reasonable rates in order that the Sub-Contractor and the Purchaser/Tenant can discuss the means of best protecting the Sub-Contractor in the absence of such insurance. As and when it is reasonably requested to do so by the Purchaser/Tenant or its appointee, the Sub-Contractor shall produce for inspection documentary evidence that its professional indemnity insurance is being maintained.

7   This Agreement may be assigned twice by the Purchaser/Tenant by way of absolute legal assignment to another person taking the assignment of the Purchaser's/Tenant's interest in the whole of or any part of the Premises without the consent of the Sub-Contractor being required and such assignment shall be effective upon written notice thereof being given to the Sub-Contractor. Further assignments of this Agreement shall be permitted with the prior consent of the Sub-Contractor which consent shall not be unreasonably withheld or delayed.

8   Any notice to be given by the Sub-Contractor hereunder shall be deemed to be duly given if it is delivered by hand at or sent by registered post or recorded delivery to the Purchaser/Tenant at its registered office; and any notice given by the Purchaser/Tenant hereunder shall be deemed to be duly given if it is delivered by hand at or sent by

registered post or recorded delivery to the Sub-Contractor at its registered office; and, in the case of any such notices, the same shall if sent by registered post or recorded delivery be deemed (subject to proof to the contrary) to have been received 48 hours after being posted.

9   No action or proceedings for any breach of this Agreement shall be commenced against the Sub-Contractor after the expiry of 12 years from the date of Practical Completion of the Sub-Contract Works.

10   The construction, validity and performance of this Agreement shall be governed by English law and the parties agree to submit to the non-exclusive jurisdiction of the English courts.

IN WITNESS whereof the parties have entered into this Deed the day and year given above.

EXECUTED as a DEED
by [*name*]
on behalf of the Sub-Contractor
in the presence of:

EXECUTED as a DEED
by [*name*]
on behalf of the Purchaser/Tenant
in the presence of:

BILD: LATENT DEFECTS POLICY

In consideration of the Insured paying or having agreed to pay to the Insurers named in the Schedule the Premium mentioned in the Schedule the Insurers agree (subject to the terms, exclusions, definitions and conditions contained herein or endorsed or otherwise expressed hereon) to indemnify the Insured against the cost of repairing, replacing or renewing or at Insurers option by reinstating the Property Insured following the discovery of:

(a) actual physical damage to or threat of imminent collapse of the Property Insured caused by an Inherent Defect in the Insured Elements

(b) damage arising from the ingress of water through the enclosing elements which form the external envelope of the Property Insured

(c) landslip, heave or subsidence affecting the land on which the Property Insured stands

and notified to the Insurers during the Period of Insurance.

For the purpose of this policy (a) to (c) above shall be referred to as DAMAGE.

The proposal and any information provided by the Insured shall be incorporated on and shall form part of the Policy. The Policy, the Schedule, any Endorsements and any Memoranda shall be considered as one Contract.

Provided that Insurers liability shall not exceed the Sum Insured at the time of the discovery of the DAMAGE.

From the date of first notification of each and every claim to the Insurers the Sum Insured shall be reduced by the amount of each and every claims payment.

EXCLUSIONS

This Policy does not cover:

(1)   the Excess amount shown in the Schedule in respect of each and every loss after application of all other terms and conditions of the policy.

(2)   DAMAGE resulting from:

(a)   the failure to effect any requirements contained in the Certificate of Practical Completion or other similar documentation.

(b)   any defect discovered prior to the commencement of the Period of Insurance unless remedied to the satisfaction of Insurers.

(c)   any process of ageing or staining or change in colour, texture or opacity.

(d)   the use of the Property Insured for any purpose materially more onerous than that for which it was originally designed unless otherwise agreed with Insurers.

(e)   inadequate maintenance of the Property Insured.

(f)   normal shrinkage or expansion of the materials used in the construction of the Property Insured.

(g)   normal settlement or bedding down.

(3)   DAMAGE which appears within a defects liability or maintenance period and which is the responsibility of the contractor(s) under the terms of the building contract(s).

(4)   DAMAGE to:

(a) Decorative or reflective coatings which are applied by brush or spray but which do not form part of the Insured Elements

(b) non-structural screeds or floor finishes within the building which do not form part of the Insured Elements

unless caused by an Inherent Defect in an Insured Element.

(5) wear and tear.

(6) DAMAGE arising from the ingress of water:

(a) during the first twelve months of the Period of Insurance through the enclosing elements which form the external envelope of the Property Insured.

(b) After the first five years of the Period of Insurance through any roof with less than 6° pitch from the horizontal.

(7) consequential loss of any kind.

(8) any DAMAGE caused by or resulting from:

fire, lightning, explosion, aircraft, sonic bangs, earthquake, storm, flood or escape of water from tanks, apparatus, or pipes.

(9) DAMAGE caused by:

(a) war, invasion, act of foreign enemy, hostilities (whether war has been declared or not), civil war, rebellion, revolution, insurrection or military or usurped power.

(c) Nationalisation, confiscation or requisition, Seizure or destruction by the government or any public authority.

(10) loss or destruction of or damage to any property whatsoever or any loss or expense whatsoever resulting or arising therefrom or any consequential loss directly or indirectly caused by or contributed to by or arising from:

(a) ionising radiations or contamination by radioactivity from any nuclear fuel or from any nuclear waste from the combustion of nuclear fuel.

(b) the radioactive toxic explosive or other hazardous properties of any explosive nuclear assembly or nuclear component thereof.

(11) Loss or destruction or damage caused by pollution or contamination but this shall not exclude destruction of or damage to the Property Insured, not otherwise excluded, caused by:

(a) pollution or contamination which itself results from DAMAGE.

(b) DAMAGE which itself results from pollution or contamination.

DEFINITIONS

Insured Elements: those elements of the Property Insured intended to support and transmit the combined dead load, load and windload together with all enclosing elements which form the external envelope.

Inherent Defect: any defect in design, workmanship or materials used in the Property Insured which existed but remained undiscovered at the commencement of the Period of Insurance.

Insured: the party or parties shown in the Schedule or any party or parties who may acquire an insurable interest in the Property Insured during the Period of Insurance and whose interest is notified to the Insurers.

EXTENSIONS

1.   Indexation of Sum Insured and Deductible

(a)   In line with General Building Cost Index

Subject to the payment of an additional premium the Sum Insured and the deductible amount will each be increased in line with the General Building Cost Index of the Royal Institution of Chartered Surveyors on each anniversary of the inception date.

The Insurers will advise the revised amounts and the additional premium due at that time.

For the purpose of any loss settlement the Sum Insured as adjusted in accordance with the foregoing provisons shall be regarded as the Sum Insured at the time of the discovery of the DAMAGE.

If for any reason the above Index ceases to be published or cannot be used to adjust the Sum Insured in the manner described then the Insurers reserve the right at any time to substitute any other index considered relevant.

or

(b)   *Compound by an agreed fixed rate*

Where the Insured has elected and paid the appropriate premium for the Sum Insured to be indexed annually by a specified percentage, the Sum Insured shown on the schedule and the amount of the Deductible will each be separately increased by % compound on each anniversary of the commencement of the period of insurance.

For the purpose of any loss settlement the Sum Insured as adjusted in accordance with the foregoing provisions shall be regarded as the Sum Insured at the time of the discovery of the DAMAGE
N.B. Only one method of indexation will apply.

2.   *Removal of Contents*

Insurers will pay costs necessarily and reasonably incurred with their consent in

(a)   dismantling and/or removing
(b)   temporarily storing
(c)   reinstating and re-erecting

any contents or fixtures and fittings at the Property Insured which require to be removed to allow reinstatement or repair provided that the Insurers liability for any one loss shall not exceed 10% of the Sum Insured.

3.   *Removal of Debris*

Insurers will pay costs necessarily incurred with their consent in removing debris, dismantling, demolishing, shoring up and propping portions of the Property Insured but excluding costs and expenses incurred in removing debris from outside the site of the Property Insured other than from the area immediately adjacent thereto.

4.   *Public Authority Requirements*

Insurers will pay additional costs necessarily incurred with their consent in complying with building regulations or local authority or other statutory requirements first imposed on the Insured following discovery of DAMAGE and relating thereto.

5.   Professional Fees

Insurers will pay Professional Fees incurred with their consent in the reinstatement of the Property Insured but not in the preparation of any claim.

6.   *Automatic Reinstatement of the Sum Insured*

In consideration of the Sum Insured not being reduced by the amount of any loss the Insured agrees to pay the pro-rata additional premium on the amount of such loss from The date of notification of a claim to the date of expiry of the Period of Insurance.

CONDITIONS

1.   *Under Insurance*

(a)   Following DAMAGE if at the time of repair replacement or renewal the sum representing 85% of the cost which would have been incurred in reinstating the whole of the property covered exceeds the sum insured at the time of the discovery of DAMAGE, the liability of the Insurers shall not exceed that proportion of the amount of DAMAGE which the said sum insured shall bear to the sum representing the total cost of reinstating the whole of such property at that time.

(b) The liability of the Insurers for the repair or restoration of property damaged in part shall not exceed the amount which would have been payable had such property been wholly destroyed.

2. *Alteration to Risk*

If any material change shall occur varying the risk as proposed to the Insurers the Insured shall give immediate notice to the Insurers of such change with full details and the Insurers shall have the right to vary the terms of this Policy.

3. *Misrepresentation*

This policy shall be voidable in the event of misrepresentation, misdescription or non-disclosure of any material fact.

4. *Claim Procedure*

(A) *Action by the Insured*

(a) On discovery of DAMAGE the Insured shall

(i) notify the Insurers immediately.
(ii) carry out and permit to be taken any action which may be reasonably practicable to prevent further DAMAGE.
(iii) deliver to the Insurers at the Insured's expense
(a) full information in writing of the property destroyed or damaged

and the amount of the DAMAGE

(b) details of any other insurances on any property hereby insured.

Within 30 days after the discovery of the DAMAGE.

(c) all such proofs and information relating to the claim as may reasonably be required.

(d) if demanded a statutory declaration of the truth of the claim and of any matters connected with it.

(b) No claim under this policy shall be payable unless the terms of this conditon have been complied with.

(B) *Insurer's Option to Reinstate*

If any property is to be reinstated by the Insurers the Insured shall at his own expense provide all such plans, documents, books and information as may reasonably be required. The Insurers shall not be bound to reinstate exactly but only as circumstances permit and in a reasonably sufficient manner and shall not in any case be bound to expend in respect of any one of the items insured more than its sum insured.

(C) *Insurers Rights following a Claim*

On the discovery of DAMAGE in respect of which a claim is made the Insurers and any person authorised by the Insurers may without thereby incurring any liability or diminishing any of the Insurers rights under this policy enter the premises where such DAMAGE has occurred.

No property may be abandoned to the Insurers

5. *Fraudulent Acts*

If any claim is fraudulent or if any fraudulent means or devices are used by the Insured or their agent making the claim to obtain any benefit under this Policy or if any DAMAGE is caused by wilful act or omission or with the connivance of the Insured all benefits under this Policy and vesting in the Insured making the claim shall be forfeited.

6. *Non-contribution*

The Insurers will not be liable for any DAMAGE insured by any other policy in the name of the Insured except in respect of any excess beyond the amount that would have been payable under such policy or policies had this Policy not been effected.

7. *Arbitration*

If any difference arises as to the amount to be paid under this Policy (liability being otherwise admitted) such difference shall be referred to an arbitrator to be appointed by the parties in accordance with statutory provisions. Where any difference is by this condition to be referred to arbitration the making of an award shall be a condition precedent to any right of action against the Insurers.

8. *Recovery Rights*

Any claimant under this Policy shall at the request and expense of the Insurers take and permit to be taken all necessary steps for enforcing rights against any other party in the name of the Insured before or after any payment is made by the Insurers.

9. *Jurisdiction*

This policy shall be construed with English Scottish or Northern Ireland law and shall be subject to the exclusive jurisdiction of the appropriate Court of England and Wales Scotland or Northern Ireland and any arbitration hereunder should be held in the United Kingdom of Great Britain and Northern Ireland.

The Insurers shall not be liable to the Insured for exemplary or punitive damages in any circumstances whatsoever.

SCHEDULE

The Schedule referred to in Policy No ....

Period of Insurance: From ....   To: ....

Premium   :   £..

Insurance Premium Tax @   :   £..

Total Premium   :   £..

The Insured:
(as more fully described in specification (i)
attached)   Interest in the Propery insured

....

....

The Property Insured:
(as more fully described in specification (ii) attached) ....

....

Sum Insured: ....

Excess: ....

Indexation Factor:
(applicable to sum insured and
excess per annum)

              Insurers: Proportion %   Reference No:

....

....

Signature for and on behalf of:

....

SPECIFICATIONS

Forming part of Policy No ....

(i) THE INSURED   INTEREST IN PROPERTY

NAME ....

ADDRESS ....

....

....

NAME ....

ADDRESS ....

....

....

NAME ....

ADDRESS ....

....

....

NAME ....

ADDRESS ....

....

....

NAME ....

ADDRESS ....

....

....

(ii) THE PROPERTY INSURED

The building situate ....

occupied as ....
and all ancillary works including permanently installed fixtures and fittings and services.

MEMORANDUM 1

Payment of any claim for DAMAGE to ancillary works including permanently installed fixtures and fittings and service is conditional upon payment being made or liability being admitted to a claim for DAMAGE to the building.

[*Reproduced by kind permission of Griffiths & Armour.*]

Index

References are to paragraph numbers; *italic* **references are to Appendix page numbers.**

ISBN 0-85308-415-7